How We Made A Million Dollars Recycling Great Old Houses

Sam & Mary Weir

CONTEMPORARY
BOOKS, INC.
CHICAGO

Library of Congress Cataloging in Publication Data

Weir, Sam, 1943-
    How we made a million dollars recycling great old
houses.

    Bibliography: p.
    Includes index.
    1. Dwellings—Remodeling.   I. Weir, Mary Patterson,
1943-   joint author.   II. Title.
TH4816.W44   1979   643'.7   78-73682
ISBN 0-8092-7427-2
ISBN 0-8092-7426-4 pbk.

Dedicated to our fellow recyclers.

Published by Contemporary Books, Inc.
180 North Michigan Avenue, Chicago, Illinois 60601
Manufactured in the United States of America
Library of Congress Catalog Card Number: 78-73682
International Standard Book Number: 0-8092-7427-2 (cloth)
                                    ⁃ 0-8092-7426-4 (paper)

Published simultaneously in Canada by
Beaverbooks, Ltd.
150 Lesmill Road
Don Mills, Ontario M3B 2T5
Canada

Contents

Foreword

In doing this book, we feel we are not in competition with other how-to books, either those on financial independence, or on house remodeling, or renovation. These books are basically general, whereas our book is specifically set to a certain lifestyle, the one we have been lucky enough to have as our own for these past ten years. Use of the term "recycling," for all of the various "how-to" in rehabilitating older houses was original with us. Others have since used the word in the same sense, to "rehabilitate" older houses. But, whatever you call it, recycling is what we've given our lives to doing, so far. And we've loved it.

We now want to share our experiences and our know-how: it was obvious to us from the first that we very likely could do much better financially by devoting the time we've spent on this book to recycling more houses. But we made the commitment to the book. It was a new challenge, and it allows us to do what we'd been wanting to do, share our knowledge.

Acknowledgment

We want to acknowledge and commend the help of a professional writer, Morten Lund, who had the temerity to take on our experience and help us get the vast subject of recycling into print, a job which required, off and on, over a year of sometimes very exacting work.

Sam and Mary Weir

THE WEIRS' TEN-YEAR TRACK RECORD

House No.	House Location	Year Purchased	Purchase Price
1	18 Beach St.	1966	4,500
2	265 New Ocean Ave.	1968	17,000
3	32–32A Riverdale Ave.	1969	13,800
4	30 Shrewsbury Dr.	1970	20,000
5	5 Griffin St.	1970	15,300
6	1 Riverview Ave.	1971	8,000
7	12 Main St.	1971	11,300
8	Route 100, Vermont	1971	21,500
9	559 Manahasset	1971	24,500
10	78 Ocean Ave.	1972	26,500
11	Goldencrest	1972	45,000
12	71 Victor Ave.	1972	9,000
13	1–3 Ocean Ave.	1973	35,000
14	34 Washington Ave.	1973	26,500
15	5 Maplewood Ave.	1974	15,000
16	477 Ocean Ave.	1974	50,000
17	477-A Ocean Ave.	1974	25,000
18	91 Rumson Rd.	1974	80,000
19	The Lindens	1975	90,000
20	Linden Pond	1975	30,000
21	141-A Rumson Rd.	1975	30,000
22	57 Hathaway	1975	50,000
23	16 Locust Ave.	1976	11,700
24	18 Locust Ave.	1976	11,800
25	59 Sea View Ave. (Lot)	1976	—
26	Manhassett (Lot)	1976	—
27	10 Acres, Vermont	1976	12,000
28	114 Ocean Ave.	1976	20,000
29	114-A Ocean Ave.	1976	10,000
30	25–27–29 Monmouth Rd.	1977	44,000

APRIL 1966 TO DECEMBER 1977

Misc. Expenses & Material Costs	Total Expenditure	Rental Profits	Selling Price or Value	Wages & Gross Profit	Equity: Wages & Net Profit
14,314	18,814	30,000	31,000	61,000	42,186
31,157	48,157	40,000	106,000	146,000	97,843
12,775	26,575	17,000	48,000	65,000	38,425
9,800	29,800	10,000	36,000	46,000	16,200
2,410	17,710	5,000	46,000	51,000	33,290
3,000	11,000	3,000	18,000	21,000	10,000
10,561	21,861	9,000	42,000	51,000	29,139
8,072	29,572	2,000	55,000	57,000	27,428
7,691	32,191	8,000	35,000	43,000	10,809
8,680	35,180	8,500	55,000	63,500	28,320
26,272	71,272	5,000	180,000	185,000	113,728
8,256	17,256	—	26,650	26,650	9,394
5,000	40,000	13,500	95,000	108,500	68,500
5,000	31,500	—	37,000	37,000	5,500
7,200	22,200	—	30,900	30,900	8,700
9,680	59,680	30,000	135,000	165,000	105,320
5,000	30,000	10,000	50,000	60,000	30,000
21,000	101,000	—	150,000	150,000	49,000
65,000	155,000	—	177,000	177,000	22,000
60,000	90,000	—	185,000	185,000	95,000
2,000	32,000	—	50,000	50,000	18,000
9,000	59,000	—	60,000	60,000	1,000
4,000	15,700	—	25,000	25,000	9,300
4,000	15,800	—	30,000	30,000	14,200
2,000	2,000	—	25,000	25,000	23,000
1,000	1,000	—	20,000	20,000	19,000
2,000	14,000	—	18,000	18,000	4,000
16,000	36,000	—	95,000	95,000	59,000
5,000	15,000	—	46,000	46,000	31,000
50,000	94,000	—	172,000	172,000	78,000
					1,097,282

part 1

What Recycling Is All About

1

The Recycling Lifestyle

Take two people with energy and enthusiasm, add some great old houses, and what do you get?

This is a book about a certain lifestyle.

It's a book about the two of us, and how we learned to live extremely well—and in one piece—within the present economic and social system. It is a book about how we developed our way of life, so that our occupation was both a rewarding business career and creatively satisfying. And we began it all while we were still in our early twenties.

It took us ten years to go all the way to our present level of success. But, the first sign—of sorts—that we had definitely "made it" came two years ago, just after we'd moved into our present house, when the delivery man who came up our walk to the door asked Mary, answering the doorbell, "Would it be possible to speak to your mother?" The delivery man was no fool. He knew that no one who looked as young as Mary could possibly be the mistress of such a mansion. Right? Wrong.

Our present home *is* fairly impressive, a symbol of what we are and what we do. You enter it through Doric porch columns and, from there, a huge walnut door leads into a spacious tiled foyer, featuring a sweeping double balustraded staircase at the other end. It's a lovely entrance. The house is equally elegant in each of its other twenty-five rooms.

If we now leave this scene, and look at our scene some ten years ago, it's as if we were looking at ourselves and our surroundings through the wrong end of a telescope. Everything back then seems restricted. The two of us were living in a small modestly furnished apartment, with a baby on our hands. We were a typical couple who had started out on the typical route through the system.

The modest apartment is a traditional first step for two young people who have married recently and who have no money. Five years and another child later usually comes the first "little house." Ten years after that, something in a modest split level . . .

What We Did

But that's not what happened. Instead of being content to climb slowly hand over hand, we sprinted up the ladder of success, and now we are asked on all sides, "How did you ever manage to do it?"

We've decided to sit down and tell all.

The process is simple enough. We can tell you how we did it. And, exactly how you can do it, too.

To start, you must get out of the rut. We did that first a bit more than ten years ago when we bought a house before we could "afford" a house. Price, $4,500. Location, 18 Beach Street, Sea Bright, New Jersey.

We borrowed the whole $4,500. We made that all back within less than two years.

The significance of that little financial coup went right over our heads because we'd been mentally tuned for the traditional goals, in which "junior executive," "four weeks paid vacation," and "a good pension plan" were key phrases. Other phrases, not spoken but strongly implied, were "Keep your nose to the grindstone"; "Don't aim too high"; and "Move up slowly."

A fortune was staring us in the face. All we had to do was look up.

All around us on the Jersey coast great old houses were being torn down. No one would live in them and no one would fix them up. Commercial builders weren't interested.

We saved these houses. We became professional recyclers.

That's how we did it.

Recycling Defined

We want to explain "recycling."

Recycling clothes, bottles, and metal is in great vogue. How do you recycle a house? Recycling a house means bringing it back to marketability from a worn-out unfashionable condition, making an older house comfortable, modern, and extraordinary. As recyclers, we buy, remodel, repaint, refurnish, restore, and modernize anything from mere bungalows to huge "architecturally significant" white elephants. We sell them as unique and highly marketable homes.

Recycling goes far beyond "home improvement." It is a different *kind* of thing. Home improvement means making changes regardless of whether they add a cent to the market value of the house or not. It is spending money without considering the financial return. By contrast, the word "recycling" includes making a substantial profit, as well as rehabilitation.

And make a profit we did. We got more and more expert at it. The professional pinnacle of our first ten years as recyclers was the rescue of Goldencrest, a historic Stanford White mansion in Ocean, New Jersey. We spent lots of money on expensive and authentic materials. We restored one dozen marvelous Victorian bathrooms, including the gold-leaf sinks. We replumbed the bathrooms very economically by getting our piping at the Englishtown, New Jersey flea market. In all, the changes did not cost us that much. When we were all through, neither did Goldencrest. It was not only beautiful, but a bargain.

We prefer Victorian houses, because it's easy to make them worth more by modernizing in a few key places. Moreover, we love working on the authentic restoration of fine Victorian carved wood ceilings, wainscotted walls, and parquet floors. It's great fun to polish and rehang original brass wall sconces and chandeliers and to figure out what furniture would go with what decor for forty-odd rooms. We always keep in mind the challenge of the bottom line: no sale, no recycle.

Recycling, therefore, is outside the scope of the contractor who renovates for an owner, for a price, and cares less whether or not the price is reflected in an increased market value for the house. What we do is also outside the scope of conventional restoration, because restorers have a "patron," even if it is only their own bank account. An authentic restoration isn't widely marketable. Who wants to cook in a Victorian kitchen? We have never had a patron, nor put money into a house we could not get back out. We have always been serious real estate entrepreneurs, producing houses that sell the day the house goes on the market.

So much for defining recycling. We will get into recycling in much detail—its defining characteristics—later on in the book. For now, let's turn to another subject, that of the attitude toward professional trades' skills necessary for success in the recycling business.

We decided early on to take the attitude—successfully, it now is obvious—that there is nothing essentially mysterious or unapproachably mystical about plumbing, electrical wiring, Sheetrocking, or any of a hundred related skills. We read the directions that came with the package. We asked a million questions. We were never too proud to say we didn't know.

In the end, we made a lot of money by asking questions. We always learned what we needed to know, in a practical sense.

What about money and our attitude toward it? Our attitude toward money was and is simple. We didn't take money as the reason for recycling. We took the recycling as a satisfying way of life.

The Ten Commandments

Then, the question is, since we were more interested in the recycling, the work, than in the money, how did we come to make so *much* money? By following rules we'd extracted out of our experience. We call them the Ten Commandments of Recycling.

Here they are:

1. Figure out where the sure profit is in a given house.
Somewhere there has to be a particularly profitable factor, or the house will not recycle well. More on that follows.

2. Make sure that the house recycles so economically that it can sell below the market price.
It's no good coming up with a house above market. It takes too much time to convince people it's worth buying. You want to be able to say with conviction, "This is a fantastic buy!"

3. Keep recycling after the first house.
If we'd hesitated very much when we saw what a gold mine our first house was, we still would be living there. We recycled 18 Beach Street and moved smartly on to houses two, three, and four.

4. Start to think big.
We started out redoing two-family dwellings, and today we do mansions. The profit on a big house is correspondingly big. A house worth $50,000 will ordinarily bring $5,000 to $10,000 profit, but a $250,000 mansion easily can bring in $50,000. A mansion is not all that much more work.

5. *Make a quick turnaround.*

Anybody can recycle a house in unlimited time. The trick is to do it fast and well. Doing three houses a year is more profitable than doing two. Recycling only one house a year is to work at a low rate of pay with no time off. You would be better off punching a time clock.

6. *Prefer the beauties to the beasts.*

We picked, when we could, houses with architectural status. We restored the fine irreplaceable architectural detail, which resulted in houses that were unique, irresistable, and profitable.

7. *Do the whole thing yourself, at least at first.*

There are some exceptions to this rule, as noted in the text later on. However, if you redecorate, restore, repaint, refurnish, rebuild, and redesign yourself, everything is under your control, and nothing gets out of hand. You learn enough so that later on you can supervise others without losing your profit.

8. *Do it full-time.*

There's a case for starting off with one or both people involved having a steady job, but that case gets weaker as the recycling profits build up. Without the distractions of a nine-to-five job, you can tackle any particularly nasty problem and get it out of the way reasonably quickly. Your overall recycling skills go up geometrically as you spend full time at it.

9. *Go in with one other partner.*

It is not always easy to make all your own decisions. A partner who can take an objective view of your ideas is invaluable. There are other advantages. In our case, we shared all the work equally, including housework and raising kids, and that sharing boosted our morale.

10. *Build a "creative identity."*

Be proud of what you are doing: recyclers save houses that

would otherwise have been lost, some of them iridescent gems of architectural art. Other houses would have lingered as decaying shells. A recycled house doesn't use up precious open space. It adds to community wealth. Be proud: you contribute to every community in which you work.

Do all these things and you will be a prosperous, happy recycler.

2

Recycling to Reverse the Money Drain

Our whole recycling enterprise was based on a theory, which we called the Definition Theory. Without it we'd never have reversed "the money drain" successfully. To see how this theory works, let's take a look at us—Sam and Mary Weir—a bit more than ten years ago.

We were fresh out of college, Penn State. We had a bank account that fluctuated from minus to zero. We certainly didn't look like system-beaters.

Now watch.

We were living in our small apartment. Sam had a job in chemical engineering. Mary was the childrearer (but was itching to get on with her career as an interior designer). In the previous twelve months, we had graduated, gotten engaged, married, and had our first son, Charlie. In November, 1965, we moved to Sea Bright, ninety minutes' commute from New York City.

Our apartment at 1390 Ocean Avenue was newly repainted,

bright, and airy. It had two bedrooms and a large living room and kitchen. Nobody lived above us. Nice quiet quarters. After a couple of months, we couldn't wait to move out.

Both of us loved to do things with our hands. The projects multiplied. Mary soon had a hard time finding room for her painting easel. Sam's Sprite engine parts were lying underfoot. Scattered about were furniture refinishing projects, knitting work—twenty things going at once. There was room for the projects but not for entertaining our friends, too. Social life was difficult.

Then we bought a baby grand—and found out the hard way that we didn't have the room for it. We got it in the door, but we had to leave it standing on end.

Finally, there was the family in the next apartment. They hinted from time to time that Mary really ought to clear off her paints and Sam should get his engine off the floor. We realized that we could use less intrusion.

We made up our minds to buy a house.

This was where we split from the norm. There was no *way*, in conventional terms, that we could afford a house.

We found out how to do it.

This jelled into the Weir Definition Theory.

The Definition Theory

In school, teachers define problems for you to solve. We decided that *defining* the problem is where you *solve* the problem. Defining is a lot harder than solving. There are more people who have problems they don't know how to define than there are people who can successfully define the problems they have. If you can successfully define it, you can solve it.

The trick is to define the problem in various ways until one definition *points to the solution.*

One way of defining our problem was that we didn't have enough money to buy a house. The going price of a modern two-bedroom in Sea Bright was $15,000 at the time, which meant a down payment of about $6,000 or $7,000, which meant, forget it. No chance of getting our hands on that kind of money. Two thousand, *maybe*.

Another way of defining the problem: we lacked the money to buy a house deemed suitable.

The solution, then, slowly but surely dawned on us. It was to find the kind of house that we *could* buy—forget about what was suitable. What could we buy for $2,000? We went to a real estate agent, and found out that we could afford a $4,500 house, $2,000 down. Was there anything in that range?

Well, yes, but of course we wouldn't want *that* kind of house, would we? It was a fisherman's row house. It had no basement, a frequently flooded first floor, no heat, no insulation, and some no-good plumbing. A charming vacation shack at best, unfit for year-round habitation. We bought 18 Beach Street.

We then defined our next problem. We didn't know enough *yet* to make this house livable. But we learned. In logical order, we built a higher foundation, put in a heating system, insulated the roof and walls, replaced the plumbing. Instead of being intimidated by the messiness of the house, we made it our turning point.

Plenty of young people have taken on a house that was on its last legs, rehabilitated it, and then stopped. We decided to do more than that. And we weren't going to have one foot in an office job for very long. If you look at where we started—college, intellectual pursuits, paper shuffling, corporate orientation—you will see that we had a long long way to go. We'd stepped gingerly into a world we didn't know. But it had been the right move. Thanks to the Weir Theory of Definition.

We started operating in the real estate field, first solving problems by creatively defining them, then lining up all the solutions, and starting to work on the solutions in logical priority.

Two years later, we'd practically paid off our loans on 18 Beach. We had a tidy income-producing resource. We could have moved out and rented the house at what we originally paid for it—making back our purchase price every twelve months. We said, "My that's nice," and continued for a while doing what we'd been doing. Sam devoted his energy to his work, which had to do with the purification properties of clay soil.

Life Plans

One thing that pushed us out of the rut was our planning sessions during our first year of marriage. We were used to planning. Our school careers, which consisted of getting through on minimum money, depended on good planning. We were getting along on almost nothing in our first year of marriage because Sam's pay wasn't all that good and we had college debts to repay. Consequently, we did not get into a morass of installment debt that makes newly married couples prisoners of the system. (It does make you eager to do your job, but for the wrong reason.) Even so, as we sat down that first year and figured out optimistically what Sam would make as he rose in the ranks, and what we needed for a decent house, and, allowing for inflation, what we needed for our two kids' education, we came up with the sure prediction that Sam would be working forever, and Mary, too, on a nine-to-five job to pay for all this. We couldn't have afforded to retire.

What a prospect that was to us, in our twenties!

We had started out with the idea that once we had gotten married, had kids, and Mary could get to work, we could be living comfortably ever after. Our figures showed no such thing. "Comfortably ever after" wasn't automatic at all.

We decided then that the system is geared to slowly drain off your savings, leaving you to die just as you become a certified pauper. This is hardly a joke. We know today formerly well-to-do couples who just can't wait, now that they are retired, for their Social Security checks to come around every month so they can start eating well again.

It looks easy to save up for your old age, when in point of fact, it is not. The usual retirement plan is based on bank interest; and the devastating effect of inflation is ignored. Inflation reduces the value of a retired person's savings to the point where he sees poverty setting in after a few years. On the other hand, people still working have the leverage to bid up their wages, increasing inflation still more.

If you are not working, the system discards you. That is the clear message.

When you invest in a retirement fund, it's simply like having dollars in a bank. The bank gives you a long-term interest rate, which the bank hopes will be less than inflation, since if the bank pays out more in interest than inflation rises, the bank loses. Nine times out of ten, the bank wins. Thus, retirement plans work only for people who retire with so much money that it doesn't really matter if the dollars they get per year slowly lose a bit of buying power every year.

One alternative is to try to make it big in the stock market. This entails risk of losing the whole thing. Most people can't afford that risk. (Never put anything into the stock market you can't afford to lose!) In the era right after World War II, when you had to be terribly unlucky to fail to make money, the investment in stocks and bonds was another thing. But that time will never come again. The market now, like the roulette wheel, causes more people to lose their shirt than to get rich.

Surely, though, with a good college education and enough dedication to the job, your salary will increase through the years sufficiently for you to put away enough money so that you have a comfortable old age? Right? Wrong!

A New Age of Less

What is happening now is different from what has been happening through the country's history up to now. The free land into which the country's growing population could expand and put down roots has gone. The world market begging for our products, the condition right after World War II, is gone. In a sense both our country and our world frontiers have closed.

One of our favorite authors, J. Phillips Johnston, has written in his fine book, *Success in Small Business is a Laughing Matter,* that what used to be opportunity has now turned to frustration. To back up his argument, he quotes Stephen Dresch, chairman of the Institute for Demographic Studies: "In a traumatic reversal of historical experience, children born to parents who entered adulthood in the 1950s and 1960s will, on the average, experience relatively lower status than their parents. This will reflect both the declining educational attainments induced by the saturation of the highly educated labor market and contracting career opportunities facing those who do in fact complete education programs."

Johnston argues that if you work it out properly, you can have a small business and thus shelter a lot more income for your retirement than if you work for a corporation all your life in an unequal battle with the money drain.

This is where recycling came to our rescue.

As we advertised our spare apartment for rent at 18 Beach, we got into the habit of looking through the real estate sections. It was obvious that out there all around us were lots of good "fix up" houses begging to be bought. Not at the ridiculously low price for which we had bought 18 Beach, but still at prices that (knowing what 18 Beach could now be remortgaged for) were well within our reach. We figured out one night what we'd be able to make if we could take on, and fix up, a second house; we extrapolated that into the future in terms of successive houses we could buy. And *then* a light went on.

Recycling allows you to invest your time now for big future profit. If you have no capital, you can still better your future position without putting in a cent, if you recycle houses. If you stay on your job, your future is all in your boss's head, and who knows *what* will come out.

So we risked our time. And we won. Easy.

Our life style has meant such a great decade for us that we're glad to share our enthusiasm and know-how. If you don't believe that after finishing this book, come down to 91 Rumson Street in Rumson, New Jersey and watch us work.

Everything you'll see there is here in this book.

3

Recycling Beats the System

House recycling works such miracles financially only because recycling works through a "multiplier" in the system.

The system is set up to allow a married couple to make money eventually on one home—but not until they're nearing their so-called golden years. The couple is to be motivated to buy their home and keep it until such time as they are ready to retire. A mortgage loan allows a couple to borrow money on their house at low interest until they finally sell it. Inflation increases the price of a house faster than almost any other kind of goods. And so the couple has, to a limited extent, beaten the system—up to retirement. Then, as we've seen, the system beats them.

The way around the system is to get into more than one house at a time. By getting into a number of houses at the same time, you take the leverage offered by society for one house and make that leverage work for your own purposes in a *multiple* way, in many houses.

Just to show you how this "multiplier effect" works, we've

made up the chart of the thirty houses and land parcels we've recycled in our first ten years and inserted it at the beginning of the book.

Step-by-step, our "net worth" has risen from house to house; reinvesting the profit from the one to the next, we pyramided it until we've gotten to be worth a real pile of cash, if we should sell it all. It's a record that any intelligent, competent couple can duplicate. Everything you need to know, you can learn.

The table shows "equity building." Equity is what is left after you subtract all the money owed on a house from its current value. Once we got started, we "built equity" fast. Bankers who had been lukewarm when we wanted our first mortgages were positively charming when we came in for our fifth, sixth, and subsequent mortgage loans. Banks *love* to make secure loans. That's the way they make money.

And now we come to a salient point.

Equity is the best kind of net worth to have, because *equity is not taxed until the house is sold.*

The profit and loss we're showing in the table is partly in cash but mostly in equity which turns to money when we choose to sell our properties. Some of the houses we own we won't sell now because we don't need the money.

Our enterprise is one of the few small businesses where the owner can exercise the pleasant option of not selling while still having income (rent) from his product, and taking advantage of inflation and increased demand (appreciation) through having made a good choice in the first place. You're *always* guaranteed against the ravages of inflation, since the market value of a properly recycled house rises as fast as inflation.

And, you can borrow money on the *increased* value of your house. You can, in effect, expand your business without having to take the profit and pay the taxes. You simply remortgage the house at the new inflated value and use the money to buy more houses.

There is some risk in having your money tied up in houses. If you suddenly need cash and don't have any, you can't sell a house overnight. (If you're not mortgaged to the hilt on every house, of course, you can raise cash with an additional mortgage.)

We always have an emergency cash reserve for contingencies such as sudden sickness, and for living expenses, of course, in case we can't sell our houses as fast as we planned.

On the other hand, if you have a savings account and want to get top interest from a bank (and top interest is the only rate worth earning), you have to tie up your money for six or eight years. If you pull out before then, you get penalized back to the lowest rate they offer. If you own a house, you can certainly sell it in less than six months; in the meantime, you'll earn a higher amount on the money invested than if you'd gotten the top bank interest.

The housing market is always on the rise. There just aren't enough houses to satisfy the demand. People compete with one another for every decently-priced house that comes up for sale. A house is a lot nicer to you than a bank.

Recycling Advantages

To sum up:

There are six great advantages to investing your time and money in recycling.

1. You get "paid in houses," so your total net worth rises with inflation. As the cost of living goes up, you get an automatic compensatory cost-of-living raise—a raise in the amount of value in the house.

2. When you *sell,* your profit is greater than if you'd put the same amount of cash into a bank for the same number of months.

3. You can *rent* out a refinished, recycled house for more per year than you'd get in interest from putting cash (the value of the house) in a bank.

4. Your risk is very much less than in the stock market, and your profit much greater, on the average.

5. You have a choice: build up your equity by living frugally, or sell out soon and pick up an immediate profit.

6. You pay a capital gains tax at half of the average income tax rate.

Compare the situation of the corporation executive who gets handed a raise. If he's upped $10,000 a year, the government nicks him for half of that. In recycling, if you make $10,000 profit, you can avoid that nick by carrying the house, instead of selling it, as its value goes up. Recyclers can keep postponing taxes all the way down the line until they stop working, by choice or necessity. When you do sell the house, you only get hit for a quarter of the $10,000. That's why we say that if you make $10,000 recycling houses, it's like making $20,000 punching a time clock.

Is this fair? You bet. It's the heart of the American system.

The tax laws encourage people to become entrepreneurs, to do creative, innovative, or at least profitable things. It's the government's way of saying, "If you are ambitious and smart, and you can create wealth in your community, we are going to exempt you, for as long as you choose, from the taxes others have to pay. When you do pay them, it will be at a lesser rate and at a more favorable time."

On the question of increasing a community's wealth: This gets to be a bit abstract in the case of a corporation executive, because while he conceivably does help create community wealth by his activity, the connection to any community is remote. But, in a house-recycling situation, the figures are black and white. We take a house worth $5,000 and make it worth $20,000, so we've definitely created $15,000 of wealth in that community. And the community can now take increased taxes, based on the increase in the value of the house. So the community is getting more into its treasury, year by year.

Not only does a recycler make money for himself but for the community, without requiring increased investment in public services or taking up open space. From a civic standpoint, you are an asset. And you are rewarded accordingly.

4

Making Recycling Profitable

Our kind of recycling is keyed to *specific* dollar-and-cents profit rules.

We have what we call the Weir Chain of Eight: eight links that have to be forged to make certain you're going to profit as much as you should.

The goal is to give yourself the breaks. You can't afford to go bust. One really bad mistake *can* do you in. If you're not absolutely certain you can make money, pass up the deal and keep looking. Another deal will come along.

Chain of Eight

Here are the eight links:

1. Bargain location: a house that can become worth a lot more just because of *where* it is.

2. Positive cash flow option: the monthly mortgage payment, plus the monthly cost of your personal loan installment (for the

down payment) plus the monthly home improvement loan installment (for materials) plus monthly carrying cost (tax, insurance, utilities) have to total *less* than the monthly rent you can conservatively expect when you finish recycling. This applies when you intend to rent your recycle. In your early recycling, you always recycle a house you can rent. You keep the renting option open, even if you eventually sell.

3. Appreciation potential: the house as it stands has to *lack* one or more important things. When the lacks are filled by recycling, you get a great increase in value *right away*. If a third bathroom costs $2,000 and it only adds $2,000 in value to the house, you *don't* put it in. But if the house lacks a second bathroom, and it's likely to raise the value of the house by $6,000 on resale, you put the $2,000 bathroom in real quick.

4. Minimum outside labor input: if you pay too many others to help out, you only come out even. You have a limited number of houses you can do in your life, and you want to make a substantial profit on each. Outside help eats up profits.

5. Minimum cost materials and furnishings: this doesn't mean inferior materials. But it does mean you go to the flea markets and estate auctions, that you tear down old buildings for lumber and fixtures rather than going to your local hardware or lumber store, where prices are bound to be the maximum. Most people don't have old buildings standing around, but sometimes their friends do, or sometimes you can find out who owns an old building and offer him a modest sum for the salvage rights.

A plumber friend of ours rebuilds and then rents houses. He used to buy his plumbing at his regular discount. When he saw the prices we were paying for "distressed" plumbing, he quickly switched to the flea market circuit and halved his investment in plumbing. (And he was in the business!) If we'd started out learning from him, we'd probably never have thought of getting our plumbing at the flea market.

6. Special appeal: give a house appeal as, for instance, an appeal to an expansive life style; "special features" make any house worth a lot more to the right buyer. For instance, we were able to sell very profitably a ski house to a skier because we

divided it into three apartments. The rentals on two units carried the third, which meant he could ski free.

7. Stable municipal tax rate: your buyer isn't going to be happy if he knows the town tax rate is spiraling, particularly if he's buying a retirement house. If you rent out a house where taxes are rising, you are going to have to charge more than landlords in any nearby town which *does* have a stable tax base. So you are put into a bad marketing position.

8. Favorable zoning code: if the local code prevents you from making the house profitable, you are better off not buying in. Subdivision laws are particularly important.

That's the Eightfold Way to big profit per recycle. And a big profit per recycle is not only nice but necessary. You are not a production-line builder. You have to make your living on a regular basis on at most, two, three, or four houses a year.

Let's have a look at profit. It's a simple concept. You need to be able to handle the concept so that you have some idea of whether you are making money or not.

To figure profit, add up (1) the cost of the house, (2) the cost of your own labor figured on a union wage scale (when you do work on a house, figure that you "pay yourself" the same amount that skilled labor would earn working for you), (3) the cost of the materials, and (4) miscellaneous costs (legal, closing fees, outside labor, cost of advertising or brokerage fee, etc.). Add the four. Subtract the total from the current market price (plus any rent you've collected through the years). That's profit.

Take a $15,000 house into which you put $8,000 of labor, $2,000 in materials, and $2,000 in miscellaneous. That adds up to costs of $27,000. If you can sell the house for $30,000, then your profit is $3,000. In addition to wages you paid yourself ($8,000), you were paid profit for cleverness, a bonus of $3,000 for using your head.

Pick a profitable situation to begin with. Follow the Weir Chain of Eight. A series of profits equals success!

Let's take a look at a couple of links in the Chain of Eight, just to expand the ideas in them.

No. 4: minimum of outside labor input.

This is an important one. Psychologically, the recycler who

envisions running a big labor force right away is in the wrong business. If you don't like doing things yourself, you won't be good at figuring out how to do them cheaply. Someone else is going to have to figure it out for you. If he could figure things like that out, he'd be in recycling for himself. So you aren't going to have a cost-effective, top-quality job unless you know how to do it yourself.

The minute you get an army of working people around, your efficiency can go down if some people are sitting and waiting for other people. The costs can get out of hand. If you are not working your crew *very* efficiently, you end up selling at a much smaller profit, or even losing money. We work hard for ourselves; but, we don't expect that the outside electrician or construction worker we hire is going to work *as* hard. Why should he? The harder the hired labor works, the more profit we make. He doesn't get a cent more.

Let's take another one of the factors, one that isn't quite so simple.

No. 1: bargain location.

There's the old story about the Down East mechanic who sometimes could take a hammer and hit a balky auto engine on the right spot, close the hood, and the engine would start. He charged $10 a hit: 2¢ for wear on the hammer and $9.98 for knowing where to hit.

Just buying any old house and saying you are going to recycle it doesn't mean you are going to make money. You have to know "where to hit."

If you live in a modern suburb where all the houses are less than ten years old and have all the standard modern conveniences, unless there's an aircraft plant going in south of town, it's impossible for you to make money there. There's very little you can do to a tract house that will raise its market value, regardless of how much more comfortable and fun the house will be. A three-bedroom, $50,000 model isn't going to become worth $60,000 no matter what you do, including adding a swimming pool and salting the flagstone patio with gold dust.

You get the idea. You can't just blindly pick a house in any town. You have to have the right house in the right part of the right town. Location is so important that even if you have other unfavorable factors, the location in and of itself can compensate and make the house extremely worth recycling.

Recyclable Locations

Here are some typical indicators of "recyclable locations":

Blocks where some houses are renovated, others not. When you recycle, your house's value will take on that of its renovated neighbors.

Any location near a college, army installation, or a big factory complex. These are good rental situations.

Near a park, playground, or school: people like the convenience.

Sometimes you can find a whole town that is a "recyclable location."

A resort town, particularly one with a fashionable high season. High season rental can very nearly carry the house, and the rest is profit. Aspen, Colorado, comes to mind, and East Hampton, New York, back about fifteen years. And Sea Bright today.

An expanding artists' colony. Traditionally, the artists are closely followed by the young and by people who want to be part of the excitement. Aspen and East Hampton developed that way; Sea Bright hasn't yet, but, its day may come. Even so, we lucked into a great "recyclable location" in Sea Bright and in nearby Rumson. (Rumson had a good many beautiful old houses, "unmodern" and deteriorated.) Yes, we were lucky.

But, what you *do* with luck is everything.

What we did was keep on buying houses, and as we became more experienced, we found we could pick out a "potentially recyclable" house almost on sight—in the newspaper ad. And, we could quickly confirm it by going out to look. We were cautious, and took our time. We looked at fifty houses for every one we bought. When we *found* one, we would hock every bit of our "remortgagability" (the added value of our houses since the last mortgage) to get our hands on the house before it was sold or torn down.

After ten years of learning how to make a profit, when we added the profits up, we found ourselves in our present situation.

Rich.

5

You Have to Like It

This chapter is about attitude.

Let's start out with the observation we've made of other recyclers. We've seen some who go into it because they think they can make money, but they don't really like the work. They don't do well. You always have to keep the bottom line in mind, but if the reason you are into recycling is only to make money and, frankly, you'd rather be sitting down with a group of brokers to talk stock market all day, you are not going to make out as a recycler.

Not only is recycling something that you have to think about logically, and be clear about in financial terms, you also have to *want* to do it. It's tiring, even tedious, unless you get a big bang out of it. If the idea of rehabilitating a house you've saved from the wrecker's ball and selling it to a grateful new owner at a fair price doesn't turn you on, then forget it.

Recycling is a trade, a craft, an art, and even a science, but it's not for dyed-in-the-wool white-collar workers. You get your hands dirty. You can't get your fingernails clean every night. Some nights you are too tired to take a bath. There has to be something to keep you going, and that has to be pride in what you are doing, and pride in being able to create with your hands.

If you don't like it, you won't be in a creative frame of mind. If you are not in a creative mood, you will make many decisions that don't work out. Being in recycling for money is like playing tennis only to win. If that's all that's on your mind, you won't play your best tennis. You have to love tennis itself, enjoy the actual physical process of the game. A good recycling job *is* like a good game of tennis. You do things that surprise your co-workers, even surprise yourself. You think, wow, I really did it! And you're not even sure of where those lifesaving moves came from. Without that kind of inspiration, recycling is dull and very likely not profitable, either.

Let's talk about physical risk.

Recycling requires long hours and a certain amount of danger. No more, probably, than riding around the block in a car. But, as in driving, you have to be alert. Otherwise, recycling can be hazardous to your health.

It's hard to be careful when you work on ladders all the time, or have to stand in awkward, narrow confines to finish off a job. Even if you keep your mind on what you are doing, there's danger. Once Sam tested a ladder we had decided to use, and just to make sure, he jumped up and down on every rung while the ladder stood against the house. Mary, being five-three to Sam's six feet, had to go up *one* more rung on the ladder than Sam had tested. That rung cracked. Mary caught herself after dropping down to the next rung, but it was a real scare. She was at second-story level, and a fall from that height would have been serious.

Sam actually did fall once. The ladder had given way, and dropped him right to the lawn. Mary was unaware of what had happened, but she heard a sound and looked down to see Sam making some somersaults down the lawn. She thought Sam was just fooling around. But it was Sam trying to break his momentum by rolling out of the fall. The neighbors came running across the lawn to help Sam. Only then did Mary realize that it hadn't been a game. We now use only aluminum ladders.

Still want to be a recycler?

If physical work and some physical risk really give you pause, then don't do it. On the other hand, there are benefits to physical labor. The manual work is hard, sure. But it also puts you in top physical condition. You don't need a gym membership.

Priorities

Let's talk about priorities.

One of the reasons we succeeded right from the start was our ability to put the houses first. Our success wasn't due simply to willingness to ask questions, do the hard work and financial figuring. It wasn't just the fact that there were all these great real estate buys around. It was that our entire lifestyle centered on houses. This meant that the lifestyle was spartan.

Every cent we earned that was not immediately needed for subsistence was ploughed back into the houses to keep the recycling momentum going. We'd find houses that fit the recycling formula, houses we simply felt we *had* to buy as they came up. Somehow we raised the cash needed. We did it by living on the edge financially. Some would say over the edge. To us it was exciting. And rewarding.

So many houses kept coming up that we *knew* were potential gold mines, we hated to let a single one of them go, even if we were currently working on three other houses—and our cash flow was down to a trickle. It was the time to buy. We bought and bought. We dickered with owners to make down payments as small as possible. Until the house could be recycled and sold, we ran up our bills and lived on credit. Then we sold, and the cycle would start all over again.

At one point, in 1970, we had signed up for a European ski trip—a rare luxury. Then, 78 Ocean Avenue came up for sale.

We knew that we had to get this one before anyone else, but we had no money. We cancelled our trip, remortgaged three houses, and raised the needed $26,000. That's commitment to the priority of recycling. The technical knowledge and skill needed to be a successful recycler are important, but the commitment is even more important.

The biggest force acting against commitment was advice by well-intentioned friends who thought that we were not doing what (1) a good parent or (2) a good engineer or (3) a good housewife *ought* to be doing. It's very hard to avoid being overwhelmed by other people's ideas on how you *should* be spending your time. Or how they spend their time. They spend forty-five minutes over coffee and the paper every morning: maybe you feel you need it. But, what about financial security? Which do you need most?

It's a question of priorities.

It was soon evident to us that we had to look hard at everything we were doing and evaluate any activity in terms of: (1) Is this project worth doing at all? (2) Is this project being done in the most effective sequence? (3) Is this the fastest and best way to do the job?

If the answer to all three was "Yes," then we proceeded with the project. This is discipline.

Everybody Else

Our parents, who were nearest and dearest to us, did not understand what we were doing at all. This was very hard on us. We came from traditional families: all were solid citizens. They were all upset because our lifestyle didn't follow their example.

Either you set yourself up in your modest house and job, then spend five years leisurely saving money to put down on a somewhat more substantial house, or you set your goal as a priority and go for it. You can't do both.

We lived in eight houses in ten years to reach our goal: financial security and finding a satisfying career. Now, we are at the point where, if we wanted to, we could sit around all day, drink vodka gimlets, and worry about our golf score. But the moments we feel most alive are those when we get up in the morning to face a series of problems, a series of "fascinating opportunities cleverly disguised as complete impossibilities." If there is one very marked change in us over the ten years, it is that, ten years ago, we worried about whether we could solve those problems or not. Today we know we can.

Before you decide to recycle as a career, take time to think over the tradeoffs. The plus side is very rewarding; the minus side is there, too.

The plus side is that you control your own time. If you want to go skiing, you decide when you do it. That is a plus. You usually have to work harder to give yourself the free time to do it in—that is the minus.

We make sure that we make time every year to spend three or four weeks skiing Aspen, Vermont, or Europe. We both love skiing, Sam loves sailing. He makes sure that he gets time to sail his catamarans, redesign rigs, build experimental hulls, and attend seminars for multihull sailors. A sparkling morning on the Atlantic off the New Jersey coast, whipping along in a terrific breeze, is worth a few late nights spent finishing up a plumbing job.

Mary makes time to do things that give her pleasure. She loves classical music and is an accomplished pianist. She is currently studying voice. During working hours, it isn't unusual to hear Mary, from her perch on a painting ladder, singing arias while stenciling a border design. Besides developing Mary's technique, it keeps whoever else is around entertained.

In recycling, the choice of tradeoffs is constant. You don't have the decisions resolved for you in terms of weekends and vacations from your job. Our life is freer than most, more fun than most, and has tremendous flexibility. We love it. But you *have* to love it.

part 2

Five Basic Recycling Decisions

6

Finding Sure-Fire Recycling Opportunities

This is the first chapter of a section dealing with making some basic decisions in your recycling career. The first of these is finding the right kind of house, the "sure-fire" profit-makers. The second is almost as vital: once you have your house, what are the things you should do to it, and what are the things you should *not* do to it?

Beyond that, there is the question of whether or not you should go full time into recycling, and if so, when? This is one that we faced, and decided positively, quite early in our careers.

The final two chapters in this section cover decisions on making use of the law and picking a lawyer. Nowhere is the chance of tripping up as great as when dealing in legal matters. It counts heavily whether or not you decide right away in your career to make the best use of the law, and to find a lawyer who will help you do just that. This is a decision you will make whether or not you are aware of it. If you more or less ignore the decision, you have then decided negatively, with all the consequences that might follow legally.

Here we go with the first of the basic recycling decisions, then:

The prime decision in recycling is picking the right kind of house to recycle. At first in our career, we picked houses that sort of *looked* like they would be good recycles. We were stung a couple of times, and we quickly learned to distinguish between "sure-fire" situations and marginal ones.

We wanted to be able to spot sure-fire recycles at a glance; so, we sat down one day and put on paper the factors that make up a profitable recycle. They are: (1) low original cost before recycling, (2) potential large amount of "added value" in recycling, and (3) high automatic appreciation of the property thereafter.

Sure-Fire Types

These three factors in various combinations make for what we have called *The Five Sure-Fire Recycling Types.* These are the five where you make real killings, and the size of the killings is in ascending order, from Type I to Type V.

Type I is distinguished by factors (1) and (2). It has an especially low cost and large "added value." This is ideal for rental, so we call Type I the "Rental Recycle."

It's ideal for beginner recyclers because of the low initial cost, and because on a *per property* basis, it's more profitable than Type II, where you recycle to sell. We spent the first five years of our career in rental recycling. Rentals are also called "income property."

The reason for beginning with a low-cost house to recycle for rental is that if you start with an expensive house you are then into high rents, competing with apartment builders dealing in luxury apartments. A recycler has no business being there. The apartment builders have too many advantages, including access to capital at low interest, and very likely good political connections, as well. Also, if you are offering a house or a large floor-through apartment in the high rental market, you are getting into a price range where it pays a potential renter to buy rather than rent.

On the other hand, since almost no one is building low-cost rental houses and apartments these days, there's a terrific demand for them. You have no trouble and waste no time getting your place rented. If you can buy a house for under $30,000, you can recycle it into a rental worth $40,000 in six months. All you'd have to charge for the house would be about $350 a month to make it worth $40,000 on the market as "income property."

There is one exception to avoiding high-price rentals: in a resort area, "high season rentals" over three months or so can carry the whole mortgage. Here, commercial builders are often at a disadvantage because of the high cost of getting the materials into resort areas, or they may be restricted as to the kinds of apartments or condominiums they can build.

To summarize the Type I recycles:

1. low-cost single-family house rentals
2. low-cost two-family house rentals
3. high-cost resort single- or two-family rentals

OK, so you have found a house that *seems* suitable for a rental recycle: it's a low-priced building and you can see how to improve it to charge a healthy rent without getting out of the modest rent bracket. How do you know whether it's a Sure-Fire Type I or not?

There's a quick way to find out. (Terms used will be defined shortly.)

First figure out what your monthly costs will be. The monthly costs are the monthly *mortgage loan* you will pay off, plus monthly payment on the money you borrow to make the down payment, plus the money you borrow (or raise) to pay for *materials* (figured on a monthly basis for the duration of the recycle), and the monthly *carrying charges*. To make a Sure-Fire Type I, you should see at least 50 percent *more* coming in monthly in rent than you have going out monthly in costs during the recycle.

This is the *Weir Fifty Percent Rule.* Here's the way it works.

Let's take an example where your monthly mortgage payments on the house are $200, your loan to take care of your down payment is $100 a month, your materials during the recycle period (figure twelve months if it's your first recycle) will be $100 a month and your carrying charges (taxes, etc.) will also be $100 a month.

This means your recycle has a $500 a month "nut."

In this case, you should see $750 in rent coming in a month in order to make this a Sure-Fire Type I.

Defining Terms

Since some of the terms here may be unfamiliar to you, let's have a look at them:

Mortgage: this is a loan in which your house is a security. If you don't pay off the loan, you lose the house. The rate of this loan is low.

The bank will only give a mortgage for two thirds to three quarters of the cost of the house. The rest is the down payment.

On a $40,000 house, the bank will usually lend at least two thirds, or $26,000. You have to find the $14,000 difference (down payment) and pay it when you take over the house.

If you make a good salary, or have sufficient assets (not pledged for any other loan), the bank might well lend you the entire $14,000 but it would be a personal loan, at a higher rate than the mortgage.

Suppose you have the $14,000. You still should figure in what the monthly payment on a $14,000 personal loan *would* be, because you are lending yourself the money, losing the interest you would have gotten if you invested the money elsewhere.

When you take out a personal loan, find out how much you get back if you finish the recycle ahead of time, that is, before your loan runs out at the bank, because you can save some money by paying the loan back early. Some banks have better pay-back-early setups than others. That is, some banks give you more credit for paying back early than others. Shop around for the best deal. As you get better known in the bank, you can ask for an even better deal.

Materials

Later on we get into estimating the cost of recycling materials. But assuming now that you can estimate the cost for the house, then divide that cost by the number of months you will be recycling the house, and you get your monthly materials cost figure. You may be able to borrow this amount from the bank on the basis stated above. If you can't, then you *must* raise the cash somehow *before* you're committed to the recycle. Otherwise you may get held up in the middle of your recycle, and not be able to finish. Then you are in the home improvement business, where time is not of the essence. If you take three years to redo a house, you have a hobby that may pay off, but it's not recycling, as we see it. (In a later chapter we get into raising cash.)

Carrying Charges

Add up the property tax for the year, the utility bills, a year's insurance premiums, plus the legal fees. (See Chapter 9 to get your total carrying charges and divide by twelve to get your monthly carrying charges.)

OK, so you now have four monthly costs all figured out. When you add these up, take 50 percent of their total amount and add it to the final amount. If this final figure is equal to or less than what you expect in rent, buy it!

The Weir Fifty Percent Rule is a rough measure, but it's easy to use, and we have used it successfully to make our recyclings come out profitably for us, time after time. You can make logical objections to the rule, but as for whether or not it works, well it does work. And if you can't see that much, 50 percent more coming in, then don't buy.

If you do buy something that doesn't make the grade (later on we tell you how to figure what kind of rent a place will bring once recycled), then you are liable to end up having a place that costs you let's say $20,000 to buy and $10,000 to recycle and getting $30,000 for it, in terms of rent and an eventual sale. In that case, what's missing are wages for your labor.

And it's pretty hard to have three square meals a day on zero wages.

On the other hand, if you do pass up all the tempting places that don't quite make it to Sure-Fire status, and wait for that one house which makes it, then you are in good shape. You will make money.

Believe us.

Type II

Let's go on to Type II, the Buy-Sell.

You buy the house, recycle it, and sell it, rather than holding it for rent.

Why would you buy and sell when you could first buy, then rent and eventually sell and make more money than just buying and selling?

Well, above a certain figure, somewhere around $50,000, you have to charge so much for rent that you are then competing with people who build high rent apartments, and you are in no position to compete there. So if you have an expensive house, buy it, recycle it, but don't expect to rent it. Sell it.

The advantages to the Buy-Sell are:

First, there's no bother with renting out to people.

Second, if you get good at recycling, you can make more money in the Buy-Sell. Because, even though you make less money on each house, you can recycle a bigger number of houses. Selling four recycled houses in two years makes more money than renting and selling two houses in two years.

Spotting Type II

How do you spot a Sure-Fire Type II?

If you can see that the house will sell for more than 50

percent more than you paid for it, plus the amount put into it, then you have Type II!

The Weir Fifty Percent Rule applies.

For example: You see a $50,000 house (mortgage plus down payment) that will cost $15,000 to recycle in materials, and has $12,500 in carrying charges over the period of the recycle (by the time you are into Buy-Sell, your recycle period should be down to six months), then you have a $77,500 "nut."

In order to buy that house you should be certain that after recycling, you can sell this house for $116,500.

If you are not sure, let it go!

We often look at three or four *dozen* houses before we find one to fit the Fifty Percent Rule.

And we wait for it.

Question: What kind of profit are you actually making?

Answer: Quite a bit.

Profit is figured on the money put up at risk.

The money you are putting up at risk is your down payment, your materials costs, your carrying charges, and your own labor (which is worth cash). Your mortgage money is not at risk because all that happens is that you lose the house and you really didn't own it anyway.

In order to figure your labor, you figure it at union wages, which is about $2,500 a month per person for the average construction work. If there are two of you, and you have a six-month recycle, that's two times $2,500 times six, or $30,000 worth of labor. (Some of the labor, you might hire others to do, of course.)

Now you add to that (to take the example we were working with in this section): $10,000 in down payment, $15,000 in materials, and $12,500 in carrying charges, over the six-month recycle. That means you are putting a total of $67,500 at risk.

And what was your actual profit in money?

Well, it's your "nut" ($77,500) plus your labor ($30,000) subtracted from the sale price. And since you sold for $116,500 your arithmetic is $116,500 minus $107,500, or $9,000.

And $9,000 is roughly 15 percent of the money ($67,500) you put at risk. This means you had a 15 percent profit. And that's about what any entrepreneur gets from putting money at risk. (The only hook is, we practically never take a risk because we follow The Fifty Percent Rule.)

Profit is not the same as wages.

Profit is what you get for using your head.

If wages are $30,000 for two of us, and with our profit, we two are making $39,000 for six months work. Not bad.

It's even better if we work faster.

Let's say the two of you finished in three months instead of six; then you are free to apply your labor to another recycling for the next three months. For the sake of argument, say that you went on to recycle a second identical house. Your labor remains the same, $30,000, because you still worked only six months. But, your profit *doubles.* You have an $18,000 profit. Labor ($30,000) plus profit ($18,000) comes then to $48,000.

Most important of all, wait for the Weir Fifty Percent Rule house! The recycler can't afford even *one* loss in buy-sell situations.

Here he is different from a commercial building contractor who has ten times the annual gross and a big organization behind him. The contractor can risk getting into a situation where the profit is slim. If he loses on one deal, he can carry the loss through to the next deal without going bankrupt. He's got a lot of cash flow—cash going in and out—and that's how he can carry his loss. He just pays out and keeps going until he makes more.

The recycler can't risk a slim profit margin. It may *become* slim, but in the beginning it should at least *look* very fat. We inspect fifty houses for every one we buy.

We once ran into a woman at a cocktail party who told us, "You know, my husband and I have been trying to buy another house for a year now, and just when we get ready to buy, and make a bid, we are told, the Weirs just bought that house. It's happened to us three times now."

When you look at fifty houses per buy, you really get the best ones, and usually get them first!

After you have looked and found a house where the Fifty

Percent Rule applies, you can go ahead and buy! Forge ahead. Don't let big figures throw you. If a house is worth $100,000 now, and you can make it worth $150,000 in six months, buy it! Don't be afraid to go into more than one house at a time because that runs up your total mortgage and bank debt.

We started out small, and borrowed $10,000 at a time. Then $20,000 at a time, and suddenly realized that we owed the banks a quarter of a million dollars!

In the next second, we realized that every one of our buys was a solid Type I or Type II. We had absolutely nothing to worry about.

Before we go on to Type III, let's distinguish Type I from Type II situations again.

A Type I rental is usually a low-priced house that can be upgraded to double or triple the rent through adding bedrooms, baths, or converting to a two-family. These are usually not particularly distinguished houses. They are primarily a low-rental housing deal. With the exception of the high season rental, you want to keep to low cost rentals, out of the luxury market.

A Type II situation is where the house is more expensive, and where the rent would be so high, if you tried to rent, that you would be competing in the luxury market. There, you know when you buy that you are *not* going to rent. You are going to sell. In terms of 1978 prices, the dividing line is somewhere between $40,000 and $50,000, depending on the neighborhood. Under $40,000 you have an advantage in rental, a big advantage over any other kind of recycle use. Over $50,000, you want to sell.

As said, in the long run, you get more *per property* from Type I, Rental Recycle. You buy them, fix them, rent them, and then sell them, you get rent income plus eventual capital gain. It's good for the beginner recycler, who is unsure of being able to make a quick turnaround.

The quick turnaround is the key to Type II, the capital gain type. Your profit per year goes up very rapidly as you get in and out faster. Turning out three to four Type IIs a year can bring *a lot* of money. The more money you have, the more expensive property you can buy, the bigger the profits.

So it's Type I "income property" for beginners—maximum profit for a given house.

And it's Type II "capital gain property" for advanced recyclers—maximum profit for a given year.

Type III

Now let's look at Type III, "investment property."

This is property that features factor (3) automatic appreciation, appreciating faster than inflation—say property whose value rises at 15-20 percent per year—because of its location or other factors. It could be waterfront property, or in a rapid-growth area. Everyone, of course, is out looking for this kind of property, since it's a solid form of investment, more secure than stocks and more remunerative than bonds.

The inflation rate for the last decade has been something between eight and ten percent. The appreciation percentage that makes any property a Type III then *has* to be in *excess of fifteen percent,* or it's not really Type III. You can get nearly eight percent risk-free by buying a savings certificate; so, to take some risk, you *ought* to be seeing 15 percent anyway.

Type III property is like a go-go blue chip stock; if you see one, take it! You don't need the Weir Fifty Percent Rule behind you.

Let's now go to the last two Sure-Fire Types:

Type IV is a combination of II and III. This is a house that is expensive, in the first place, but can be profitably recycled, that is, can have its value jumped at least 50 percent by recycling; beyond that, it's gaining on inflation by appreciating at 15 percent or more per year.

Obviously IV is better than any one of I, II, or III alone, so this is one to be on the lookout for. Our recycle at 78 Ocean is a Type IV: we recycled an expensive, beautiful house that was in such bad shape and had such outmoded baths and kitchen that we could jump the price 50 percent in a recycle. In addition, it was near the waterfront, in an area where property was going up at 20 percent per year automatically.

Type V is a combination of I and III. This is a house that will recycle to make a low cost rental. The property also is in an area where the price of properties is going up at 15 percent per annum or better.

Again, you can make an awful lot of money here: after you buy Type V, you can rent it after recycling; then you get further gain.

On a per property basis, it's the best money-maker of all. As it happened, our two first houses, 18 Beach and 265 Ocean, fell into this category, and gave us a jet boost into our career. (We sort of lucked into them by instinct; and then we looked back to identify the factors that made them so profitable.)

Success in recycling depends on your honing your perceptions so you can spot these five types. Often you will have a choice between a number of houses, and if you can see what types you are dealing with, you come to a quick decision. V is better than IV, III than II, etc.

Success depends in all, I to V, on getting good *estimates,* both as to added value after recycling and as to cost of materials needed to recycle.

Hereafter, in this chapter, we deal with value after recycling. (To get our thinking on the cost of materials estimating, turn to Chapter 11, on making estimates.)

Brokers

First, let's talk about the good side of brokers.

It can be tremendously helpful to cultivate one broker. A real estate broker can keep an eye open for property suitable for recycling, once the broker knows what that is. And, as you become a repeat customer, you get preferential treatment. The broker will soon realize that it's smart to act in your best interest. The broker will give you first crack at real buys. All this is good: your "regular broker" is a regular gold mine.

Second, let's talk about what can be bad about brokers.

As mentioned in the later chapter on the legal side of recycling, a broker who is not your "regular broker" can be carried away by the fact that there is a commission in the offing. The broker can "puff" the property—a certain amount of "puffery" is something you should expect. It's not that the broker is sneaky, just that the broker is trying to sell a property before another broker sells it, and under that pressure, the broker's judgment isn't something you should rely on totally.

Check everything that a broker says with another source. Check a broker's estimate of what the house would sell for (when properly fixed up) in newspapers, by comparing ads for houses in similar situations; check other brokers and, most of all, other recyclers in the neighborhood, if there are any.

Check any statements glossing over the functioning faults in plumbing with a local plumber, if you're not a good plumber yourself. Check any structural defects mentioned with the local building inspector. And so on.

We once took an agent's word for the fact that the potential sales price of a recycled house would be $40,000. What we found out was that, although the house itself was in the right class, it needed an acre of land *with* it in that neighborhood to sell for $40,000. We *actually* got $37,000, which means $3,000 came right out of our labor—it was work we did for free, just because we didn't do our homework. That hurt.

These few preceding paragraphs are an important *caveat,* or warning. *Caveat* is Latin; the Romans had a famous phrase: *caveat emptor.* "Let the buyer beware."

7

What to Do and What Not to Do to a House

A second set of decisions faces you once you've picked a Type I, II, III, IV, or V house: decide what to do and what *not* to do to that house.

We defined profitability as working on those things that raise the house's market value before anything else.

Again, a simple definition. It points to a solution. But it wasn't an *obvious* definition at all. We learned the hard way on that one.

Let's go back to our first venture. The fisherman's cottage at 18 Beach was a marvelous "classroom." There was—as we later saw—plenty of room for making mistakes. And we made them. But, under its shabby exterior and distressing problems, 18 Beach was a Type V!

It was recyclable as a low cost rental; it was also near the Jersey shore waterfront, where property appreciates if you just let it sit there at 15 percent and more. To maximize our profit, the best course was to recycle as a rental and then hold it until

45

we felt that we could use the sales profit quickly for an even more profitable recycle. This is precisely what we did.

At the early stage in our recycling career, we picked our buildings more by instinct than by reasoning. Our instincts, however, weren't all *that* sharp, yet. Where our instincts lacked refinement was in knowing—once we'd lucked into 18 Beach— what to do and what *not* to do with it.

We like to blame our lack of sharpness on the kind of "home remodeling" magazine reading that we were doing. Such writing lacks "dollar sense." The writer is going on the assumption that there's no important *investment* involved. For us, and for most families, that is simply not true.

Architects, too, can mislead. We work with some very good ones, architects who *understand* that renovation is a *family investment program.* We've also had some architects who ignored the fact completely. Such architects suggest things like adding rain gear lockers, garden tool storage, and outside basement access. All "very nice." But you can do all those things and *not increase the value of the house* on the market one penny.

The architect who says, "These poor people have no place to store their garden tools and rain gear" should be saying instead, "These poor people need a renovation that increases the house's *market value.* Their house is their big *investment.*"

Increasing Market Value

Let's turn to the subject of how to increase a house's market value then. For starters: add bedrooms, up to five in number. This goes whether or not *you* need the five bedrooms personally. It will still increase the market value of the house.

What else? Add bathrooms. For more than two bedrooms, a second bath adds market value. For more than four bedrooms, a third bathroom adds market value.

What else? The third market-value raiser is to redo a one family house so that it becomes a two-family house. Again, this seems pretty obvious; but, most people don't think about the option. (Making a house a *three*-family house may get you into a whole new set of rules and regulations; you may be under a "hotel law" or "multiple dwelling law" that you might not want to be under—so check that out before you go making a house more than two-family.)

The fourth most effective market-value raiser is to modernize the kitchen.

The kitchen is the place where offering the ultra-modern adds a lot to the potential value of the house. You may have to lay in a new electrical service (see Chapters 29 and 30) to offer a dishwasher, but it probably is worth it.

What all the foregoing comes down to:

In opposition to the usual idea, the time to worry is if you have a House Beautiful on your hands. Then there is not much you can do to it to raise its value on the market. But, if you have a house that's not so hot, you *should* feel reassured.

18 Beach

For instance, our first place at 18 Beach was a mess when we walked into it. The twelve-inch tiles on the kitchen floor, for instance, had warped because of the wetting action of the occasional storm tide that crept through the front door. The four corners of each tile had lifted and were pointing nearly straight up! In the pocket thus formed in each tile lay a musty pile of gunk. Sam's mother, who saw it before we got to it, is still talking about *that*.

We moved in on the day we took ownership papers because our apartment lease was up. It was on a cold April day; 18 Beach was damp and unheated. The plumbing had not been operative for years. Our gear lay piled in the middle of a very dank living room. We searched around for a faucet, preferably one that worked, to quench the considerable thirst worked up by carrying and hauling. We finally found one: the garden hose tap in back.

We weren't fazed. We just told ourselves, okay, so we haven't any water or heat, so we'll have to do something about that.

The thing we remember most is how super it was to have *space*. It was the first adequate space we'd ever owned. Happily, our joy did coincide with reality. We'd made a good investment. The one thing you could say about 18 Beach was that almost *anything* you did would make it worth more.

The first thing we tackled was the threat of a tide invasion. Eighteen Beach was about a foot off the ground, on four low cement piers. We hired an experienced "house-jacker." He raised the entire place six feet. Now we could build a full headroom basement which in a pinch would make a whole apartment floor, if we cared to go that far.

The process was a bit hairy. We had to go in and out the front and back doors on ladders until the jacking was finished. We would be lying in bed during a "jacking week" and wake up feeling the bed tilting (our man got to work on his house jacks early every morning). We'd glance up and spot a new crack making its way across the bedroom ceiling, like watching a crack grow in the ice on a pond.

Foundation Raising

It wouldn't have made sense for us to jack the house ourselves. That is a specialist's job. On the other hand, the new basement foundation wall was something we *could* build ourselves. Laying brick (or cinder block) is easy to learn. If you make a mistake— a brick or block is out of line—you can knock it off and reset it. There's nothing irrevocable about cementing.

The town building inspector, whom we had consulted on how to go about getting final approval, also turned out to be a contractor. He lent us his transit, a device that allows you to level off your wall properly by sighting through it. Between his advice and a how-to book on masonry, we learned enough to be able to tie off guide strings so the blocks would line up. We built the foundation quickly.

Mary insisted on doing an underpinning for the new front stair, using cinder block and doing it all herself; she mixed the mortar; she set each block. Several times, men driving home from work stopped off to help Mary mix a wheelbarrow full of mortar.

We never turned down help. And there's a lot of it around, if you look. Among the helping hands on the mortar-and-cinder block phase of the 18 Beach recycling were Sam's in-laws, the aforementioned strangers on the street, and the neighborhood kids.

Sam organized the neighborhood kids to play a game in which they went down to the beach with their tin buckets, brought up sand to mix in the mortar, and helped smear the resultant mix on the cinder block, which Sam would then chunk into place. When it got late, Sam would take all the kids down to the beach, go swimming with them, and always make sure they got all the cement off their skin before sending them home to their parents.

The front stairs became a marvel. There was no room for a straight stair up from the street to the front door, so Mary laid out a spiral stairway. To do the spiral stairway, a construction company would have had to bring in an architect, a blueprint man, a carpenter, a mason, and a helper. It would have cost a fortune. It cost us next to nothing. One reason it cost next to nothing was that we got the wood for the steps themselves off the beach: deck planks that had drifted in. Salvage.

The Weir Salvage Principle: *very often, you can take nothing and make it into something*. We turned what was firewood into an imposing addition to the house. We've since salvaged wood from old barns, out-buildings, and even abandoned farmhouses.

A recycler develops a "salvage eye" that enables him to find money in the street. We developed it; we had to, because we didn't have any money. A salvage eye can make the difference between some profit and a good profit. A salvage eye is priceless at an auction or a flea market.

Two things that every habitable house *has* to have (and 18 Beach, thank goodness, didn't have) is heat and plumbing. Your moderately knowledgeable buyer is always going to look at the plumbing carefully. And he's going to want a furnace that runs when you push the button.

We'll get into plumbing and heating at greater length later. But for now, we're just pointing out you can't start showing someone around a house saying, "Well, the furnace is off today but it usually works," or "Well, we have a little leak over in the corner of the basement from these pipes but it can be fixed." If the buyer has any sense at all, he's already starting for the door.

The same goes for electrical wiring. If your floor is a tangle of extension cords because you didn't put in the proper number of outlets, you'll be lucky if you don't trip up your prospects before you make your sales pitch.

Insulation: you might get away with renting a badly insulated house if you rent only in the summer. But if you're going to rent, you get back every cent that you put into insulation in reduced winter heating bills.

Wrong Moves

We finished the bottom apartment at 18 Beach by June, 1967, and rented that out. We moved upstairs. We put in a new kitchen there and finished off the apartment upstairs by January, 1968. Not too speedy, were we?

Well, what do you expect from beginners? At least, we were well into our careers as recyclers. We'd done a lot of things right. But we did a lot, too, that we didn't *need* to do.

For starters, we tore out a narrow thirty-inch-wide staircase one Saturday night and Sunday morning, easily the most emotional, least logical thing we did to the house. We had a huge pile of debris on Sunday to get rid of, and had no idea how to do *that*. Then, by the time we realized we were going to have to get a van to take it to the dump, we had wasted some more time casting around for alternatives. (The van we bought to truck the wood away was terribly useful, though.)

Today, we simply would not replace the stairway. It was serviceable. Rebuilding it cost us several hundred dollars, which was not going to show up in the increased value of the house. And the new stairway took us two weeks to build. All wasted.

Then there was the next most foolish thing we did—ripping out all the interior walls. True, we were then able to insulate very quickly; but there are ways of insulating *without* tearing down the walls.

Our misguided motive in tearing down the interior walls was to redo the house in pine paneling, as per *House and Home.* It took us three months, and much of Sam's salary, to get the interior looking properly suburban. Paneling is a really precise fitting job, and there's always so much more wall to a house than you think there is. The plaster walls we had replaced were adequate, and we could have made them look fine with wallpaper and a good spackle job, a rugged coating that will practically glue a house together by itself. Now we know!

The third mistake was replacing the windows. We took one look at the leaky window sashes, with their shabby-looking surfaces and decided we must have new windows. Replacing them took forever. It was expensive. Finally, we got smart. We looked at the last window and said, "That doesn't look too bad. Let's leave it in." And we devised a way to make *any* sash airtight. (See Chapters 23 and 24 on insulation.)

Doing Things Right

Even with all our mistakes, we did a great deal more right than wrong at 18 Beach. And yet that particular fact wasn't obvious.

At the time we were working on 18 Beach, one of our neighbors was at work on his house, too. He worked as hard as we did, maybe harder. He actually dug a basement for his house and cinder-blocked a new foundation for himself just as we had. But, in his case, the basement foundation he had was *already* adequate; his floor was never flooded on any tide. Second, he put a roof on his house when his present roof was perfectly good. By the time we'd moved out of the neighborhood, he'd put in a minimum of $3,000 in materials and an enormous amount of time. He'd raised the value of his $16,000 house to maybe $18,000. He'd lost money, on a cash flow basis alone, not to mention the value of his labor.

The standard price for a one-family house in that neighborhood eight to ten years ago was about $16,000. We had taken our $4,500 place and made it livable for $5,000 in materials. Our house now came up to the standards of the houses around it, so it was easily worth $16,000. Since our cost on paper was only $4,500 plus $5,000 in materials, our paper wages-plus-profit was the $16,000 it was now worth, minus the $9,500 cash we'd put into it, or $6,500 gained for two years' part-time work.

The Worst House

The neighbors we had in Sea Bright, however, couldn't see the difference between what we were doing and what our neighbor was doing. In fact, they felt he was working on a "nice" house while we were wasting our time working on a "shack." One of the neighborhood kids came by one day to tell us, "My mother says you were nuts to buy that house. It's the worst house on the block!" It was. But that was just *it*.

As a rule of thumb, we never buy the best house on the block. We are much more interested in the worst house on the block. Recycled, it will, at minimum, take on the average value of the houses around it.

When we moved out of 18 Beach two years after we bought it, we were able to rent the two apartments in the house for more than $3,000 a year net after expenses. Thus, over the ten years that we kept the house (we just sold it), we took in $30,000 on it just in rentals. Subtract from that our original $9,500 cost, and you have more than $20,000 in profit. With inflation, Type III (Investment Property) appreciation, *and* recycling's "added value," we sold it for $31,000. We made more than $50,000 on that one little house!

That's what you get for buying the worst house in the neighborhood.

8

To Quit or Not to Quit Your Job

Another basic decision in recycling is whether or not to quit your job. Quitting your job is something you do if you really want to recycle full-time. If you have serious doubts about going full-time, stick with your job. Some people find recycling too chancy, and that spoils the fun. Some don't like to get their hands dirty.

You have to like challenge and have the desire to get into recycling so deeply that the external circumstances don't really bother you. If your frame of mind is this affirmative, then quitting your job is primarily a matter of timing.

You can't quit your job if you don't have a sufficient bank account to tide you over the transition from part-time recycling to full-time recycling. Recycling provides at first only deferred income. Usually you can help tide yourself over by taking out a personal loan *before* you leave your job. Make it at least a three-year loan, so that you do not have to pay large installments.

Say you need $8,000 to make it through one year before your

first recycles pay off. You have only $5,000. You borrow $5,000 over three years, and at the end of a year you've only had to pay, let's say, $2,000 back. That still leaves you $5,000 plus $3,000, or $8,000 to live on. You pay the personal loan off with rent from recycled houses. Pretty soon you can remortgage the recycled houses and live off that. A remortgage rate is cheaper than a personal loan—by a country mile.

Breakthrough

Our second recycle at 265 New Ocean in Long Beach was our "breakthrough" house. We signed contracts for it practically on sight. We were shown the house, and we couldn't believe it! There it was, right on the Atlantic Ocean in New Jersey, going for $17,500. Amazing. Because we were Johnny-on-the-spot, we got it.

Anything on settled waterfront is Type III, "investment property," for starters. And 265 New Ocean needed insulation, badly, and central heating—two biggies that would raise the price considerably once they were installed. We could then get a healthy Type I rental for it in the summer. So we really had Type II plus Type III—another Type V house!

Rent from our first house, 18 Beach, was by then coming in, so the timing for quitting the job was right. We could do it, financially, and we knew it. Sam quit.

Why doesn't everybody quit and do something "better"? Most people wind up talking themselves out of it. There's the retirement pension or comfortable working conditions. There are the many words of caution from friends and relatives. There are your own fears. Security is always seductive.

Take a careful look at your present company: where are your fellow workers and colleagues who now approach retirement age? Most jobs look pretty good when you are young. What lies ahead? Is it a trailer camp in Florida? Maybe that's what you want. Or maybe you want to get into full-time recycling to retire in style.

Job Trouble

In our case, finally, what decided us was disillusionment about Sam's job. Sam had taken a position with the idea that he could show talent quickly and win recognition quickly. In fact, Sam did show considerable talent. He invented a new purification process, but, he didn't get the recognition.

Sam's proposed improvement in the company's purifying process could have saved the company $2 million a year. When Sam brought the idea to his supervisors though, he learned that all business is not run by logic. The company had just bought a whole new set of purification equipment, and they couldn't face junking that. It wouldn't look good on the books. Too many questions would be raised, even if they would make more money after a year.

There was another thing: Sam was 25, just hired. To their way of thinking, Sam wasn't "ready." He hadn't paid his dues yet. This put Sam into a blue funk. He was having trouble keeping focused on the work. Sam felt, at 25, that almost half his healthy life was used up. He wanted to leave some footprints. The personnel administrator just that week had told Sam that after four years he would be eligible for the company retirement plan.

Retirement? Sam felt that if he couldn't retire on the money he had saved by the time he was fifty, he would rather walk off into the ice floes to die, like an old Eskimo.

So Sam and Mary had the right "mind-set" for the big break. Let's turn to the importance of "experience." We don't advise recycling full-time for anyone who has no experience in it. There's a knack to working quickly with tools and materials.

By the time we were moved into 265 New Ocean, we were completing in a couple of weeks the kinds of recycling tasks that had previously taken us months. Our physical moves in painting, scraping, nailing, and sawing became relaxed and sure. We were in good physical shape from our work. Where we used to pause for breath to saw through a wide plank, now we did it without effort. So we were in the right state of body to make the "great decision."

Once you do it, going full-time has tremendous advantages. The amount of work you do expands geometrically with the time available. You now can concentrate and leave distractions aside. You have time to plan your work, ordering materials well in advance. It's another level of productivity.

Productivity and problem-solving come more easily with increased involvement. Once you "live" with a house, the solutions start coming; all you have to do is stay free of distraction. This happens only after you have a backlog of experience. You may be reading the paper or putting the kids to bed, but your mind, without your knowing it, is focusing on the problems and solving them.

Another big advantage is the freedom. When Sam came home that first day after he'd picked up his final paycheck, he said to Mary, "You can break off that little alarm clock bell dinger." We never set an alarm thereafter. If we work late, we sleep late. We awaken fresh and ready to go.

When you go full-time, you can utilize help efficiently. At 265 New Ocean, we hired our first co-worker. That helped us measure time in money. Whatever idled our helper cost us money. It was great discipline.

Money Jobs Make Efficiency

Last, we found that by having an array of jobs underway, we could shift from one job temporarily held up to one that was ready to be taken on. Not only did we have one house at 18 Beach and one at 265 New Ocean, but we shortly bought 32-32A Riverdale and 30 Shrewsbury Drive. Now we had a larger assortment of jobs ready to go at any one time; it made us even more efficient. We could just turn to a waiting task while waiting for the missing piece to be delivered.

To handle multiple houses, you have to be adept at keeping

the various jobs well in mind. We found that, after a while, we did that automatically, even though there were fifteen or twenty projects going on simultaneously in four different houses.

Our four houses were, in a sense, self-supporting. The rent coming in from the first house, 18 Beach, paid our general running costs. Thus we could work on the second and third houses, and afford to keep the fourth house in "drydock" as a rental until we got ready to work on it. By the time we'd finished making a two-family out of 265 New Ocean, we had rental income there and could afford to drop the fourth house off the rental market while we worked on recycling it.

We had put our amateur days behind us, and we looked ahead to a substantial income. Quitting was the beginning.

9

The Paper Trail: Using the Law

Making best use of the law and of lawyers is basic in recycling, and it takes a bit of doing. Some see the law as a tiresome process of pursuing fine legal points for petty advantage, but law can be far more productive than that.

One of our friends told us a true story which makes a relevant point. It is about a salty admiral during the Korean War. The admiral walked into the wardroom one day as his junior officers were complaining about the pettiness of the war's naval action. "Dammit," growled the admiral. "Don't complain about the war. It's the only war we've got. And we damn well better make the most of it!"

The law is not perfect, but it's the only legal system we've got, and we damn well better make the most of it.

In recycling, you run into legal processes all the time. Property and law have always been closely intertwined. Transfer of land, even in primitive societies, requires formalities. Civilization multiplies that need. Every state and county in the U.S. requires a set of formal signed documents for transfer of real property. In addition to those formal documents, there are the informal records which may become important in determining the intent of any parties involved, in case some conflict arises. We call the total set of documents, the "Paper Trail."

Formal Papers

First let's look at the formal documents. There are four initial documents that are universal in this country: (1) the deposit, or "earnest money," usually a check given by the buyer, (2) a receipt for the check, given by the seller, (3) the contract of sale, and (4) the deed.

The contract of sale is an agreement, referring to a description of the land contained in a deed to the land up for sale. The buyer usually can enforce this agreement in court *only* if it is signed by the seller. Whoever signs the contract first gives the other party a chance to back out: the first signer is committed. If you sign a contract of sale and mail it to the would-be buyer, he can sit on it until he sees whether or not he can get a better deal. In the meantime, you cannot legally sell to anyone else. That's the reason why most "signings" are simultaneous, face-to-face.

The Deed

The deed is the most important piece of paper. The purpose of a deed is to describe in a useful fashion the boundaries of the property.

Our "fee simple" concept of ownership stems from English common law. The premise is that a man's home is his castle. Even today, an owner has considerable freedom to do what he wants with his land. If you own a piece of land, you could cover the entire property with a foot of sand if you wanted to.

In this form of ownership, boundaries are important, and boundaries are not always obvious. Let's assume that you say to someone, "I'll sell my motorcycle to you for $500." The other person says, "I'll take it." Even though nothing has been put in writing, you have a legal contract. If you want to enforce the contract, then you have the right to take the other person to court. You may bring in witnesses, and proceed to prove the contract, and thereby collect any damages the other fellow's breach of contract may have caused.

But, if you and the other man happen to be talking about a piece of land instead of a motorcycle, even fifty witnesses will not make an oral offer and an oral acceptance an enforceable contract. The courts can't take the case. And for good reason.

A man who offers his "home on Elm Street" orally doesn't settle the question of just what that "home" consists of. The land boundaries may be different from what the seller honestly thinks they are. The boundaries of land are not as definite as the boundaries of a motorcycle.

To reduce the possibility of a difference between what the seller and/or buyer thinks the bounds are and what the bounds *really* are, the law requires a transfer of a "good and sufficient deed," a document properly spelling out the actual boundaries. Whether a deed is good or not depends on whether boundaries are spelled out in sufficient, up-to-date detail.

Some descriptions in a deed may be very crude. ("The corner of the lot lies fourteen feet approximately SW of a large boulder five feet from the road.") Or, the lot may have been diminished by a road project occurring after the existing deed was filed; the lot is five feet shorter from front to back than in the existing deed.

Sometimes a current deed merely repeats descriptions of the previous deed without anyone having gone out and looked at the present state of the land at the time the current deed was written. Sometimes "easements" (rights of outsiders to the land) will not have been recorded.

For instance, if the people of the neighborhood have beaten a path across one corner of the lot for years, usage alone may entitle the public to use the path, a "public right of way." In addition, existing power lines or pipelines across the property can constitute legal easements. If so, you can't get them off; they have a right to be there.

For all these reasons, it's important to "walk the lines." Take a walk around the boundaries of the property with the owner; if the owner is not available, then ask the neighbor whose joint boundary it is. That way you get to see any obvious easement problems, and you get to see if the description in the deed fits the facts.

A Survey

The most accurate property descriptions are those prepared by surveyors. They work from permanent marks; they deliver the boundaries in precise directions and distances. Today, if a property has not been surveyed, we suggest strongly that a survey be taken and that the survey results be contained in the deed. Even if the property has been surveyed once, unless it's a recent survey, your most solid procedure in buying or selling is a "resurvey."

The final session of a transfer is the "closing." The transfer is formalized in the "passing of the deed" to the buyer and the passing of the purchase money from the buyer to the seller.

Transfer procedures vary from jurisdiction to jurisdiction. Only your lawyer knows. One purpose of this chapter is to help you talk semi-intelligently to a lawyer. In a property deal, you need a competent lawyer to lay out the proper formal documents. (In the next chapter, we'll discuss how to pick a lawyer.)

Informal Records

Laying a proper paper trail also calls for an informal record of all the smaller steps you take, a record of the conversations you have with any of the people involved. The people you deal with in a legal sense in land transfer can include buyer or seller, renter, broker, lawyer, judge, building inspector, town councilmen, and city planners. Any one of these can make statements they later forget; or you may mistake the meaning of a conversation. A record of a conversation is not legally binding, but it certainly can be persuasive in court.

Suppose you've asked your lawyer to be present with certain documents at a closing, and he doesn't show up. You, in consequence, lose the sale. You certainly would want to fire the lawyer and maybe even sue him if your deal was potentially a good one. If you have a carbon of a "memo letter" you sent the lawyer confirming your phone call asking him to bring the papers to the meeting, your paper trail is complete. You may then be able to recover damages in settlement, or—at least—not have to pay the lawyer his remaining fee. This may sound a bit tough, but as a recycler, working from one project to the next, you cannot afford to be left hanging on a limb by someone's carelessness.

The paper trail not only sets the right legal tone, but it sets the right psychological tone. Follow up face-to-face conversations and phone conversations with a brief memo saying, "Nice to talk to you. Here's a note confirming our conversation," containing the essence of the conversation, will cause people with whom you deal to realize that you are serious and well-organized, that you intend to do what you say, and that you expect the same from them. There will be less temptation on anyone's part to reduce their commitments. Creating a "willingness to cover commitment" is important. It's both difficult and expensive, as well as chancy, to try to make someone do something he has decided he might not have to do.

Brokers Again

Let's have another look at real estate brokers, this time in relation to the law. Legally, most real estate deals begin with brokers. The broker advertises the house for sale, and he conducts tours of inspection. The broker isn't legally supposed to misrepresent the property outright, but he may exaggerate its glories a little (known as "puffing"). A broker once told us that the road past a house "dead-ended a few miles down," implying that the traffic was light. *We knew* that a few miles down *before* the road dead-ended there was a subdivision of a thousand people. Don't count on your lawyer to rectify moves you made because of "puffery." This is a "gray area" where you are on your own. It's too hard to treat "puffing" as outright misrepresentation.

It is important for you to go back to the property at different times of day, so you can observe what happens. A broker might take you down at the most favorable time, when the smoke from the nearby dump isn't drifting across the land; or when the tide is in, rather than out, so as to hide the mudflats; or during a time when none of the local freight trains are rolling by.

It's a good idea to set down in a memo what you understand the good and bad points of the property are and mail it to the broker, keeping a carbon for your files. If nothing else, the broker may decide that you desire exact information in the future.

Not all brokers are looking out for your interests; the best ones do. Some brokers have a favorite tactic of giving an impression there are other buyers in the wings. This means that the broker is trying to rush you. Don't be rushed. Take your time. If others want to get in, let them. There are always deals to be made where you have sufficient time to think. These are the ones on which you make money.

Let any broker know in conversation (and writing) that if he does well by you, you will have more business for him. A broker and a recycler can create a relationship that cuts through a lot of potential problems, avoiding people the broker knows are unreliable, or property that looks desirable but really isn't. If he sees you could be giving him much future business, he'll be that much more helpful.

Three Lawyers

Let's turn to the "lawyers you'll meet." Generally in a real estate deal there are three lawyers: yours, the bank's, and the other party's lawyer.

The bank is really mortgaging the *building,* not the *land.* The bank's lawyer is not as concerned with the accuracy of the deed's description of the boundaries as you are. If the land, indeed, is *not* exactly as described in the deed, you probably can't sue the bank's lawyer. You didn't hire him. He isn't legally responsible to you.

Federal regulations (for member banks of the Federal Reserve System) require Federal Reserve banks to hire a lawyer of your choosing—a regulation widely ignored by banks. They would like to hire a lawyer of *their* choosing, usually a staff or retained lawyer.

Even if you can choose the bank's lawyer, it is best from all viewpoints to hire your own lawyer for any land transfer. There are three things a good lawyer will arrange for you: (1) the agreed-upon money at (2) the agreed-upon time, for (3) the agreed-upon matter. Money, time, and matter. Let's look at these in detail.

Money

Money: if you are buying, the lawyer should enable you to get the property for the amount agreed upon, plus reasonable costs in closing the deal. (Definitely get the lawyer to outline all the "costs of closing," including his fee, in advance.) The other side should sell—as agreed.

If you are selling, the lawyer should get you the agreed-upon price from the buyer without incurring a lot of unforeseen costs.

If the lawyer conducts a solid series of transactions, it should be hard for the other side to wiggle out. It should appear certain that any lawsuit would go your way, and any damage you have suffered would have to be compensated by the other side.

Time

Time: you should get possession of (or get rid of) the property *at* the agreed-upon time, or close to it. Not two weeks or a month later. If you plan to recycle immediately, then you need "a time is of the essence" clause in the contract. A delay causes you to lose time in starting work on the house by idling your work force (even if it's only you), thus putting off the date when you finish the recycle and can start renting it for money. Even more acutely undesirable is a delay when you are buying a house to put up for seasonal rental. A delay can cost you some or all of the total income for the year.

A seller or a tenant in the house you are buying can simply refuse to move out. It will take the owner time and trouble persuading someone who doesn't want to leave (even though legally he hasn't a leg to stand on) that he *should* leave.

Therefore it's important if you are the buyer to have a "time is of the essence" clause in your contract of sale. This means the seller is on notice that any delay will cost you money, and he will be *liable* for that cost in case he's not able to deliver. You are on notice that he *may* have trouble delivering if he refuses the clause.

Matter: once a property's bounds have been determined to the satisfaction of your lawyer, he should then agree either to give you a "title opinion" or get you "title insurance." Either way, you are protecting yourself if his legal work is sloppy.

Title Opinion

A title opinion is the lawyer's written assurance that he has indeed investigated the soundness of the deed's description of the land. A title opinion costs more than an ordinary lawyer's fee, but it's worth it—if you don't want to go to the greater expense of title insurance.

One way of saving money (if that is very important): ask the bank if they will have their lawyer's title opinion "run to you," as well as run to the bank. If the bank is anxious to give the mortgage, it might grant you that favor. This means that the bank's lawyer writes you a note assuring you that in his opinion the title is good. Then the bank's lawyer is responsible to you, as well as the bank.

A bank may take out its own title insurance on the property to be mortgaged, but that insurance only covers the amount of the mortgage, not the full value of the house and land. As you pay off the mortgage, the bank's title insurance covers less and less of the actual market value of the house. Thus, for maximum safety, you should take out your own title insurance. It's much better to go this route than try to save money. If you blow a big one, you blow your career as a recycler.

Title Insurance

A title insurance company is bound by the terms of the insurance to defend your title in court, which a lawyer who has given you a title opinion isn't bound to do. In other words, suppose someone shows up with a deed to "your" property. (It can happen.) A title insurance company will go to court for you. Otherwise, you may have to go to court twice, once to get satisfaction from a lawyer who has given you the title opinion; once against the claimants to your land.

Title insurance protects you against having your buyer find flaws in the title you've passed to him, and rescinding the deal. If there is one thing that you don't want in recycling, it's to go backwards, or even lose momentum. Your title insurance is momentum-insurance.

Now, having talked mostly about the law, let's talk some more about lawyers—in the next chapter.

10

The Paper Trail: Picking Your Lawyer

So far, in this section of the book, we have been through some basic decisions in recycling: (1) what kind of house to pick, (2) what *to* do once the house is picked, and what *not* to do, (3) whether to quit your job or not, and (4) how to best use the legal system. Now we come to (5) how to decide on your lawyer.

The first thing you look for is experience. A lawyer with little or no experience who offers you friendly help in closing a real estate deal may *not* be doing you a favor. Real estate is a tricky area of the law. Only a locally-experienced lawyer can give you the best odds; an inexperienced one can get booby-trapped. Fifty percent of all legal malpractice suits filed in this country are filed against lawyers in real estate deals by clients convinced that their lawyers did not do a good job. Often, the client is right.

Only a lawyer with a lot of experience can help you lay a paper trail that goes from the beginning of the deal to the end, so that your profit becomes sure. In that framework, the experienced lawyer's fee is worth every penny.

Next to experience, you want a lawyer who is open and

willing to list all the details needed, from the beginning on, to make the deal click.

Slow Lawyers

Back when we were new to the business, we were astounded at the slow service we got from lawyers. We finally came to realize that, in the end, it was *our* responsibility to expedite things. What happens with lawyers is what happens with everybody. They get very busy from time to time, and some of the things they are supposed to do slip into the cracks and disappear.

Today—even with a top-notch lawyer—we make sure that we know the scheduled steps of every particular transaction. We make sure that the timetable is kept. We check with the lawyer as each step is due.

We write down the legal steps with a target date on each. If our lawyer gets bogged down, we will step in and do the paper work ourselves; we will take the papers to the proper government agency to be filed and get the approvals from town and city officials ourselves. Whatever action is needed, we are prepared to take it. Once we have a deal going, we want to keep it going.

The second quality you look for in a lawyer is a lawyer who will willingly help you lay all the necessary legal documents in a row, making a clear paper trail.

To digress for a bit from lawyer-choosing: the paper trail, we want to repeat emphatically, is not just the legal documentation you get through working with the lawyer but also all the intermediate steps, the things you do yourself—recorded in a orderly fashion.

The Memo File

Part of the paper trail is your memo file. If we have a conversation or get in touch with someone over the phone, we follow up with a note typed on our battered typewriter, saying, "Glad to have talked to you today, and here's our idea of what we and you decided to do." This includes summing up visits with and phone talks to the lawyer, as well as significant telephone calls to buyers, sellers, and brokers.

Nothing can substitute for a paper trail constructed this way, for your own clarity as to "what happened when" and to apprise the other party of your thinking. Some people create ambiguity deliberately, assuming that if the other side is not sure of what is going on, this will lead to some advantage. That is a very poor process. What ambiguity leads to is confusion, delay, and loss.

Follow up conversations with a memo summarizing the content. You'll be amazed (we have been) at the large differences in interpretation that can exist between two intelligent people after talking to each other in a presumably intelligent way. Second, keep carbons of the memos arranged by date in every particular transaction. This is a very solid kind of evidence in case something goes wrong. A judge or jury is going to favor the view that you would never go to all the risk of forging a series of carbons in order to give yourself an advantage. Therefore, legitimate carbon copies are likely to be believed.

About lying. No good lawyer will coach you to come into court to construct a false story. Social life condones polite fibs, but lying for your own advantage *in court* usually becomes very transparent. No one should count on being able to lie convincingly at length. Besides, lying in court is perjury—a crime.

Rental Laws

As an example of a paper trail, let's look at renting. There are comprehensive rental agreement forms that you can buy. Let your lawyer see your form, or have him recommend a form with which he's familiar. There may be things that the law requires you to inform a tenant. Ask your lawyer to let you know.

We don't believe in making rental deals by withholding information from the tenant. Say that we know there's a pothole outside the apartment and that the trucks hitting it make a loud rumble. We let the tenant know by memo. This is better than just hoping the tenant won't mind. An angry tenant can simply decamp and leave you the job of quickly filling his place. If you have had a reasonable up-front relationship, he will be more likely to let you know ahead of time, rather than leaving you to discover his flight. All in all, we try to give our tenants a good rental buy and keep them happy by truth-telling—and by attention to their expressed needs, recorded on paper.

The way we feel about renting is that we didn't go into recycling to spend our lives dealing with unhappy people. We like an impersonal but good relationship with tenants.

Making Repairs

We are capable of making repairs ourselves, so we do give prompt attention to the tenants' requests for repair. This cements a reasonable relationship. We also bend a little. If a tenant says he did not get adequate heat last month, we go in and do a caulking job on his windows and put down some big rugs to help him keep the apartment warmer. And we record all that.

One landlord we know takes an opposite view. One of his tenants once volunteered to fix a malfunctioning heater, and did. The tenant sent a bill for the new parts to his landlord. The landlord refused to pay, saying that the rental agreement called for the tenants to pay for repair. The next week, the tenant moved out without saying anything. The heater soon went out of order and all the pipes froze so the whole house had to be abandoned for the winter.

This brings us back to lawyers, and the third quality you want in a lawyer: he ought to be a good negotiator.

Every sale or rental requires some negotiating. You may or may not be a good negotiator, but a lawyer has to be as a matter of course, or he wouldn't have lasted long as a lawyer. A good negotiator sizes people up quickly and can make suggestions that will appeal to both sides. You can learn a great deal about negotiating from a good lawyer.

The fourth quality: local knowledge. A lawyer should know who the local good guys and bad guys are: this spares you dealing with someone known to be a con man. A lawyer who has been around a long time will have an idea of what local buyers, sellers, and renters are good risks.

In some places, young single renters are good risks; they are either working at steady jobs or attending school. In other places, particularly where you are dealing with college rentals, young singles' sense of responsibility is low.

Local Knowledge

A good lawyer with local knowledge also will help you avoid getting stuck with property that's undesirable because of local social, civic, or environmental circumstances. We once almost bought a mountain property until the lawyer we talked to told us that the particular section had bad-tasting water in its artesian wells. Local people had to import their drinking water. We would have ended up in court.

Good real estate lawyers don't make their money going to court. The good ones keep you *out* of court. We figure our time is worth $300 a day a piece at least. If either one of us has to go to court, it costs us more than just a lawyer's fees.

Once you *find* a lawyer with the right experience, openness, and local knowledge, hire him *before* you make a move. Before you put down "earnest money" or even talk to brokers, consult a lawyer. Once a deposit is down, a lawyer will hesitate to "break up the deal" since that gives the lawyer a local reputation as a spoiler. If you haven't negotiated seriously yet, the lawyer is much freer to tell you his reservations on the deal.

There are some other advantages you may acquire along with a lawyer. A good lawyer is often well-connected with banks, and he can tell you where you can get mortgage money. In time, when he comes to know you, he can recommend you himself. Once you become a steady client of a well-known lawyer in town, one who's respected, you get the advantages of both good legal advice and of financial credibility in the community.

Last, another advantage: a well-known lawyer is often able to help with the town or city council and planning board, if that becomes necessary.

We once went into a strange town cold and bought a lot that

could be legally subdivided. This is usually a good opportunity for a profit because once a piece of land is subdivided, a house can be built on one part, and sold off with its land, and the original building can be sold with the remaining land. In this case, however, we didn't know anybody in town; we used an outside lawyer. The planning board stalled our application for subdivision, treating us as if we had come in to rip the town off rather than to increase its taxable property values. Here's where a good local lawyer could have helped us; he could have made us palatable to the planning board, and thus paved the way for subdivision. As it was, we had to go to court. It cost us $5,000 out-of-pocket plus valuable time to get an approval to which we were legally entitled in the first place.

Lawyer's Delay

At least occasionally, you will be dealing with lawyers on the "other side" who feel they have to justify their fee by "getting something extra" for their client. At the signing of the contract, they want extra furnishings, extra work on the house—before they agree to the sale. Their lawyer is probing to find out how anxious you are to sell the house. If you give way on small details, he will keep pushing for concessions, even if his client is willing to go through with the deal anyway.

When we sold our first "new" house (one we built ourselves on a parcel of land subdivided from a larger piece), we asked $175,000, and a buyer agreed orally to meet the price. At the signing of the contract of sale, his lawyer started asking for additional features—until we said that we had another offer (which was true) for $185,000. It took the until-then balking lawyer about 30 seconds to agree to go up another $10,000. His client not only wanted to go through with the deal but—in fact—was willing to go up another $10,000.

Building Inspector

Now we come to a man with whom you will have as close a

legal relationship as you will with your lawyer, but in a different way: your building inspector.

You want to keep on the right side, and also be legally sound, in your dealings with the building inspector. Keep your lawyer informed if you have trouble in your dealings with the building inspector, beginning with your contact initially to get a building permit.

In most towns and all cities you have to get a building permit to build or to make substantial inside or outside improvements. This is usually done by submitting a plan for improvement that conforms to the local code. The building inspector comes in. It is his job to come around every so often (after advance notice, usually) to make sure you are following the approved plan. While he's there, a number of other hitherto undiscussed things may come up, such as the grade of lumber you are using, and so on. If the building inspector feels you have ignored the approved plan or are using unsound materials, he can stop you from going further until you make corrections.

First of all, the building inspector is a social being. The legal process is only in the background. We welcome the arrival of the building inspector because he's usually got some useful advice. He usually isn't going to pin us to the wall with fine-honed interpretations of the building code. We foster a good working relationship with the inspector, and we value what he says. He's trying to make sure, after all, that what is done is done right. Rather than argue points with him, we'll bend to make him happy.

Back to lawyers. Do you ever need "the best lawyer in town"? There is one situation where a top lawyer on your side is worth more than his fee. That is where the title to the property you want is "clouded" by being in litigation or part of an estate. The fact that there is a complex legal situation surrounding a property may present an opportunity, rather than an obstacle, if you have a top lawyer.

When we contemplated buying our first mansion, Goldencrest, we faced an "estate problem." The estate of a deceased person owned the property. Anything to do with estates, wills, and inheritance is always complex. A number of people later told us that they had considered buying Goldencrest, but their lawyers had advised them not to touch it. Our lawyer, however, rolled up his sleeves and waded into the problem; he is a creative lawyer who is willing to make things happen. We ended up buying Goldencrest and making a lot of money on it.

An older, more expensive lawyer isn't necessarily better, however, for run-of-the-mill deals, even if he is more experienced than a younger lawyer. The younger lawyer probably has more time to give you for the money. Talk to other recyclers who have had a particular lawyer and ask them what their experience was.

Final Points

Here are some final pointers in dealing with your attorney:

Tell him what you expect. Then he can tell you if what you expect is realistic. Some lawyers as a matter of course give *only* legal advice and no practical advice. If you *want* practical advice, tell your attorney so at the start.

Tell your lawyer whether or not you are experienced in dealing in real estate.

Ask beforehand what his fee will be. Ask whether it will be a percentage or based on straight time. Offer to put some money up front as a retainer against the eventual fee. That will set a businesslike tone.

If you are in a money pinch, tell him you want minimum service adequate to making the deal work and are willing to do legwork yourself. Or, if money is not a primary consideration, tell him you want maximum service and minimum bother with details.

Discuss with him the advantage of moving promptly on the deal and the risks of delay, so that you both know how urgent the time factor is.

Finally, when it's all over, thank your lawyer. Surprisingly few people do. A lawyer who gives good service deserves a thank-you.

part 3

How to Plan and Finance a Recycle

11

Cost Estimating for Profit

This is the first of five chapters which set up the financial side of recycling, of which we have sketched a few parameters already. There is a good deal of very interesting and remunerative detail in this subject, and we get into in this section as much as we feel you need before you go out and get your own practical experience.

The first is "cost estimating" which you do the very first time you look at a house. You need to have some sort of idea right from the start of what it's going to cost to recycle the house. Otherwise you can't decide whether or not to buy it. Even though it may be one of the Sure-Fire types, some Sure-Fire types are more profitable than others. The cost estimate is one key to deciding.

The next two chapters cover figuring the other financial factors that go into profit, including how much cash you can raise, how big a mortgage you can get, and how much money you need to live on until the next recycle is complete.

The last two chapters deal with the design that you make for the recycled house, which may be a completely different design from the house as it stands. The design enters strongly into profitability.

Let us start with the first, the art of making a cost estimate. The "rough cost estimate" is a deciding factor in buying. In previous chapters, we assumed that you could make a proper rough estimate. In this chapter, we are going to make sure you can.

The rough cost estimate is the cost of materials (and possibly furnishings) that you estimate it will take to recycle when you first consider recycling a house. Rough estimating is a fascinating combination of seat-of-the-pants feelings and precise figuring. It's crucial to finding a profitable house.

You can't use the original cost of the house as a guideline to determine the cost of fixing it up. We've recycled houses where we put in materials costing five times the buying price of the house, and we've recycled houses where we put in one-fifth.

Obviously, the greater the potential *added value* of the house after recycling, the more you have to spend on materials to fix up. *But,* just because there is a big added value, don't feel you have to spend a lot fixing it up. Take the added value in profit rather than putting more into the house than you need.

Three Cases

Ideally, you pay *low* for the house and put very *little* into it. We call this our "Case I house."

Case I—The house is low-priced and needs little. Ideal.

Case II—The house is low-priced. It needs lots of materials but is still profitable.

We started our career doing Case II houses. Our first two houses were really low-priced, but we put a good deal of money into them. We had a lot of margin between our buying price and our selling price, however, so the two houses were both very profitable.

Case III—The house is priced somewhat under the market, but needs little, so it is still profitable.

Case III houses are fair game for the recycler. We never turn down a chance to make quick money by buying just under the market and selling almost right away, with a few added cosmetic touches. Don't turn down a house simply because it is relatively high-priced or because there's not enough work to do on it to challenge you. You can use that money to set up greater challenges the next time around.

Case IV

Case IV—The house is low-priced and needs more to make it marketable than the market will pay for.

You can get burned on a Case IV house. Never pick a house simply because it's low-priced. Do your arithmetic. If you make a thorough rough estimate, you will spot a Case IV house for what it is—and you'll look elsewhere.

A couple of friends of ours bought a house for $30,000 and put $10,000 into it to bring it up to marketability. The market price for that house was only $40,000. In effect, our friends got nothing for their labor. If they'd bothered to make a rough estimate, they would have been forewarned: Case IV house!

A house that is low-priced is not automatically recyclable. Once or twice we have had friends insist that we buy a particular house because it was so "ridiculously low." Our estimates showed that materials needed to recycle were ridiculously high in relation to the potential market value after recycling. Yet our friends kept insisting that such a low-priced house was "our kind of house." Our kind of house, first of all, makes money for us.

Details of Rough Estimate

Now to the details of making a rough estimate. Begin making your rough estimate as you walk through the "potential recycle." Keep a pad in hand. Put down anything you see that can stay— furnishings, moldings, floor finish, etc. Put down in another section anything that will have to be supplied, together with estimated price. To give you an idea of what kinds of sums are involved, here are some rule-of-thumb average costs for a 12-by-15 foot room:

Carpeting—$150
Paint for ceiling—$50
Wallpaper—$100
Spackle and paint for walls and moldings—$50
Total for the room—$350

If you have an average size house, say seven rooms outside of kitchen and bath, that comes to $2,450 for the house. There's more usually. Allow $4,000 for kitchen renovation (including dishwasher, stove, and refrigerator). Two bathroom renovations will cost $2,000, bringing the total to $8,450. You have to add to that any costs for central heating, new wiring, and insulation. As you can see, it's easy to spend $10,000 recycling a house.

In general, you can almost count on carpeting and wallpapering or painting most rooms in an old house; also on installing new fixtures, and—almost always—renovating the bathrooms and kitchen. These last two are where the average householder's expectations have risen the most in the past twenty years. People expect a dishwasher and freezer in the kitchen, low toilet, vanity sink, and shower in the bathroom.

There is, as well, a second series of changes that nearly always has to be undertaken: increasing the size of the rooms. People today want a spacious feeling, even if it means combining living-dining or study-bedroom. You can almost count on moving a wall or two. That puts you well over $10,000.

Becoming a good rough estimator depends somewhat on your experience. Get help at first from experienced people. Once you get to be a good rough estimator, you also become a better detail planner. That in turn feeds back so you become a better rough estimator. It's a round of experience that experience improves.

Once you have the rough estimate, you have *the* key figure in "financial fit," a more complex calculation, which we go into in the next chapter. (Financial fit tells you how good it is for you to buy this particular house.)

If there is one core idea in rough estimating, it is to "estimate high."

Estimate High

The Weir Materials Estimate Rule is: *add ten percent to the rough estimate.* That's going to be close to your real cost. Nobody can forsee all the costs. You have to give yourself a margin.

By estimating high, you avoid two traps that trip up new recyclers. First, there is the "running out of gas" trap. Running out of gas (money) and consequently having to wait until you raise cash before continuing to recycle is unprofitable. It's not just marking time, it's getting hung up while your talents go to waste.

Trap two, the "penny ante" trap, is more subtle and therefore a bit more deadly, even if caused by the same mistake of a low rough estimate. If you have to recycle the house too cheaply because of a too low rough estimate you are in the penny ante trap. The house will look cheap.

A recycled house which is *not* solidly good-looking wastes your time and your psychic energy. It wears on you to show your house again and again. *You* have to put so much of yourself into it, you will react personally. Even if a broker is showing it, you lose time: you could have had the money to go on to another recycling.

There's a flow to recycling, just as in everything else. When you break the flow, you lose momentum—and creativity. Every additional showing—all the time spent unrented and unsold—is a loss of momentum.

Using Good Materials

It's chancy to make an estimate "come out right" by using inferior, tacky materials.

Using materials and fixtures that have current vogue makes a house saleable and rentable quickly. Your house may not have more to sell than the others on the broker's list, but if it sparkles with a fresh, modern look, you'll get the first sale.

Tough materials, easily cleaned, appeal to the people who are going to buy, particularly those with experience in housekeeping combined with careers, a large part of the market these days. Also, kids and renters raise hell with delicate stuff.

Some materials are easily installed—sand paint, for instance. It paints over a wall that would otherwise take lots of patching and finicky repair, and it fits the two categories above, as well. Cork ceilings are squares that paste into rough ceilings quickly. These are just a few examples of good materials.

Determining Costs

How do you determine the cost of each particular item? It's a bit like learning to dance. You go to a dance studio and work with a real live teacher; you ask questions and learn fast. Books are the long way around. You can learn to dance from books, but not fast.

By going to real live experts and asking the questions, we got the answers. Beginning recyclers who read catalogs and builders' guides will get the right questions if they read with care, but not necessarily the right answers. You see a new miracle cement described: but why are builders still using good old Portland? (The answer is that when you experiment with things, half the time it turns out wrong. Builders are not into product development. The recycler, however, has some leeway to experiment.)

Another reason for going to experts: practical materials buying depends on location. What is cheap in Detroit may be expensive in San Francisco. One immediate source of information on materials costs is another recycler. If you see a house being worked on by one man alone, stop and talk. Any lone builder can be a source of much wisdom, even if it's just finding out what he's doing that won't work for you. Going over a house with another recycler is great: he is proud of what he is doing. He sees his as an alternative to less rewarding life styles.

He is really willing to talk and share his experiences. Find out where the lone builder got his materials, what they cost, and how big the job.

Extension Courses

Another source: formal adult extension courses. They are not always *practical,* but you will meet kindred spirits and get sources of information on interior design, carpentry, cabinet-making, power tool use, real estate, and building methods. Just don't take everything you "learn" for gospel truth. There's more creative innovation outside formal classes than there is inside. Still, you *can* learn in a formal situation. Just don't get brainwashed.

Another source: the "recipe," the directions on the package or bag that the materials come in. They will tell you how much ground the materials will cover in many cases. That, plus some collateral reading from your how-to-do-it library, will give you a rough idea; at least it will give you a list of questions to ask the first real live expert you run down.

Another source is the suppliers of the materials. The building material supplier—be it hardware clerk or lumber salesman—has a stake in your success. He wants successful, productive customers—if he's smart. He may be willing to help you sort out the options, the procedures, and costs.

One of our hardware sales clerks pointed out to us—just to take a small example—that wood filler in powder form was more for the money than filler in putty form. It can be mixed thick for filling up wide seams between boards and mixed thin for spreading into small cracks, whereas wood filler sold as putty is all one consistency. He said further that if we applied a bit of linseed oil in the cracks to prime the wood beforehand, the bond between wood and filler would be more permanent. He was right on all counts.

We won't detail here a million and one tips on house construction. There are hundreds of resource books. (We've listed our pick of the lot in the appendix bibliography.) We do want to tell you that there are things that you won't think up by yourself—just as there are things you will. You want to work both sides of the street.

Professionals

Now we come to another source: the professional workman, plumber, insulator, carpenter. You might find it more profitable to hire a pro for an estimate than do it yourself. If you find the estimate reasonable, hire him. Make it clear that you want to watch; some pros don't like being watched. Others welcome a reasonable amount of spectating and questioning. You can find out who is willing to work while being quizzed by talking to suppliers or other recyclers. Professionals with good reputations are a *must*.

Another approach is to get estimates from several pros, then hire the one you want to work with. At any rate, hire at least one pro after getting estimates, or you will get a reputation of trying to get free estimates, and you won't get many people who want to do that for you.

Furnishings: it's worth the effort to furnish well if you rent. You get back more in added renting price than you put in, by far. You can charge 20 percent more. Furnishing a house makes it inviting. You get more selective and, therefore, better-behaved renters.

Furniture Not for Sale

Furnishings for sale: unless it's a great house, where you're selling restored furniture, do not include furniture in the asking price. It *can* sell a house if you furnish it, for appeal, but list the furniture separately. Make sure, though, you have a place to store the furniture in case your buyer wants to buy without. Sometimes you will list separately a number of special items—chandeliers, wall hangings, and so on. This gives the buyer an option of buying at a lower price—or buying high-priced fixtures.

Conversely, anything attached to walls, ceilings, or floors *is* by law part of the house and sells with it, unless listed separately.

The trick to estimating furnishing costs is, first of all, to see what there is in the house that you can keep. Second, know the cost of what is left to buy at the flea markets.

When you have come up with your "furniture needed to buy" list, you will have completed the work for your rough cost estimate.

12

Financial Fit: Raising the Cash

Once you have your rough cost estimate, it's time to go on to the rest of the "financial fit." This is the set of figures that tells you what house you can best afford. It is the same as knowing what *particular* house is going to be *most* profitable. The process outlined below is simple arithmetic: it takes the previous information in this book and applies it to fit your situation before you decide to buy, or not.

The financial fit involves relating nine figures:

1. Cash you can raise.
2. Cost of materials (including furnishings) you need to buy (rough estimate).
3. Size of down payment you can afford.
4. Size of mortgage loan available to you.
5. Price you pay for the house (house cost).
6. Carrying cost: mortgage payments, insurance, taxes, interest, utilities, legal fees paid during the recycling.

7. Price the house will sell for after recycling (minus commission). This is Recycled Market Value.
8. *Added value* of the house over house cost once you have finished.
9. Your next six-month income needs: wages and profit in sale, or remortgage.

Here are the three important arithmetical operations:

I: (1) equals (2) plus (3) plus (6).
II: (5) is no more than (3) plus (4).
III: (9) equals (8) minus the following: (2) and (6) together.

If these three equations work out, then all the nine factors will relate properly. Then, it's a financial fit.

Equations Explained

In words, the equations say:
  I: Cash you can raise has to equal cost of materials plus the size of the down payment together with carrying costs.
  II: Price you pay for the house should be no more than size of down payment you can afford (in the light of I, this depends on how much cash you can raise) plus the size of the mortgage you can afford.
  III: The added value you create by recycling has to be big enough to cover cost of materials and carrying charges and still leave you enough profit in sales or rental equal to your income needs until you finish the next recycle, six months from now.
  Let's take a specific example.
  Say we have a house we can buy for $40,000 and we can get it for $10,000 down, and it will cost us $8,000 in recycling materials, and $2,000 in carrying costs.
  That means we have to raise $20,000 in cash before the end of the recycle, and half of that *before* the recycle. Now whether this house is a financial fit or not depends, in the first place, on

whether we can raise that cash or not. OK, let's say you can raise it.

That satisfies 1, above.

(For ways to raise it, see the rest of this chapter.)

But let's say that you can't get it for $10,000 down. The banks want you to put down a third, rather than a quarter, or $13,000 rather than $10,000. In the light of your financial fit figuring then, you find you can't afford this house. Look for another at a lower price, or where the cost of recycling materials and carrying charges are lower.

The last step in figuring financial fit is whether or not the house will yield a profit sufficient to your needs until the next recycle.

We deal with that in the chapter following.

So now let's turn to the initial hurdle in financial fit, raising the cash.

Finding the Money

Cash is how much money you can raise in time to buy and recycle the house in dollar bills and personal loans. How much you can raise depends on what you can see as cash sources.

The most obvious form of cash is dollars in your wallet, in a purse—or in a mattress, for that matter. These loose dollars are a prime source because they are losing value at eight percent per year due to inflation, at the average during the past decade. A bundle of cash may seem comforting, but try to think of it as being squeezed dry, like a sponge. That's what inflation does.

Next: your savings account. The dollars here, unless you are getting eight percent or better, are also losing value. They are not gaining on inflation. If you need them, take them.

Retirement funds also might be a source. A good retirement fund that is contributed to by only you is okay, but once you retire, your income from it contracts every year in relation to prices. You need something else. Unless you have an employer-contributed plan, or your own tax-deductible plan (an IRA or a Keogh plan), count your retirement fund into the potential kitty, too.

Second Source: Equity

Another source of cash is "equity." This sounds as if you have to be in stocks and bonds, but such equity (the present market value of stocks and bonds) is only one kind of equity. Stocks and bonds on average are not beating inflation. You may want to cash them to help you meet cash needs. Other kinds of equity are: life insurance (redemption value), present nonrecyclable house (market value minus remaining mortgage), your second car (market value) and your vacation trailer. All of these things are nice to have, but not as nice as a house that can be recycled for a lot more money.

If you have youth and not too many obligations, life insurance is only savings in another form, at a low rate. If you already have a good cash reserve, one that's making more than eight percent, you don't need life insurance.

Your present "little brown house," unless it's recyclable, isn't going to make you more money; it's only going to keep pace with inflation. You don't need to sell your house. You can "get the equity out" by remortgaging to make it a cash source, or by getting a second mortgage on it, if it's already mortgaged to market value. Your second car may only be costing money, not making it for you. Your vacation trailer is only standing there.

There are some hard choices here; but, out of hard choices comes gain—if only because so many people aren't ready to *make* hard choices. It's more risky in the long run to have a lot of nonprofitable equity lying about than to "go for it," and get into recycling.

Third Source

Third cash source: credit. Nearly everyone who works regularly or has regular income has a "credit line" with the banks, credit cards, and store charge accounts. These may not be more than $500 each, compared to an affluent person's credit line of $50,000, but you may have potentially profitable credit lines all the same. A credit line, in other words, is what you can get on your signature (without hocking the family jewels) as opposed to on your car (as in a car loan), or in a mortgage on your house.

You can spend your *cash* on recycling and *charge things* (use your credit lines) for a while. If you make $10,000 a year salary, let's say, the bank may be happy to lend you "on personal credit" ten percent of that. It all adds up.

In the recycling framework, a personal bank loan is usually called a "home improvement loan," but basically it's available whether you have a house or not. It's what the bank thinks you can pay back in a couple of years if they just hand it to you. If the bank has done business with you before—or any bank has—you are in a better position to have a larger credit line.

The rates of interest on personal credit are high, but it isn't so costly in actual dollars if you recycle your house quickly and neatly. You're only paying interest for part of the year, hopefully, so the total cost isn't all that prohibitive. Only if you lose the flow of the recycle and have to wait for more cash does it mount up to expensive interest in actual dollars.

One thing about personal bank loans: they are not as hard to get as other loans for a very good reason—the interest is so high. The personal loan is often "discounted." That is, the loan you get already has the interest for the full term of the loan taken off. A $2,000 loan for twelve months will get you only a check for $1,800 and change from the bank. The interest for the twelve months is taken out. This actually means that you are paying at an effective rate of up to 18 percent. If this is the only kind you can get, make the loan for as short a period as you are able—six months at the outside. You can always get another loan if the recycle runs beyond the period of the loan and you are not able to pay back yet. You either get a new loan or extend the old one. This way you are not paying interest for any time beyond your actual need for the money.

FFL Loan

Finally, you have friends and family for the "FFL" loan. The "friends and family loan" is a time-honored way of getting cash. We began our recycling career on a $2,000 FFL loan; we think it's a good source. It gave us the necessary leverage. Don't overlook it.

These are the most readily available cash resources for the beginning recycler.

There's another that becomes more available when you have a track record, and that is credit from your building materials supply source. The supplier wants his money back in thirty days. After that, he starts charging interest. What happens thereafter depends on how financially sound he thinks you are. He may sue to collect if he doesn't think you are a "going concern," and that dries up a materials source. Plan on paying your supplier promptly on the first go-around; on subsequent ones you have more leeway.

Bonus Cash

There's one more. BC, bonus cash: If something in your purchase—say extra land—can be sold off immediately, or if there is a second house on the land that can be subdivided off and sold, that's a "bonus" you can add to your cash total. If you buy a two-acre lot with house, you may be able to sell an acre of land; you can look for that situation if you need it.

Add it up. Your cash sources:

Loose dollars
Equity
Friends and Family
Suppliers
Bonus cash

To summarize: If you can't handle the cash required by down payment and carrying charge, come down to a recycle where you can. Be sure you have the cash.

Cash is what's available now—not over the next ten years. If you spend ten years on a house, it's not recycling. It's a great hobby. So, plan on turning your house around within a year, maximum. A six-month turnaround is much more profitable, of course. Nothing is more depressing than having to pay out mortgage interest and other carrying charges you'd have avoided paying if you had a good fast turnaround.

Now you have item (1) of the list of nine figures at the beginning of the chapter. You already have (2), estimated costs, the first cash item, from the previous chapter.

Let's look at (3), down payment, another cash item. (The down payment, as well as materials, *has* to come out of cash.) The down payment on a house is usually figured by the bank as one-third (33 percent) or one-quarter (25 percent) "down." Before you go to a bank, see what the present owner is willing to do. He can give you a 10 percent down mortgage or whatever percentage he likes. Ten percent down is better than 33 percent. He might give a standard mortgage (33 percent to 25 percent down) with less hassle than a bank.

Mortgage Factors

That takes us to (4), the size of the mortgage the banks are willing to let you have. Don't take this personally—the banks are only trying to make money, just as you are. You have to be persuasive and confident about it, as well as meeting the banks' standards—you may be able to make them want to bend a little, if necessary. Usually banks don't want to give you a mortgage where monthly payments are more than 25 percent of your monthly income.

There's also a "big picture" factor. Some years the banks, due to the financial picture in general, want to lend you $50,000, where the year before they wanted only to lend you $25,000 for your mortgage of two-thirds or three-quarters. The state of current bank thinking is, of course, a thing which concerns all brokers. It tells them whether they'll be selling a lot or a little, to some extent. They keep in touch and can tell you what your chances are, and with what banks.

Even if one bank turns you down, another may not. One bank may need to make some *more* loans in a given month or, conversely, may be over-the-top on mortgage loans this month. Just because a bank lent your friend Joe $25,000 last month (he earns what you earn), the bank may not give *you* $25,000 this month. Again, nothing personal: be of good cheer and keep applying to different banks, several months in a row. You never really know.

The bank's willingness to mortgage for a certain amount equal to two-thirds or three-quarters of the house price depends not only on *your* salary or income but on how much the property is *worth,* in the bank's eyes. They send out an appraiser. In some cases, the asking price may be higher than the bank appraises it for. That doesn't mean it is a bad buy. For instance, in case of a condemned house, even if it is recyclable, the bank will appraise it only at the value of the land (minus what it might cost you to tear down the building). The house, in effect, is appraised at less than zero. This was the case with Goldencrest, our premier mansion recycle.

Opportunity

The fact that the bank may not give a full three-fourths mortgage may be an opportunity. The owner is in a spot. He wants to get rid of the property. He may then be willing to give a full 100 percent mortgage at reasonable terms. Or he will take a second mortgage to make up the difference between what the bank will give and what he wants to get from you. In these kinds of situations, therefore, the owner is going to want to take a chance on giving credit. He's not as concerned as the bank with your income in relation to mortgage. He doesn't care, in a sense. He *has* to take a chance on you (or somebody) to get his money out. The situation where there's a persuasive case for an owner-mortgage (take-back mortgage) or second mortgage is often a place where you really make out.

We've gone to an owner and said, "Give us a 90 percent mortgage, and a year to pay." In that year, we easily recycle the house. In effect, we get it for ten percent down. This is real leverage; it gives us terrific margin, a chance to buy more in materials to make it sell, to make that proverbial big killing which starts a recycler up from the ground floor to the higher levels of recycling.

13

Financial Fit: Making the Offer

This brings us to (5) on the list of "financial fit" items—what you pay for the house. It is *most important* to feel you don't have to meet the "asking price" simply because your "financial fit figures" say that you can meet that asking price. That should be clear. In fact, if you want to continue recycling, you'd better *not* meet the asking price most of the time.

Asking price isn't, of course, necessarily what the owner will get. He usually will get less. How much less will he take? Make a low offer and find out. Sometimes a low offer will buy the house. The owner may not get the kind of inquiries he expected. What you do, ideally, is go around making a series of low bids and haul in the one that bites.

In order to keep making low bids, we usually buy three or four houses *ahead;* these stand ready to recycle. That gives us a chance to look around without feeling we *have* to have a particular house. The "have to have" feeling is death to profit, year in and year out.

We usually offer as low as we can without actually insulting the seller. (We don't want to get him mad, of course.) If he wants $60,000, then offering $40,000 isn't an insult. It's a substantial offer. Offering half or less might be considered insulting.

Often we then get a turndown—but, believe us, most sellers do not spend much time playing cat and mouse: either they jump for the money or they really mean they will hold out for their asking price—or nearly all. You might—and probably will—luck out on some of your low bids.

After a turndown, if we do need another house to work on, and if nothing better pops up on the horizon, we'll make an offer closer to the asking price—if we can see that we can afford it via our financial fit.

When we make a low bid, we specify, "no contingencies, immediate closing." That means we'll pay without asking for any special extra considerations, such as having the seller throw in the furniture or give a little extra land. And we'll go right to the closing whenever he's ready. There are so many so-called buyers who like to fool around, make an offer, and—when it's accepted—start haggling for extras rather than close. The broker in the sale will recognize the value of our clean offer. We get some spectacular big profits that would have been only average size had we met the initial asking price. When you get a big one—on a low bid—you are really in business!

Now we come to item (6), carrying costs.

This is pretty straightforward. Make sure you include these cost figures in your thinking, because it's easy to overlook them. Just add them in.

Now for (7), the price the house sells for, *after* recycling. Chapter Six has told you how to find out what a house will sell for once recycled.

The added value is (8): simply the 50 percent or thereabouts that you predict the house to rise in value under recycling. You *picked* it so that its value *would* go up 50 percent, as outlined in Finding Sure-Fire Recycling Opportunities, Chapter 6.

The Crux

Now we are getting down to the crux of the matter:

We can start to figure out whether or not our profit and wages on this house that we can "afford" are going to be enough to cover our needs for the duration of the next recycle.

Let's say we need $8,000 to live comfortably for the six months after we finish a recycle, while we are doing another recycle.

Then let's take a concrete example: the $40,000 house of the preceding chapter.

To see if the profit and wages meet our needs (9) then we take the cost of the house, which includes the mortgage ($30,000), the down payment ($10,000), our materials ($10,000), and our carrying charges ($2,000). Our cost of the house exclusive of labor and profit is $52,000.

Now we sell it for $78,000, or 50 percent more, as planned.

Our yield has within it, the needed $8,000.

So here is a house we can afford to buy, and which also will produce enough profit and wages to enable us to live comfortably through the next recycle.

Suppose that the profit plus wages had come to only $6,000. That would be calling it too close. We don't want to live on short rations just to recycle, when we know by waiting for the right house to come along, we can live comfortably.

(Ours is a business, not a social service.)

That way of figuring works even if you keep the house and rent it, instead of selling it, because you can "get the added value out" by remortgaging it at its new higher value.

The plus for *renting* is that you have an income with which to establish a higher credit line, particularly mortgage credit rating. As a beginning recycler you may want to sacrifice the higher profit on the first few houses to increase your "loanability" by renting out houses. This leads eventually to bigger recyclings. That is what we did.

The house you keep to rent increases your "loanability" more than the house you sell. A rental house can also be remortgaged as it appreciates. When you are renting out three or four houses, the banks will lend you money with a big smile. They then know you are successfully *in business,* that you can keep collecting rents.

For most beginning recyclers rental is the choice. If you hate the bother of rental (it is a bother) so much you'd rather not and you have substantial salary or other resources, so that more current income is not necessary for needed credit, then you can go into buy-sell right away.

14

New Plans for an Old House

This chapter is about the detailed planning of the recycle *after* you buy.

The way to profit is to *control* the money required by the detail plan so that you stay *within,* and preferably *below,* the rough estimate. This control is a discipline. It's frustrating, it's challenging but, above all, it's necessary. Lose money by over-spending on materials, and you lose at least some of your motivation in recycling.

Let's say your rough estimate (which includes a margin of ten percent, remember) is $5,000. You may change your whole rough plan after buying, but you still have to stay within the $5,000 figure. Good creative detail planning will even drop the actual cost below the rough estimate.

When you carry out the detail plan, you have to spend enough. But not too much. It does sound like Polonius' speech to Hamlet ("Neither a borrower nor a lender be. . . . "). There *is* a balance to be struck to make things flow. You can go to the extreme in art but not in business, and ours is a commercial enterprise. You have to take a middle course.

Here are the specifics of redesign:

Changes dictated by a detailed plan for the old house can be roughly grouped into three kinds: exterior, interior structural, interior nonstructural. The least expensive plan is one in which all changes are nonstructural interior changes. This catagory yields the highest market value per dollar invested.

Exterior: the less done, the better. Exterior changes are always expensive. All exterior materials have to be rugged and weather-proof. If you buy a house with a downright ugly exterior, you had better realize that a defaced, weathered, frazzled exterior won't sell *without* extensive exterior changes. You *can* get renters, if the rent is low enough, without extensive exterior changes.

Exterior Changes

Sometimes there *is* a case for extensive exterior change. We once got hold of a couple of garages that had been joined to make a house. In order to give the house a unified look, we built a roof between the two garages. This by itself doubled the value of the house. It was an extraordinary opportunity in which extensive exterior changes paid off.

Competing in the neighborhood is also a case for exterior changes. If you are recycling to sell, you must have a recycled house that competes—in appearance and in the way it makes maximum use of its surroundings.

Take surroundings first. Let's say you have a beach-front house. Here the ocean view is money in the bank, and certainly a case for picture windows. You don't sell the windows; you sell the magnificent view. It's irresistible. (There's a salesmen's adage that you can resist the steak but not the sizzle.) A house competitive in the neighborhood means making good use of any spectacular landscape around. Nobody's going to fall over themselves to buy a house if something else nearby is scenic and delightful.

Appearance

Appearance: let's say you decide to recycle a house in a neighborhood where there are several modern houses with skylights and dormers. Your house has none. There you have a case for putting in skylights and dormers. No matter what you do inside, you do have to have a house that has "curb appeal." If you already have an otherwise attractive house, and there are no other houses around with skylights, forget skylights, however much skylights would improve the design.

On the other hand (here we go again), if such a place has nothing *special* going for it, you may find that skylights are just the thing to make it competitive. A skylight costs about $150 for a big one and as little as $30 for a small one. At 16 Locust, a small, not very distinguished cottage, we put a four-by-four skylight in the main bedroom which gave the house that extra touch. We figured it increased the value of the house a couple of thousand in the final sale. That's what we like: spending a morning's labor and $150 in materials to make $2,000.

Now, let's digress for a minute and look at the process of controlling those dollars going in. The process is "frequent accounting." Be up-to-date on what you have been spending. This works in two ways to help you recycle profitably.

First, by knowing how much you have already spent, you have a psychological deterrent to overspending. Temptation is met by reality. You also have a basis for rational decision-making. Do you or do you not spend amounts as specified in the detail plan? Do you start cutting back? (If you are running over, you start cutting back, immediately.)

You see a wallpaper that is good *enough* for $4 a roll, and you look at another that is terrific for $8 a roll, and you think, oh boy, what a great impression that would make! Do you or do you not get the expensive type? Well, here you can depend on one thing. If you always make the decision to get the better stuff, you end up spending too much. Your house isn't going to sell for enough to make the profit you need to keep going. Alternatively, you are going to have to put it on the market for more than the average going price for this kind of house. This will waste time and psychic energy while you try to get it sold or rented.

It takes experience to convince yourself that you can't afford $14 sink handles when the $4 ones are available and are good enough.

On the other hand, if you are running under, you can well *afford* to spend on something extra. At 78 Ocean, we had been running under our estimate. One day we saw a $250 Tiffany-type chandelier that would go just splendidly in the dining room. We could afford to buy it, according to our accounting, so we did. We sold the house the day we hung the chandelier. The prospective buyer took one look, and we knew that he just had to have that dining room with that chandelier.

A weekly tally of what you have spent—exactly—is good. Daily is better. (Incidentally, the Internal Revenue Service is more likely to believe a daily accounting than any other form of deductible-expense accounting. And, of course, all materials are deductible.) Without a good expense record, you are making decisions in the dark.

Interiors

First, the plans. When do you do the interior plans? The answer: get right into the house and start cleaning it up. That's how you start the detailed plan.

That surprised you, right? What's cleaning got to do with planning? Everything. In the cleaning process, you get to know the house thoroughly. You get the feel of the house, its "personality." Cleaning the house is when the really creative ideas start stewing. Start from the top floor and work down. Throw the junk down the stairs ahead of you, and out the door. Behind you is a clean set of rooms ready to work on.

Don't cart anything *away,* at first. Let it stand around in the yard under cover for a few days. You may come across moldings that have fallen down and were never replaced; you can't find them duplicated today. Those you must save. Furnishings that originally appear worn out may suddenly find new uses. Once you have all the available furniture in mind, you can get combinations going.

Sometimes you can use parts of one piece to complete another. If you have a broken chair that has good arms, you can put them on another chair that needs arms. Once we threw a bureau away. A good friend of ours took it, removed the top two drawer spaces (where the drawers were missing), and replaced the bureau top on the lower section to make a beautiful low bureau.

At some point, you know what's really junk; and then you get rid of it. Sometimes you can get charity organizations or thrift shops to take some of it away. That's a deduction. What's left is all the scrap that's gone too far to refinish, the old linoleums, bad rugs, and a hundred badly broken chairs. (Get the local sanitation department to take it away. That's free, maybe.)

Some towns have a rule that you get one free "junk trip" for every change in ownership. Most cities and towns will pick up trash—once—that you throw out during renovation. Others charge a fee. One-shot junk take-away can be a real lifesaver. At Goldencrest, we had nine dump truck loads standing there waiting, and they came with nine dump trucks and took it all away free.

Now you've cleaned.

Do the room plan.

This is the overall plan for rooms on each floor. Where do you want to remove walls, and what spaces go with what other spaces?

After that, you do a detailed floor plan for each *room* in the new configuration; draw in where the doors and windows and major furnishings go.

Between the overall plan and the detailed room plans you can set an optimum traffic pattern, allowing people to flow through the house without invading certain sections set aside for privacy.

The interplay of traffic and quiet is different in modern interior design. The Victorians seemed to think of each room as a closed space without relation to the rest of the house—not just walls, but walls within walls. It's amazing how opening up two little rooms to make one larger room creates spaciousness.

Flowing Traffic

Flow means you can enter one end of the "public" rooms and exit the other rather than having to double back. It means you have a minimum number of steps from the front or back door to the downstairs bathroom. It means you *have* a downstairs bathroom.

You maximize open space, short of leaving no privacy, and minimize hallways, stairwells, closets, and cul-de-sacs. You take down what stands in your way.

Here, just for a minute, let's deal with the question of whether or not you need an architect. Usually, you are working pretty much within a given set of rooms. Your changes are made in a pattern of uses that you can work from. You don't really need an architect. If you feel at all anxious, however, you can call one in, but first get your own plans down so you know what *you* want.

On the other hand, if you have a huge space that hasn't been lived in previously—say you are redoing an old barn, carriage house, or any sort of out-building, a boathouse or an old garage—you *do* want an architect to come in first and draw a plan that you can use as a basis for your further thinking. He's an expert at beginning from scratch.

Let's look at your own plan. What do you need? You need to plan three bedrooms for a one-family house; and there's a good argument for four. (If the first buyer doesn't need four, he will appreciate four as leverage to resell the house.) You need two to three modern baths. Separate adult and children's bathrooms, if possible, are terrific persuaders.

How do you find space for these rooms? Exactly so. You "find" space. What was once a pantry with windows can be added to the kitchen or even be made into a whole kitchen. We find space in attics made accessible by circular staircases or in old washrooms. Or in basements, if the building code allows, or in porches which have perfectly good roofs and which can be relatively inexpensively enclosed and made into a bedroom or a study space, or used to enlarge the living room, putting it right over the lawn. Or we combine several small closets, hallways, and rooms into one big room. The removal of a single wall adds several cubic feet of space. Taking out three or four transforms a house.

Two Kinds of Walls

Before you go wild knocking down walls: there are two kinds. One kind of wall is nonstructural, and you tear it out without harming any ceiling that needs support. There is also the *structural* wall, which does support the ceiling. Before you decide to make a wall disappear, find out which kind it is: a structural or "loadbearing" wall is three times the trouble to take out. You might profitably leave it in.

Which walls are structural load-bearing walls? Exterior walls are *usually* loadbearing. Only some interior walls are. A loadbearing wall is there, in the first place, to minimize the size of the ceiling lumber needed—the longer the span, the larger the lumber for the span—and large lumber is expensive.

On top of any loadbearing wall, one set of ceiling beams ends. If it's an interior loadbearing wall, another set of beams begins. To find out if a wall is structural, go up in the attic (or cut a hole in the ceiling). Have a look at what the beams are doing there on top of the wall.

It's a structural wall, but you must get rid of it anyway? You construct a header or support beam, that is, a support below ceiling level to take up the load formerly held by the structural wall. On each end, the header has to have a "leg." The legs can either be inside the wall or set as exterior columns against the wall.

A load-bearing wall nine feet long, let's say, can be replaced by a nine-foot header made from two side-by-side two-by-tens or one four-by-six. If the span is fifteen feet, it might take two two-by-twelves. And so on. The exact sizes are usually specified by the local building code. If not, better get an engineering manual or an engineer.

Clearing Away

Clearing away a structural or nonstructural wall is not as formidable as it looks. First, you have to see if there is any wire or pipe in the wall. Take off the floor molding and cut through the plaster all the way across the foot. This way you locate the electrical wiring the plumbing, if any. You may decide, at this point, there's too much in the wall to bother replacing the wall. You can simply rough-plaster the foot of the wall and put the molding back.

Do your wall-ripping in the daytime when you can easily find where—in the cellar—to shut off the pipes that go to the wall. Also, you can shut off all the electricity in the house in case you can't locate the specific fuse for the circuit in your wall. Once you can get to the wire in the wall, you can break it and insert a voltage tester in the wire's circuit. Turn on fuses, one by one, until you locate the controlling fuse.

Once the pipes and wires are shut off, and, if necessary, a temporary header up (you can't put in a permanent header until you take out the wall), you then go at the wall, armed with crowbar and sledge. For your own protection, wear a dust mask and goggles. This is an easy place to get debilitated by dust-in-the-lung or dirt-in-the-eye.

Reworking a Plan

Now you are at the state where you have cleaned the house and ripped out the walls. It's looking the way your floor plan and room plan does on paper. Have another session with your plans. Give them final form.

Accurately measure all the rooms as they now stand. Transfer that set of measurements to graph paper (squared-off paper) on a scale of one square (a quarter inch) to the foot. Now fill the squares to represent the way you think your furniture is going to sit and where you want your light outlets and plumbing to come through the walls.

You may come up at this point with some *daring* ideas—one-of-a-kinds. In our recycle at 1 Ocean Avenue, we put the kitchen and dining room on the *second* floor so that those rooms had a great view of the ocean. On the first floor you looked at the back of a dune.

You might at this point, want to call an architect over. An architect may be glad to tell you how *he'd* do the house, and you can show him your plans, and get some feedback. An hour's conversation with an architect, another recycler, or just a couple of friends walking about your house before you are finally committed may make you save much time and result in better planning. Or it may leave you happy that your own plan is best.

With a little practice, you develop a feel for what can be modernized and how to redesign without spoiling, say, a good old Victorian whose gingerbread charm should be kept intact. A good plan for an old house, esthetically (beauty), and a good plan for an old house, practically (it works), will zoom a recycle's profitability. You will get your money out as well as pay for your own labor at a good rate, and make a bonus (profit) too.

15

Recycling Designs That Work

Recyclers prosper because they know that each house needs an individual plan—an individual approach—to do it least expensively and to give it a unique look. The comforts have to be up to standard; the overall appearance should be something special.

After ten years, we had done some twenty-five recycles; and there hadn't been two alike. Here's how some of our best designs worked. Take 265 New Ocean Avenue, our second house; it was our early prime design example. We moved the dining room and kitchen to the second floor, we put in glass doors opening on a balcony to give an ocean view—and we did this for two apartments which we created out of a one-family house, giving us a great deal of rental income.

Third Recycle

Our third recycle, 32-32A Riverdale, consisted of two houses back-to-back on a single lot. In the first of these, we turned a rather *poor* two-family house into a *great* two-family house. In the downstairs apartment we took out a hallway which gave space for a new dining area that had not been there before. The old enclosed kitchen became a second bedroom. An outdated washroom became a new kitchen. It was more compact and efficient than the old kitchen, and nearly as large. We put in a washer-dryer downstairs in the basement to serve the laundry function. Upstairs, we removed a hall, opening the apartment from front to back to make it airy; and there was now a bay view from all points.

At 32A, we did a modern renovation in kitchen and bath. Lots of new wallpaper and paint now made this bungalow into a solid rental. The rents from 32 and 32A Riverdale both were double the previous rentals.

Fourth Recycle

Our fourth recycle was 30 Shrewsbury. We took a little old Cape Cod house, added insulation and heat to make it into a year-round house, and remodeled kitchen and bathroom. We tripled the rent.

By the time we finished this fourth recycle, we were into our third year of recycling. Our four rental recycles were giving us more than enough to live on and still create a credit rating to buy more houses and the materials to make them rentable—the Weir rule calls for at least 50 percent more rent. We'd done that and more in each case. We were looking at $20,000 gross rent coming in every year. Only half of that was going out in mortgage payments, leaving us $10,000 clear. Plus we had—rent free—our own apartment on the beach at 265 New Ocean, which counted for $4,000. We were, in effect, netting $14,000 a year without lifting a finger at this point.

We were just getting started. This was when Sam quit his job. We really got rolling. Instead of recycling a house-and-a-half a year, we started doing three or four a year and kept that up.

Fifth Recycle

Five Griffin was our fifth recycle. Our special touch here was staining the beams up in the attic where we built what was formerly storage space into four bedrooms. We almost quadrupled the rent income, converting a dingy two-family at $275 a month into a great two-family at $1,000 a month.

Our sixth recycle, 1 Riverview, was a summer bungalow with a strange narrow hallway that went almost the length of the house to a bedroom and bath in the back. We gutted it, took out all the interior walls. The tiny hall, the tiny living room, the porch, and the entryway were combined into a large living-dining-kitchen area. We still had space for a second bedroom. It was only a small house, fifteen by thirty, but we had made it *look* big. We doubled the rent on this one, too.

Seventh Recycle

Our seventh was 12 Main Street. We converted one side of a porch into a bedroom-den. We put in central heat and repainted. We added an upstairs bath, allowing us to raise the rent from $200 to $400 a month.

Then we went afield, for the first time, and bought a single-family three-bedroom house in Vermont near Stowe and changed it to a three-family, eight-bedroom dwelling, which gave us an apartment rent-free to go skiing from. We found space for two bedrooms in an attic, for two more in the basement. When we rented it all out we took in $800 a month for a house that had formerly rented for $400.

Ninth Recycle

Our ninth, 559 Manahassett, was a steal—from an estate sale, a property which our lawyer helped us mightily to get clear title to. Not only did the rent we get carry the mortgage, but it gave us two extra building lots on riverfront property. We added two bathrooms, wallpapered, and sold it for $11,000 more than we bought it for. We still hold the two building lots which at this date are worth $10,000 apiece. This was our first recycle not based primarily on rental income. We could risk holding the building for resale for a big lump sum. We had enough rental income so we didn't need any more current income.

Next we bought our first real restoration, a house built in 1895 by the Evans family at 78 Ocean. We rehabilitated it as it should be—modernized the kitchen and bath, restored furnishings and decor to the Victorian age—and we sold it for $55,000, double our buying price.

We also subdivided the property to give us a lot, 59 Seaview, that eventually sold for $23,000, money in the bank.

Goldencrest

Then we bought our first real mansion: Goldencrest, built at a cost of $1 million in 1901 by the Dixon family. It had forty-six rooms, but was in such sad shape—it had been a fraternity house in its last phase—that the building was condemned. No one wanted to buy it and pay what looked like would amount to an exorbitant price to restore it. It had been on the market for six months.

In a house this big, you don't need to knock down walls. It's got plenty of rooms to set up any pattern of uses you want. We moved the kitchen from servant's quarters in back to the former dining room and created a new dining room by simply setting aside a space in the original living room, which was fifty by seventy-five in and of itself. Shortly, our idea of modernizing this huge house while keeping its Victorian feeling paid off. Within a year, we had a buyer for $180,000; we had paid $45,000—which was the value of the land.

Goldencrest gave us a big chunk of money to play with. Now we were really in a position to buy and sell. The first purchase thereafter was almost the opposite of Goldencrest: 71 Victor. Two garages had been moved onto a single lot and joined to make a house. Pretty ugly stuff. We roofed the space between the garages; now it looked like, and was, a real home. It took us a month, and we made $9,394 when we sold, a good month's pay. The design was the key: all it needed was a little imagination to make it into a reasonable buy rather than a neighborhood disgrace.

Here's an appropriate point to get into the art of selling: how to best make your recycle sale. One of the questions is whether or not you put the house up for sale *before* the house is finished. The argument for advertising before the house is finished is that if you start getting inquiries early, you will sell the house faster. Take it from us: wait until you have finished the house before you advertise.

Any house looks cold unless it's finished, with a few amenities in place. We always hang curtains on the windows, for instance—it's inexpensive and warms the house up. An unfinished house is uninviting. If there are debris and construction around, this is doubly true.

Wait. Finish; clean up. Hang curtains. Then advertise.

Using Brokers

The second question is, do you use a broker or just advertise in the papers? We use brokers, generally, for a good set of reasons. First, the brokers know the market. They can tell you whether or not the price is too high at the moment. (There are "seasonal" and "psychological" variations.)

Second, they also know the "window shoppers."

In every area there are people who have nothing better to do than look at houses. They never buy. Well, almost never. They are basically a waste of time. The broker can handle that group.

Third, if a house proves to be not easy to sell or rent, then the broker will be there for the four or five weeks, or two months, however long it takes to find someone to take the house. They can also tell you what the potential buyers' comments are. It might be too hard on you psychologically to listen to criticism. The broker can relay them to you and tell you whether or not they have any validity.

Fourth, it's very important to *work* with your local real estate agents. The buyer reads a paper, *but* he usually also calls a broker.

Fifth, as the broker gets to know you, he's willing to vouch for you and your workmanship. Your reputation gets a chance to help you make the sale.

Sixth, in the sale itself, the broker will help make it come off. The broker's lawyer will write the contract of sale for the potential buyer, and the broker himself will help the potential buyer get a mortgage. A good broker can facilitate a sale enormously. He will keep plugging away at the detail work of making the sale until it gets made.

Another question is: exclusive or multiple listing?

Multiple Listings

A broker will work harder to sell a house he has on an exclusive, but he can not have as many contacts as can the total number of brokers in the area. Even if he works harder at it, one broker very likely is not going to make the sale as quickly as it gets made via multiple listings.

There are two kinds of multiple listings.

In the first kind, there is a "split" between the "listing broker" and the "selling broker." This means you list the house with one broker; he sends out the listing to all the area brokers; they split the 6 percent commission "sixty forty" between them, something like 2.4 percent of the sale price for the listing broker and 3.6 percent for the selling broker. (If you sell the house, you get the 3.6 percent yourself. In the meantime the brokers are all on the lookout for a buyer for you.)

In the second kind of multiple listing, you send out the details to all the brokers yourself. Whoever sells gets the whole 6 percent, and if you sell it, you get the 6 percent.

There are variations on this theme: some places you can't sell the house yourself until after a certain time period has lapsed after the initial listing, and so on. Check your local broker—or better, check several of them.

Bargaining

The final question. How much do you bargain? Suppose you have a house for which you want $49,000, because that's double your purchase price. You therefore list it high, which is usual. We list from 10 to 15 percent higher than our "bottom figure."

Let's say you list at $54,000. Now somebody offers you $47,000. Should you take it? Probably.

For one thing, "the meter is running." Your carrying charges, such as taxes and interest charges, are accumulating. If you wait for another offer, you may have to fork out another $500 to $1,000 just in those charges. Also, the buying season in the northern U.S. runs from April through September. If you don't sell within that season, you are in for a long winter of paying interest and taxes. Then there is the matter of the house being "hot." A house is always shown frequently when it's just come on the market, but the brokers lose interest somewhat in a house that has been on the market for three months.

So, take the close offer.

You can help the buyer. If he's got a problem with getting a mortgage, you may want to offer him a second mortgage or a take-back mortgage. If you accept less than 30 percent down, in cash, you can pay federal income taxes at a lower rate than if you get the whole amount on closing the sale. If you take 30 percent or more, you pay capital gains that year on the whole amount.

Designs that Sell

Now, back to our history of designs that sell. Your good designs put you in the driver's seat. After we'd been through two recycles, we were in a position to really *pick* our projects. We were also able to train a number of really good people to work with us and to start them off on their own projects. (This has become the nucleus of a "recycling community" that has developed around our work.)

We found that by planning our designs carefully, we could continue to recycle, continue training people we liked to work with, make a contribution to the renewal of the communities around us, and still make good money. A nice combination.

From our first twelve recycles, we developed a sense for buying the houses where the impact of design would be greatest, among all the possible buildings we could have bought. If we bought a huge beautiful place, like Goldencrest or the Lindens, we bought to restore for potential big killing. Where it was an ugly duckling, like our garages at 71 Victor, we bought not so much to build beauty as to design sanely—and thereby reap a good quick reward. The more screwed-up the design, the more the house had deteriorated, the greater the reward for good redesign. A good, imaginative plan can be worth a tremendous amount of money, even on an ugly duckling, if you can see the potential.

You can't design a modest house into a gold-plated high-priced home. There's only so much—at most—any buyer is going to pay for a given number of bedrooms in a given location.

On the other hand, you make a mistake if you don't put in enough solid work and materials to fulfill the recycle design of a great house—such as Goldencrest. We put $26,000 in materials into the house, and got that back six-fold. It was the result of seasoned judgment.

part 4

Making Money with Tools

16

The Unfasteners

Here begins a section devoted to tools. It's a rather detailed rundown of the relation of tools to recycling, with much more specific information than we have been giving throughout the first part of this book. The reason for this detail is that we investigated a number of tool books and none of them seemed quite relevant to the recycling trade. We wanted to be able to acquaint the beginning recycler with the tools of his trade, and to make him think closely about the kinds of things he will be doing and the kinds of tools he will need. For those who are already acquainted with tools, there may be repetition here of things they already know. But it would be surprising if an experienced craftsman did not find a few new ideas here regarding tool use and kinds of tools available.

Those more interested in the other aspects of recycling are welcome to skip this section and come back to it when they feel they need more fundamental grounding in the use of tools when faced with an actual project.

Catalogs

Any comprehensive tool catalog or a how-to-use tools book will bewilder you by the complexity of the subject. We have a tool-rich society. The recycler, ideally, buys no more tools than he needs for his work. He buys considerably fewer than a shop craftsman would. He buys used tools, as well as new ones, You have to "get your money back" on your recycling tools. Recycling is not a hobby. Think before you buy; you can lose nearly as much money by oversupplying with tools as you can taking on a house that won't recycle profitably.

The usual hobby shop is designed around heavy, stationary "bench tools" such as lathes, planers, bench saws, and shapers. These are of marginal utility in a recycling operation. Our tools have to be rugged, portable, versatile, and compact.

Portables

A recycling operation is designed around portables such as circular power saws, not around stationary bench saws; around hand-held power drills, rather than a fixed drill press. Friends who have invested in stationary bench tools have found out that recycling is not the same as building cabinets. Each house you work on is your "shop." We just store tools in our home. We don't have a home shop.

The big difference between recycling tools and home shop tools is wear and tear. The recycler is in a hurry sometimes. He's going to be hard on his tools. The recycler has to make every workday count. He can not run out for exactly the right tool on every occasion. He makes do. He may use a saber-saw blade that is too slim and risk breaking it. He may use pliers for wrenches, screwdrivers for pry bars. What breaks, he replaces.

This means he is looking, in part, for expendable, less-expensive tools rather than hobby craft showpieces. In some cases, a high quality recycling tool pays off. But, recycling is not an exercise in fine tool collecting. We can't let our tools own us. Our pride in our tools is based on results, not ownership.

Time is of the essence if a profit is to be made. The recycler will see the job through every day with tools he has on hand. The alternative is to buy enough of everything to cover every possibility. That's too much money to invest. We like to say that we recycled our first house with a saber saw. Obviously, we had a hammer, a screwdriver, and a wrench, too. But we didn't have the money to buy many tools; we scrutinized every problem to see if we couldn't solve it with the tools we had. We improvised a lot; thereafter we never got in over our heads in tool inventory.

Bargain Tools

The tools you buy depend to some extent on what you can get at a bargain. A flea market can have marvelous bargains. So can farm and estate auctions. We have some "antique" tools that drive screws and drill holes as handily as a spanking new Stanley Christmas Special. We bought a power bandsaw for fifteen bucks, and it's a marvel. It has lasted for years. But, we would have waited a lot longer to buy one of these if the price had been $250.

Building up a recycler's tool chest, then, is a feedback situation: see what bargains you can get and then fill in the gaps when you have to with "store-bought" tools.

There are other books that devote themselves entirely to giving you a look at nearly every currently-used tool. We have read a good many tool and how-to books. Sometimes we discover in one of them a useful tool we thereupon buy.

One book we found most useful is *The Incredible Illustrated Tool Book* (Pathmark, paperback, Boston, 1974, $3.00). Another that uses exactly the same pictures and text is *Tools and Their Uses* (Dover, New York, 1973, $2.00). Both are copies of the original Bureau of Naval Personnel training manual put out in 1971; the illustrations are very good.

Another book we like is Grosset & Dunlap's *Manual of Home Repairs,* published in New York in 1969. Any library, however, will have its own reference set of books on how-to and tool inventory. Do some library reading and then you will know if there are tools that will help solve specific problems.

We know what tools *can* be bought and how they work. If there is a tough job, there is undoubtedly a tool made to do it. A specilized tool may or may not pay its way, but you should certainly know those available. If you go on hacksawing by hand for hours when you could have been using a bolt cutter to do the job in seconds, your profit suffers. Include in your calculations what your time is worth. If you are recycling full time, you are worth at least $15 to $25 an hour, depending on how fast you are working that day.

We classify tools operationally rather than by species of tools. We think of "fasteners," "cutters," and "surface removers" rather than chisels, mallets, and belt sanders. Nails, bolts, and rivets compete with glue, clamps, and staples as fastening devices. Grouping glue and nails together under "fasteners" helps you make useful connections.

Here are our "comparison categories":

Unfasteners
Fasteners
Cutters
Removers and Resurfacers
Disc Handlers
Efficiency-Makers
Troubleshooters
Maintenance
Measuring

Unfasteners

Let's start with "unfasteners."

These are tools whose primary function is unfastening. Unfastening (pulling) nails, for instance, is a big part of recycling. Much unfastening is done with specialized unfasteners; but, you have to look through a lot of books before you find one with a section dealing with subjects such as nail-pulling at any length.

One exception is the *Popular Science Complete Book of Home Workshops* (Harper & Row, New York, 1969).

Some "verbs of unfastening" to help define tools falling in this category are: pull, pry, cut off, rip out, poke out, tap out, extract, unbolt, and unscrew.

Most nailed objects can be removed by the use of "claws" and "pry bars." The various kinds of claws and pry bars are worth looking into.

The claws:

The claw hammer is the most common claw and, for some situations, the most effective nail puller; whenever the nail head sticks above the wood far enough to slide the talons of the claw under the head, it's easy. To double a claw hammer's effectiveness on bigger nails and spikes, lay scrap wood under the hammer to give you more leverage. You also get a straighter nail. Financially, it may not be worth saving a nail, but, from a safety standpoint, you should remove all projecting nails and toss used nails into a "used nail bin." Either that or bend the nails over in the wood, so they won't stick into a vulnerable human.

Safety: your shoes ought to be thick soled enough and hard, so you can walk across a lying nail without getting hurt. Any loose nail underfoot may roll and cause you to skid and fall. Discard all nails into a container.

Efficiency: you may run short of a particular length of nail; if you have a reserve in the form of a used nail bin, you can save yourself time from one day to the next.

Back to our claw hammer. Don't strain the hammer. If you can't remove a nail quite easily, then substitute a "gooseneck stripping bar" or the larger "gooseneck wrecking bar" (some call them erroneously "crowbars"). Any gooseneck is a steel bar with a rounded curve on the clawed end that provides maximum leverage for nail pulling.

Even if you do take care not to strain hammers, some will break. If you have an expensive hammer, you can replace the handle later. To replace a handle, take the head with the broken end of the handle still in it, roast the whole thing in your oven (on "broil") or leave it under the grate in a fireplace. Then pick the ash out of the hammer head, insert a new handle, and drive in small metal wedges to hold the head in place.

Generally, hammers are expendable. We buy them by the dozen for a dollar each at the flea market. Hammers not only break, but get covered with glue or mastic or simply get dropped in a hole. You can afford not to fix, clean, or mourn a single hammer that cost you only a dollar. Our "buy 'em and break 'em" attitude may offend the true woodworker; he buys the best and cares for his tools lovingly. We are not specialized woodworkers or cabinetmakers; we are first of all recyclers. Our trade has its necessities.

Have a supply of hammers; don't lose time hunting for a lost or strayed one. We know someone who spends a lot of time compulsively searching for small mislaid tools. He never gives up and never gets much done. To avoid this, when we see screwdrivers, pliers, wrenches, vice grips, or even small power drills at a bargain, we grab them up.

Claws

Back to claws. Claw hammers and gooseneck claws work well on nails that are already started out of the wood, but what of those nails flush with or sunk into the wood? That's when you need a "catspaw" whose points can chisel into a board to wedge a sunken nail head to the surface. From that point on, either a claw hammer or gooseneck has to take over to pull it out. The claw itself won't pull a nail. Using a claw in tandem with a hammer, even though the heads are buried a quarter of an inch into the plank, you dig 'em out quickly.

If a nail is too deep for even a catspaw, take a cold chisel, or—if you use it carefully, so as not to strike the nail—a wood chisel. Cut the wood away from the nail head so it's exposed enough to be wedged up by a claw.

Suppose your nail head is bent over and hard to reach. Working at the nail from one side with a claw may bend it more. The best "straightener-upper" for a bent nail in a close place is a pair of wire cutters. They grab the nail from both sides and you can then bend it straight in no time.

Bending Nails

Finally, there is the option of not extracting nails at all; if you're not going to reuse the piece of wood, pry off the whole piece, nails and all, and bend the nails over before throwing the wood away. (The surest way to have an accident in a work situation is to let planks with nails sticking out lie around. A trip to the local infirmary for a tetanus shot because you punctured yourself is not an aid to efficiency.)

If you intend to use the piece of wood, be conscientious about removing every nail. The nail you leave in is the nail your circular saw will hit later on. It's less expensive to pull a nail than change a saw blade.

Pry Bars

This brings us to pry bars. They are classed as wrecking bars, stripping bars, ripping bars, chisels, and crowbars. Some have a gooseneck working end or neck, and others have a different shape at the neck. The curved end of the gooseneck stripping bar referred to previously is the most powerful nail-puller of all; the more specialized pry bars fit more special needs.

Crowbar: a straight steel rod four to five feet long with a thick chisel-pointed end; for heavy duty wrecking, breaking up concrete, etc. We call ours "The Killer."

Jimmy bar: one foot long version of above; used in close quarters to "jimmy open" cracks.

Ripping bar: has a slight bend; used to pull nails when there's an obstruction close above nail.

Gooseneck stripping bar: rounded neck; pulls nails where the space above is free.

Stripping bar: has a square neck; used where a gooseneck ripping bar won't work because of an obstruction such as a wall right beside the nail.

Floor and clapboard chisel: a short bar with a wide, wedge-shaped spade-end for hammering apart crates to open them, and wedging apart crevices between floor boards, etc., in order to pry them up.

Gooseneck wrecking bar: king-size gooseneck for pulling spikes.

Clapboard chisel: driven behind a shingle, it cuts the nails off behind the shingle, so a shingle can be removed without being broken up.

Electrician's chisel: shears nails in hardwood flooring to pry boards up for laying cable.

Molding chisel: removes the trim along the floor and along the ceiling without scarring it; you hammer it lightly to pry up the molding and then remove the nails with the nail slot in the chisel head.

All the above chisels are soft-bladed; they can deal only with wood. If you want to cut, split, or crack heavy metal, such as a spike or nut, you use a *cold chisel.* It's made of hardened steel and has a blade no wider than the shaft; it will not break even under great pressure.

That's a fairly complete list. You don't need them all. For example, unless it's imperative to work fast yet save moldings, you don't need a molding chisel. Any flat-ended prybar used carefully will do. To get all the pry bars listed would cost fifty to seventy dollars, so proceed with caution. Start with the bare minimum: the catspaw nail claw and the gooseneck ripping bar will do.

Saws

Now to other ways of unfastening. Start with "slim saws."

If you want to remove old heating pipes or get rid of a stud that won't pull out easily, the reciprocating saw is the answer. It's a portable power tool fitted with a slim metal-cutting blade that can cut pipe or studs at the floor or wall surface. The reciprocating saw is the big brother of the saber saw. It is one of the surest, fastest, and most useful of unfastening tools. We did recycle our first house mainly with a saber saw, but a reciprocating saw would have done it for us faster. It's bigger and more powerful, a professional tool, twice to three times as tough as a saber saw, worth the extra money. We pick the reciprocating saw over the saber saw as an unfastening tool.

Hacksaws and Hole Saws

The handheld equivalents of the saber and reciprocating saws are the hacksaw and the hole saw. There are times when the handheld hacksaw is the only thing you can use to get at the job; but it's a tedious way of cutting things. Make sure your blade is sharp if you have a lot of cuts to make. Even a fairly new hacksaw blade can be quickly dulled to uselessness by sawing hardened steel bolt. Hacksaw blades should be changed frequently.

Stab-saw: a handle which holds an unsupported hacksaw blade; in effect, a way to hand hold a short hacksaw blade. The stab-saw, unlike the hacksaw, can cut metal flush with any surface and saw from a start in a slot or hole. It's slower than a hacksaw. A reciprocating saw will do the job in one-tenth the time of either hacksaw or stab-saw if you can get it into position.

Shears rather than a saw often will do the most rapid job on metal. Bolt-cutters are giant, highly-leveraged shears that will snap off half-inch thick bolts of mild steel. A bolt-cutter also will shear sheet metal; it will cut through wire cable, provided the wire is not highly tempered (tempered steel wire will nick the shears; use a hacksaw). Bolt-cutters are big and heavy and expensive. They can be replaced in function by the slower reciprocating saw; yet, if you have a lot of metal cutting in a recycle, bolt-cutters will more than pay their way.

Compass saw: this is a narrow-nosed wood and metal saw which can be inserted through a hole drilled in a wall to cut the wall away. The small version is called a keyhole saw.

Sledges

That brings us to yet another class of unfasteners: sledges. The metal-headed sledge is the recycler's equivalent of a construction company's wrecking ball. The recycler can break up, splinter, or otherwise knock asunder what stands between him and the plan he's made for a particular house.

There are two types of metal sledge. The hand sledge has a foot-long handle; you use it in narrow quarters or where only judicious impact is indicated. Second, there are the three- to ten-pound standard sledges with three-foot handles. You swing these in a big arc, and they cause big damage to unwanted objects. We have a large and small sledge on every job.

A wood sledge is less destructive and more efficient for moving a wall back or knocking out a beam you want to preserve.

Two things you must not hit using a sledge: yourself or the sledge handle. A heavy sledge head tends to bounce to the side easily, so stand clear when you hit. If you over-reach the mark and hit the object with the handle instead of the head, you will snap the handle.

Wedges Help Sledges

A useful helper to the sledge is the woodcutter's wedge, as is used in splitting firewood. You can split a reluctant stud by driving a wedge into it, then sledge it in two; use the wedge to cut through nails under the foot of a stud. Whenever a really powerful chiseling action is needed to do the trick, the sledge plus wedge will do it.

There is a kind of wedge mentioned previously which is important; that is the very small wedge driven into the end of a hammer or sledge handle inside the head of the sledge to spread the wood and thus secure the head of the sledge (or hammer). A wedge can work loose. If this kind of wedge works loose it should be reset immediately in a different place in the end of the handle and an additional wedge driven in to keep the handle tight. By no means work with a hammer or sledge whose head is a bit loose. A loose head can fly off like a ballistic missile.

If you find something that doesn't give way to the sledge, use a house jack. A real tiger of a tool, it can lift 5,000 pounds.

Wedge a jack against a beam, and you can break it by jacking away. Your sledge won't do it because of the beam's resilience. The house jack is also useful for pulling up posts, holding beams to exact height alignment until they can be fastened, or for jacking the end of a beam right out of its fastening place.

One more important category of unfasteners is the screw and bolt removers.

Screws and bolts sometimes rust up. Normal attempts to remove them are ineffective. The screw and bolt extractor is a tapered righthand-threaded shaft with a handle at right angles. You take a power drill and bore a hole in the bolt or screw, then turn the extractor down into the hole. It goes in with counterclockwise turns. When the extractor sticks fast in the hole in the bolt or screw, just keep on turning it counterclockwise and the screw or bolt will unbolt or unscrew from its hole. Don't get a cheap extractor; the cheap ones break.

Extractor-aids

One great "extractor-aider" which should be applied preliminary to any removal process is "penetrating oil." This is a special lubricant which loosens rust and penetrates dirt to reduce resistance to turning. Soak a reluctant screw or bolt with penetrating oil and let it stand for a week if you have the time; this will often permit extraction easily.

If you heat the nut or bolt for thirty seconds with a propane torch, you may be able to loosen it that way—the metal will expand and break loose enough to be turned. You can do the same with a screw.

The ultimate extractor is an "impact wrench." You hit the top of the wrench with a hammer which imparts a turning effect on the bottom of the unit. You attach either a wrench or a screw blade to the bottom to loosen bolts and screws, respectively.

If the extractor-plus-penetrating oil or the impact wrench or the propane torch do not work, you can drill into the bolt or screw with a twist drill just slightly smaller in diameter than the bolt or screw. What remains is a thin shell which you can pry out with a prick punch.

A last resort in unfastening is an acetylene torch. You can use it to cut through thick metal, but unless you have been to welding school or at least have had some experience in welding, this should be best left for someone who has.

That winds up the formal categories of unfastening. There are informal categories though. That is to say, if you want to unfasten something badly enough, you will find a way to do it with what you have.

Say you want to remove a plank by pulling its nails, but you don't have a nail claw. You can sharpen a screwdriver blade (if that is all you have), dig out the wood around the head of each nail, and pull it with pliers. Or say your screw and bolt extractor isn't available. You can hacksaw through the nut from top to bottom and split the nut off with a cold chisel, then drive the bolt out with the chisel.

Some unfastening jobs are quite complex and take several rounds of pulling, sledging, and cutting out to bring about the desired removal. That's a small but satisfying challenge met.

17

The Fasteners

The simplest fastener of all is a hammer driving a nail. Nailing's advantages are speed and ease. Most important of all, nails are cheap. This makes nailing the fastening method of choice.

The claw hammer rather than the roundheaded (or balpeen) is more versatile (as indicated in the previous chapter), so we buy claw hammers a dozen at a time.

Nails come in "penny" sizes. A 3d is a "threepenny." They come in different shapes, such as common, box, brad, finishing, and spike. These all have slightly different advantages and yet to some extent can be interchanged in a pinch. The finishing nail has a small head, so it can be driven flush to leave only a small piece of metal showing. You can drive it in farther with a "nail set" and cover that with wood putty to make "invisible nailings."

Spikes

On the large end of the nail spectrum are spikes—technically, 20d nails or bigger. Where a stud or joist has to be nailed up solidly with only a couple of nails, a nail the size of a spike is required. In driving big nails, to avoid the danger of the spike splitting the wood, drill a slightly undersized hole for your nail, just as you would for a screw. When nailing paneling or sheet rock, the best procedure is to use nails in pairs, so that the first nail positions the panel, while the second holds it in place more firmly.

Hammers

Hammers are also used for non-nailing fastening jobs such as pounding a piece of paneling into place. Here, a professional carpenter would use a soft wood mallet, but you can make do holding a soft wood block to the paneling. Either way, the hammer can't mar paneling.

Besides "nailing," common verbs in fastening are: screw, bolt, glue, staple, rivet, join, sew, and solder.

Screws Fit Stronger

Screws cost more, but hold ten times stronger than nails the same wire-size and length. We buy a dozen at a time of common size screwdrivers; these come cheap. To drive a lot of screws quickly, use a drill with a screw-driving adapter. We buy half a dozen power drills at a time, given a good bargain. Power drills are relatively cheap and speed many jobs considerably. A variable speed power drill can run slow; otherwise it's necessary in driving screws by power drill to gain power by gearing down via "power chucks." These enable the standard drill to drive screws. A power drill with a power-chuck screwdriver takes the pain out of fastening with screws. (The power-chuck can also be fitted with a wrench head for turning nuts.) Other screw fittings include a drive head set at right angles and a flexible cable drive head.

A desirable drill feature from a recycler's point of view is a reversible motor; this means you can unfasten screws quickly, as well as fasten.

In hand screwdrivers, a "ratchet" feature is good. It allows you to turn the screw, and then turn the handle back to get a new purchase without letting go. This speeds up the job.

One ingenious form of ratchet, the "Yankee screwdriver," turns the screw when you push the handle down. It's the fastest of all ways to drive screws. You do have to have the footing to push hard on the handle without losing balance. (You can also fit "Yankee" with twist drills for drilling in places inaccessible to the power drill.)

There is, finally, a screwdriver which doesn't much look like a screwdriver at all—the offset screwdriver, a metal handle running out horizontally from a screwdriver blade. With this, you can drive or extract screws in a location where there's an obstacle close above the screw itself; you work at the screw from the side, the way you do with a wrench. At times, no other screwdriver will do.

Sizes if Screwdrivers

It's important to have available four sizes of common screwdrivers. Nothing will botch a job as quickly as using a screwdriver whose blade is too small for the slot in the screwhead. The too-small blade will constantly slip out of the slot, scarring the screw head in the process. Pretty soon you have a ruined slot that will force you to extract the screw somehow and replace it. A snug fit between the blade and slot is critical.

As a screwdriver wears down, the sides of its blade wear unevenly. Then, even if the blade was originally the right size, it will nevertheless now slip out of the slot because the sides don't fit snugly. Time to put it away and pick up a new one.

If you want to save a screwdriver from job to job, you can "square" the blade with a file or on a grinding wheel. It's also possible to change the size of any screwdriver blade in order to get a particular job done where you don't have the right size blade at hand; another job for the grinding wheel.

There are various sizes and shapes of screws. You can read all about them in any complete tool manual. They come in "wire sizes," the size of the shank, or thickest part of the shaft. Get an actual-size screw chart to identify the size and thread of the various screws when ordering them.

Every screw has at least two different diameters; the diameter of the lower threaded part is slightly smaller than the shank. In the common flathead screw, there is also the even larger tapered head that has to go into the wood. If you're dealing with softwood, as you are in most construction, you have no real problem. To drill the right size hole for a screw, you simply eyeball it. Hold the drill above the screw and close one eye; the right drill is large enough so that there is just a little thread showing out from under each side of the drill as you squint at the two. When you drill, pine board will compress enough so you can drive the screw shank down and the head as well.

However, in harder wood, such as maple or oak (you run into a lot of hardwood in Victorian houses), you won't compress to fit the larger shank. So you first drill the threaded diameter hole, then drill a larger hole partway in for the shank, and then use a countersink bit for the head, three separate operations.

A way to do this much faster—a way to do any screw-fastening job more easily—is to buy what are known as all-in-ones or "screw mates," little blade drills exactly the size of a given screw (like a metal cutout of the screw's shadow). This will allow you to do the whole job in one pass with the drill. The disadvantage is that you have to have one blade drill for every size screw. Let's say you have to drive twenty screws the same size; a blade drill would pay for itself right there.

Twist Drills

Most drills for small size screws are "twist drills." These consist of twisted grooves in a metal shaft. Most twist drills will go through metal; but some of inferior quality will only go through wood. From our point of view, it's worthwhile getting the more expensive twist drills so we can use them for both wood and metal as needed.

When it comes to boring large holes for fastening purposes,

however, the "flange bit," a shaft with flanges, will do the job a lot faster. Any hole a quarter inch to two inches in diameter calls for the flange bit rather than a twist drill. Beyond that size, you use an expensive bit, a blade bit which can be set for diameters up to four inches.

The only remaining kind of hole-drillers for screw fasteners are the rotary-wheeled hand drill and auger bits held in an old-fashioned carpenter's brace. Both are outmoded by the power drill and are used only in situations where you can't get a power line in or can't position the power drill.

Bolts

The bolt is a way of making a fastening job easily reversible. We use bolts (the most expensive kind of fastening) in wood construction where we want a very strong structure or want to be able to take the structure down again in the future.

Our permanent workbench can be taken down and carted from place to place; we bolted it together with large "carriage bolts" strong enough to be set so tight that a few of them will do the job of many screws or nails.

The small "machine bolt" is most frequently used in metal construction where screws and nails can't be used. We are always dealing with metal structures and so have a number of adjustable wrenches to loosen or tighten the nuts that secure machine bolts in place. One adjustable wrench does duty for a whole box of fixed size wrenches, so we don't bother buying fixed size wrenches at all. One exception is socket wrenches; they reach difficult spaces.

One of the weaknesses of nuts and bolts is that their threads are easily damaged and dirtied. Screws are cheap by comparison, so you are much more likely to discard them and use spares on hand. If we have to work with an expensive carriage bolt whose threads are dirty, we have inside and outside "thread chasers" that can scour dirty threads. For badly damaged "cross threaded" bolts and nuts (someone tried to force the nut on), we have adjustable dies (for bolts) and taps (for nuts), which are, in effect, circular gouges that recut the thread and save you a trip to the store to replace a damaged bolt.

Pliers and Vise Grips

Sometimes, you'll be forced to use pliers for removing a nut from a bolt. Standard wrenches just won't get in there; or, you haven't got the right wrench. Pliers grip a nut only under continuous hand pressure, so it helps to have a strong hand in undoing a nut with pliers. On the other hand, if you get a series of easy-to-put-on nuts, you can do it quicker with pliers than a common wrench, since you can let go and reset the pliers very quickly to turn the nut.

However, pliers tend to slip and scar nuts, so it's better to use this tool as an extractor or gripping aid rather than as a fastener. Pliers, generally speaking, will do a lot of jobs in a mediocre fashion that other tools will do better. Nonetheless, pliers are so versatile, it's handy to have several pair around.

Vise grips are pliers with a self-locking mechanism. These are very versatile and fast, but do a relatively rough job on nuts, scarring them unless a buffer is used. Vise grips also can be used to hold pipe and as temporary clamps. They do have a wide range of uses. We always have a half dozen available on any recycling job.

Fastenings for Special Materials

Concrete, plaster, mortar, and Sheetrock are nonwood, nonmetal materials that require special fasteners.

Concrete or masonry can be pierced with cement nails, strong shanked nails with fluted sides. For a more permanent, consistent fastening process, a carbon steel tipped special masonry bit will drill into cement, stone, brick, and other hard surfaces. The holes can then be plugged with anchors of one sort or another built to accept screws.

Plaster and wallboard are two cases. Where the fastener is to be sunk into a wall where a stud runs directly in back, a regular nail or screw is used. The studs can be located with fine precision by a stud-finder or "stud dowser" using metal balls or a magnetic compass. Or you can develop a knack for finding studs by tapping the wallboard.

Where there is no stud in back, the flange-type "molly" bolt is used. It's inserted through a hole drilled with a masonry bit; then, as the screwhead is turned, flanges spread out behind the wall to hold the bolt in place. A variation on this is the toggle bolt, which has folded wings that will spring into ready position when thrust through a predrilled hole in the wall. The toggle is tightened until the bolt holds firmly to the wall.

Gluing

One of the most frequent forms of fastening is gluing. Today there are glues that will stand up to damp and hold forever, provided you get them to "take" in the first place. If we restore a banister or a piece of furniture, we use glue. The general rules for successful gluing are: 1) preparation, 2) penetration, and 3) pressure.

Under (1) preparation, clean the surfaces and sand them slightly rough. Any piece of material to be glued should be sanded before gluing.

For (2) penetration, make sure there is no oil or other slippery material already on the gluing surfaces to prevent the glue from sinking into the material and grabbing hold. If you have oily surfaces, forget about gluing.

(3) Glue's success is directly proportionate to how small the gap, i.e., how much pressure you can apply to the pieces to be glued as the glue dries. A glue will lock two pieces together when the surfaces are only a hundredth of an inch apart, but may fail if they are a sixteenth of an inch apart.

In the case of a molding, we put glue on the underside and apply pressure by driving two or three nails per strip. On a banister, we'd wedge or clamp the banister pieces together so that there is pressure on the pieces while they dry.

Stapling

The modern construction staple gun is to an ordinary desk stapler as the tiger to the pussycat. The carpenter's staple gun is about the quickest fastener there is. Almost everybody uses the staple gun to bond fiberglass insulation between studs or roof or floor joists. The fiberglass roll has edges designed to take staples. Working with fiberglass is an unprepossessing job because the little glass "dust" gets in your pores; so the quicker you can do the job and get out, the more comfortable you'll be. In view of that, the stapling gun is a blessed invention.

Joining

There's a whole area called cabinetmaking or "joinery"; this is the classic carpentry-as-art field with antecedents back through the woodworkers' guilds of the Middle Ages. Decoratively putting together two pieces of wood with complex joinery isn't something that is needed all that often in recycling; our work with wood is usually fairly unarty. In the case of hardwood floors, we nail floors down with finishing nails without any attempt to pretty up the work.

There are times when you might use joinery technique to dowel-and-glue two pieces of wood together, rather than bolt or screw or nail. This simply means you buy a dowel (round wood stick), drill holes in each piece just a bit larger, coat the dowel with glue, and drive it in, thereby locking the two pieces to each other forever. You might want to do this when you have such a limited space for your fastening device and you want the fasteners to be flush with the wall. You can in a pinch use a pencil or cut the head off a spike as dowels.

Riveting

This is another ancient technique, in which a metal rod stub is thrust through a pair of matched holes in separate pieces of metal to be joined. The rod end is then bashed and spread so that the rivet cannot come out of the holes; this makes a solid connection.

Today there is a home riveting outfit you can get at most hardware stores. It consists of a couple of shaped pieces of metal. One piece is male, to pound the rivet head with the help of a hammer. The other is female; it spreads the other end of the rivet to make it stay. You have to work on both sides of the material. One side of the rivet has to be pounded, the other side spread. This makes it no better than bolting.

A more recently developed "pop riveter" is a clever system that lets you rivet from one side only, without any pounding. It's based on an elongated rivet that spreads on the "blind side," as the pop riveter shortens it. Very neat and handy. Where you can only get at one side of an object to be fastened, but need to have pressure applied from both sides, the pop riveter is indispensable.

Soldering

Another commonly used fastening method in recycling is solder. Solder is a way of joining electrical wire and small metal pieces where not a great deal of strength is required. For soldering, you need a soldering gun or propane torch to supply the heat, flux and solder metal to provide the "glue," and some patience to learn how to do it.

Sewing

For joining fabric, as you often must do in redecorating, a sewing machine is still the best device, although there are cloth glues.

Attacking the tool problem operationally, as we have here, should make it plain what fastening tools you will need for any given project.

18

The Cutters

The most important cutting tool in recycling is the saw. Following in importance is the drill as a plain hole-cutter. The other cutters are: chisels, files, planes, knives, power sanders, bolt cutters, wire cutters, shears, and razors. The cutting verbs are saw, shear, file, plane, grind, smooth, take down, and shape.

Saws

The most common hand saw is the crosscut saw, with teeth designed to cut *across* the grain of the wood. (The length of any board runs *with* the grain of the wood.) The most frequent use of the crosscut is simply to cut across a plank to fit it to a particular job. Planks seldom exceed twelve inches in width. The crosscut never has to saw very far for any one cut.

This is not true of the rip saw. The rip saw makes a "chiseled" cut so as to be able to go *with* the grain down the length of the board without getting hung up in the fiber. The rip saw often has to travel the whole length of a plank, and to "rip" a plank by hand is a long, heavy job.

Circular Saw

Almost no one rips by hand. It's done by circular power saw, using, ideally, a seven-inch combination carbon-tipped blade. The circular saw makes short work of ripping a plank. It does it well, provided you draw an accurate line to follow and have a secure way of guiding the saw.

The circular saw will crosscut, too, but on most planks it's almost as fast and sometimes less trouble to cut it off with a hand saw. It depends on how many planks you want to saw. If you have five, use the circular saw to save your arm and time.

We usually buy the carbon-tipped circular saw blade; it lasts a long time without having to be sharpened (if you don't hit a nail or metal while sawing with it).

The circular saw is one of the most dangerous pieces of equipment you work with. It has a guard to keep teeth out of your way, but the guard swings up to let the blade into the plank; the saw blade is exposed beneath the plank as it saws. You must remember that. The saw runs on a spring trigger; if the saw binds and lurches, it shuts off as soon as your finger comes off the trigger.

The key to using this saw is to make sure that it cuts absolutely straight. Don't cut by eye; use a scribed or pencil line and a saw guide if inexperienced. The slightest bit off a straight cut and the saw binds and lurches. You can minimize binding by sticking a nail or wedge in the cut. (This is true for any kind of sawing, hand as well as power.) It also helps to keep your saw from binding to support the part of the board you're cutting off as well as the part you want to keep. Set up a comfortable situation. When you use a circular saw, be balanced on your feet so you can move easily. Sawhorses, saw benches, even sturdy old chairs help out. To saw a long piece, lay it on the floor on two two-by-fours, then push the saw along easily.

The circular saw's combination blade will splinter veneer, so use a finer "plywood blade" for a smooth cut in plywood or paneling.

Reciprocating Saws

The next most-useful saw, from the recycler's point of view, is the reciprocating saw, described in the previous chapter. Here it is used as a way of making curved cuts in wood or as a powered hacksaw for metal, saving the recycler the tedium of hacksawing by hand. For heavy metal cutting, the circular saw can be fitted with a toothless carborundum metal-cutting blade that will do the job faster than even a reciprocating saw.

The power saw is a smaller version of the reciprocating saw. The saber saw is much easier to handle on lighter materials. It also makes a smoother cut and will follow sharper curves. For the ultimate in smooth, curved cuts, though, you change to the coping or jigsaw, hand-held. There is a bench jigsaw, which, although it's small and fairly portable, is not worth buying for the small amount of use you have for it. Between the saber saw and the coping saw, you can do what you need promptly.

Next on the recycler's list is a miter saw, which sits in a miter box and has an adjustable guide that can give you any angle or cut you want. Sometimes you really need an exact eighty-nine-degree cut; the miter saw is the instrument for it. It's a square, finetoothed saw that makes precision easy, even though it's hand-held.

The bow saw or "firewood saw," fitted with a plywood-cutting blade is handy. It cuts in places where other saws won't, and cuts faster than any other kind of hand saw. We use it to cut window openings through exterior walls.

Bench Saws

We have a single, stationary bench saw that is very good to have. That is our band saw. It's a real time-saver when it comes to cutting paneling or any material that is flexible. To saw it by hand, you have to support paneling. Paneling need not be supported, however, if it is being moved through the bandsaw. That is one of the bandsaw's advantages. Another is that it can cut intricate lines quickly and smoothly. You can trim a half inch off the end of molding very quickly and accurately even though the cut is zig-zag. Also, the bandsaw cuts ceiling cork very quickly without breaking it up.

The power hole saw blade fits on a power drill. It's a set of blades from one-half inch to two inches in diameter. It's the fastest way to cut a hole of one-half inch to two inches. The set is not expensive. An expensive bit and auger will do the same job, if you are forced to do a hand-held job.

The compass saw and its smaller cousin, the keyhole saw, are two of the recycler's best friends. Take any wall, make a small opening, and the compass saw will trace any shape of cut indicated by marker line. The compass and keyhole saws have a variety of blades from wallboard, to metal-cutting, to plywood-cutting.

For a really straight, fine cut, where you are fitting pieces closely, a backsaw is handy to have. It has a "spine" which stiffens it and makes it simple to cut a very straight line with it. It's the same sort of saw that's in a miter box, except that you don't have to keep taking the miter saw out of its slot.

Hack and Rod Saws

The two remaining saws are for tough, hard-to-cut or hard metal and/or glass—the hacksaw and its cousin, the rod saw. The hacksaw can be taken up a ladder and used overhead where the reciprocating saw is not so handy. The hacksaw breaks blades frequently. (You can wrap tape around one end of a broken hacksaw blade to use as a stabsaw—substituting for a compass saw; or, buy a stabsaw handle to hold the broken piece. The hacksaw cuts mild steel well, but not hardened steel. The rod saw will cut what the hacksaw won't, although it takes time, including hardened steel and even glass bottles.

We also use an electric or gas-powered chain saw. This cuts through walls much more quickly than a reciprocating saw. It makes it possible to cut through many layers: board, shakes, shingle. A chain saw will rip nails out rather than cut through the nail, so you don't dull the blade so much.

All saws have to be kept fairly sharp or they will not function well. Every hardware store has a sharpening service which you may want to use, even though you learn how to sharpen your own. For saws with replaceable blades, such as the circular, hack, and reciprocating, keep dull blades in stock for cutting Sheetrock.

Shears

You'd think with all the saws available, you wouldn't need any other kind of metal sheet cutter. However, tin shears or tin snips, particularly the double action "airplane" shears, will cut through thin metal very quickly and easily, while the vibration caused by sawing the same material makes it very hard to saw smoothly and quickly.

Another welcome cutting tool is the carpet shear, an overgrown scissors that cuts carpets, rugs, and fabrics, as well as cardboard boxes with surprising ease.

Another somewhat specialized tool worth having (if you can get it inexpensively) is the already-mentioned bolt cutter, which will snip through relatively thick metal sheets with ease because of its high-advantage leverage system.

Chisels

There are two types, the wood chisel for soft materials and the cold chisel (and its related forms such as the cape chisel), for cutting metal.

The wood chisel is used to cut slots and other recessed areas—as for door hinges and locks; it can do that fairly quickly, provided the chisel operator has some experience at it.

The motorized version of the wood chisel is the router, but since most of the wood work in recycling is simple and not extensive, you can let the router go until you feel rich. Even if you have a router, there are times when you will find it's simpler to use your hand-held wood chisel.

The cold chisel is mostly a metal-marking and metal-breaking tool, used to lop off metal that just barely projects from a surface or to make a small dimple so you can start your metal drill off at the right spot.

Files and Rasps

A plain old "file" usually means a metal file, best used only for metal. It has very hard, ridged teeth. The rasp or wood file has softer teeth and is much less fine.

Files cannot be sharpened. They depend on a file card, a metal-bristle brush, to keep them from clogging. A file that is clogged won't really file. This is true especially in filing hardened metal. The metal filings clogging the face of the file will "roll" the file over the surface like so many ball bearings, keeping the file from cutting at all. You should use your file card to clean the file every few strokes.

Files are usually "double-cut," that is, cut to make ridges diagonally across the face from the left and diagonally from the right. However, single-cut files are available and clog less easily. Finer files, particularly, gain usefulness in single-cut. The single-cut is more easily cleaned with the file card, too.

Most people file metal by drawing a file across it from tip to tail, but on larger surfaces it's more efficient to file by pushing the file sideways down the material. It's called cross-filing. In any case, never hold the tang end in your hand; hold the file ahead of the tang so you will avoid getting stabbed by it.

Planes

The most useful plane for the recycler is the small block plane. It can smooth off the sides of planks and paneling and round edges on stock. We buy only block planes. The larger joiner plane (which is used in joinery for seriously thinning and leveling down a piece of wood) has largely been replaced in our work by the power belt-sander. We use a big commercial grade power belt-sander that will work two or three times faster than the plane, although not quite as smoothly.

The commercial grade disc sander (as opposed to the sanding attachment sold for use on the power drill) is a valuable cutter. It can remove an inch of wood from the width of a two-by-four in very little time, faster than a belt-sander. In a small closed workshop, the dust from the sander is a very logical objection; but most of our work is done in big unfinished rooms or outdoors, so we can just let the dust lie.

Knives

The knife is still useful—both as a primitive plane, and to cut, mark, and whittle. It's easy to carry.

There's another class of knife, the razor blade. The single-edge razor can be bought cheaply by the hundreds, and it will cut fabric, thin plastic sheets, wallpaper, and cork. You can use it once while it's sharp, then throw it away without a pang.

The utility knife is nothing more than a handle set with a rugged, razorlike blade that costs little. The blade can be thrown away when dull without regret. The utility knife's most prevalent use is to scribe wallboard so it can be broken to size. It will also cut through linoleum and other thin plastic materials too tough for the single-edge razor.

19

The Removers and Restorers

Recyclers do a lot of work in the first quarter-inch of the siding and interior wall surface of a house. This is not to say recycling is purely cosmetic; but, the greatest amount of deterioration—scars, imbedded dirt, paint build-up in the course of the years—does take place at or near the surface. The surface is where you restore the old beauty or bring in a contemporary color scheme. To restore the old or put on a usable attractive new surface is a big part of recycling.

Let's take wood surfaces first.

The woodwork in the house to be recycled is usually flaky with dirty paint or is unpainted, discolored, dented wood. In either case, you remove the disagreeable looking surface and then resurface. The quick way to remove wood surface is to sand; to remove paint, it's quick to scrape or sand, burn or strip. Scraping paint off is the quick way to do a small surface. The alternative is the power sander, but that's heavy and is hard to use on ladders.

Scrapers

There are several kinds of scrapers; the most professional is the simple steel blade—the cabinet scraper. If you know how to sharpen the cabinet scraper, you can peel off loose layers of paint quickly. The trick is to "true" its edges with a fine file so that all edges are "square," that is, right-angled to the two faces.

Those who don't want to get into the mystique of maintaining the cabinet scraper can use the more conventional hand-held scraper, not as precise, but since the blades are cheap, they can be discarded after they get ground down to the point they can't be resharpened.

Sanding

The other way to remove paint is to sand it off. Sandpaper comes in two forms, hand-held and power. The simplest form is a piece of sandpaper held in your hand to smooth off and suitably rough a surface where most of the paint has been previously removed. The key to repainting or resurfacing of most kinds is to have a smooth, just slightly grainy surface to repaint. *Regardless* of what else you do, you *must* prepare a surface for painting by a previous sanding.

A more sophisticated form of hand sanding is to use a sanding block. This gives you twice the speed. The block is made to hold the sandpaper so you can apply more pressure on it than if you held it in your bare hand.

There are varying grades of sandpaper. The temptation is to start with too fine a grain, and this makes for a lot of tedious sanding. It's faster to start with a good coarse grain, and then smooth the job with a fine-grain sandpaper.

The common power-sanding device is the disc attachment for the electric drill body. This works pretty well. Drill bodies are relatively cheap. We have two or three lying around on the job with a different coarseness of sandpaper on each.

Every sanding device has limitations. The electric power-drill sander can't really take much pressure. If you lean on it, its motor starts to slow down, or "lug." Too much of that will burn out the motor. The more powerful commercial grade sanders such as disc sanders, belt sanders, and orbital sanders stand up under pressure. By working faster they will do jobs in half the time an electric power-drill sander takes.

Commercial Sander

The commercial grade disc sander (discussed previously) is the fastest way to remove paint. The speed is double that of the electric drill disc sander. The commercial disc sander costs four to five times as much as the power drill; be prepared to keep it clean and maintain it.

The more powerful the disc sander, the more likely the surface is going to undulate when you are finished. If it's important to leave a flat surface, the belt sander comes on strong. The belt sander is less handy, in that you are working with a sanding machine that has to contact a large surface all the time. Precisely for that reason, the belt sander will create a surface truly flat when you are through. Obviously, you can create undulations in a surface by careless use of the belt sander, too, but it's easier to make a flat surface.

The drawback of both disc and belt sanders is that they leave scratch marks. If you have to have a "show surface," absolutely smooth to the eye, then you use the orbital sander. This vibrates back and forth (oscillates) to leave no discernible sanding marks.

Burning Paint

Another way of removing paint is to burn it off. Use a propane torch (the kind we previously discussed for soldering). Burning off is quick but tricky. Hold the torch on too short a time and you won't blister the paint enough. Hold it on too long and you scorch the wood underneath so it has to be taken down afterward with sanders (you've lost the time advantage you gained). To burn off well you have to be in good practice. (Mary once set 91 Rumson on fire burning off the outside of a set of pillars.)

The last way to remove paint is with a "stripping" chemical.

Such chemicals smell bad but dissolve well. The paint softens so it can be scraped off easily with a blade. Stripping is much used for restoring furniture, the object being to keep as much of the old wood surface intact as possible. In house restoration, we strip key wood surfaces such as painted bannisters and decorative wood pieces. Otherwise, stripping is too time-consuming to make sense in our operation. First, you have to apply the chemical, then let it set so the paint dissolves, then come back at just the right moment when the paint is suitably soft to scrape it off. If you come too soon, the paint is too hard; if you arrive too late, the chemical has started to evaporate and you have lost time.

Sometimes we have to deal with curved metal surfaces, and there the stripping process can make sense, since the surface is usually limited in area but hard to get at with a sander.

Wallpaper takes a specialized steam appliance that you can rent. To buy the steamer is expensive; it's readily rentable at big hardware stores or local contractors. After you steam the wallpaper, it can be peeled off. Then you sand the wall surface before you put on new wallpaper.

For surface removal of stains and grease we lay in a supply of strong detergents. On the insides and hood of a stove, for instance, we use Easy-Off or other spray-on grease remover. We clean up kitchen walls and woodwork with ammonia. For rust spots of small size, there are chemical rust removers that work much like stripping chemicals.

Resurfacing Walls

For resurfacing, there is a time when wall paint *is* indicated. We always paint ceilings. If you have a large house and it's not in the high price range and you have to get through it soon to make a satisfactory selling profit, then you paint walls, too.

We paint with rollers, not with brushes. The art of rolling on paint takes practice but pays off. You can learn rather quickly what the consistency of the paint has to be in the pan (use paint thinner to get the right mix) and how to roll on smoothly; a roller can do in fifteen minutes what would take an hour or more to do by brush.

In making resurfacing choices, balance the pros and cons in terms of time and money. There is no need to make yourself a "martyr to house restoring" by slaving away at details that are never going to be noticed. On the other hand, it doesn't make much sense to botch up a beautiful room because you wouldn't take the time to do it right.

Good decision-making in such a matter involves calculating the balance of cost of purchase against maintenance and cost of labor (your own). You can't duck the responsibility. You do not have to decide correctly each time. You will always make some mistakes.

A third option with paint is to spray. We use this on exteriors. We have an electric compressor spray gun that we got for a reasonable cost. The deciding factor in whether or not to use a compressor spray gun is whether or not you have a job where you can "miss the edges" a bit without having to clean up the misfired spray paint. Some who use paint sprayers "mask off" the edges to be sprayed to keep the paint in bounds, but we try to avoid that time-consuming practice.

An ideal spray painting situation: you want to stain some plain plywood paneling and can set the paneling up against a saw horse in a back yard; spray it, and let it dry there before taking it in and nailing it up.

Fillers

Our last category of resurfacers is the fillers. Nearly every long-used surface will have dents and depressions. These have to be filled out before ceilings, floors, and interior walls can be resurfaced. The filler we use inside is a prepared paste called "interior spackle." (You can also buy more expensive waterproof "exterior spackle.") You use spackle to fill out sheet rock (the normal interior wall surface in today's construction) or plaster walls (the common Victorian construction). Spackle comes in a can which you have to keep closed except when you dip in for a new supply. Have some paper pots (any hardware store sells them) for your immediate supply of paste. If you leave the can of spackle open, you dry the can out in short order.

In deeper holes, spackle will not dry out. We fill deep holes with Gyspsilite or Structo-lite, pastes that mix with water to set like cement. *Then* we finish off the surface with spackle.

For filling out wood, we use a powder wood filler. Wood fillers can be bought in shades to match the wood, light or dark.

For filling out metal surfaces, we use two-part mixes, such as auto body filler or epoxy filler. Both of these work better if you dry them under a heat lamp.

Once the surface is relatively smooth, shaped to fill out a depression with the proper contour, you can proceed with the resurfacing.

Above: Mary caulking a window. *Photo by Jeff Martin.*

Above left: 18 Beach St., before. *Photo by Sam Weir.*

Below left: 18 Beach St., after being recycled. *Photo by Jeff Martin.*

Above: 1 Ocean Ave., before. *Photo by Sam Weir.*

Right: Bathroom at 1 Ocean Ave., after. *Photo by Jeff Martin.*

Above left: 1 Ocean Ave., before. *Photo by Sam Weir.*

Above right: Sam laying slate. *Photo by Jeff Martin.*

Left: Painting The Lindens. Lots of free help from friends and relatives. *Photo by Dorn Studio.*

Left: The Lindens, ready for sale. *Photo by Mel di Giacomo.*

Below left: Stairway at The Lindens, before. *Photo by Dorn Studio.*

Below center: Same stairway after renovation. *Photo by Dorn Studio.*

Below right: Sam, Mary, and Chris at new house built on lot from The Lindens' property. *Photo by Jeff Martin.*

Above: 78 Ocean—ready for sale. *Photo by Bruce Plotkin.*

Above right: 32 Riverdale Ave. *Photo by Bruce Plotkin.*

Right: 559 Manahasset, originally a summer home, completely winterized. *Photo by Jeff Martin.*

Right: Goldencrest, after. *Photo by Jeff Martin.*

Below: Goldencrest, before.

Far left: Goldencrest kitchen, after. *Photo by Mel di Giacomo.*

Near left: The kitchen at Goldencrest at the time of purchase.

Right: 91 Rumson Rd. (the White House) in 1949.

Above: Sam, Mary, and Chris restoring an old oak fireplace. *Photo by Elizabeth Gee.*

Right: Sam and Mary painting the living room at 91 Rumson Rd. *Photo by Mel di Giacomo.*

Far right: The foyer of 91 Rumson Rd., after. *Photo by Jeff Martin.*

Above: The living room of
91 Rumson Rd., after.
Photo by Jeff Martin.

Right: The living room of
91 Rumson Rd. Sam and
Mary, with Charlie on the
bookshelves. *Photo by Mel
di Giacomo.*

Above right: Dining room,
91 Rumson Rd.

Below right: Billiard room,
91 Rumson Rd. *Photo by
Jeff Martin.*

Right: 265 New Ocean Ave. *Photo by Sharon Kent.*

Below: 78 Ocean Ave., before. *Photo by Sam Weir.*

Below center: 30 Shrewsbury Dr. *Photo by Bruce Plotkin.*

Below: Mary, working on the ceiling at 91 Rumson Rd. *Photo by Tracy Ecclesine.*

Above: 71 Victor Ave.
Photo by Bruce Plotkin.

Right: Sam, Charlie, Chris, and Mary in front of The Lindens. *Photo by Tracy Ecclesine.*

20

The Efficiency-Makers

Efficiency is important. Either work efficiently or lose time that you could have taken off or turned into money.

One path to efficiency is to use tools to fit the job. We'll start off by talking about tools to handle disc-shaped objects such as rods and pipes.

Disc Tools

The premier, all-around disc tool is the pipe wrench. It has a set of jaws designed to clamp onto any rounded surface it can encompass. If you've tried to hold a rod or pipe with a regular wrench and had to give up, you will know why pipe wrenches exist. A handy substitute for a pipe wrench is the vice grip described previously. The vice grip should be used with a cloth over its jaws to keep the teeth from scoring the pipe, if you are working with fixtures that have to retain their shine.

There is a chain wrench to loosen stubborn rods and pipes at their threaded joints. The chain wraps around the rod or pipe. With it, you can get a tremendous amount of leverage.

There are special rod or pipe clamps and vices. But, for most recycling work you are well supplied if you have a small and a large pipe wrench—a twelve-inch and a three-footer—plus a chain wrench and a combination vice, as suggested below.

The reciprocating saw and the hacksaw are preferables for cutting rods and pipes. For soft metal tubes, such as copper pipe, there are neat little pipe cutters that do the job with a minimum of stress; they don't bend or damage even a soft copper. It is important not to disturb the shape, because if you flatten out the cross section, copper pipe won't "join."

The main means of joining rods and tubes is threading. There are dies which cut an outside thread, and taps which cut the inside thread. Once threaded, the pipe or rod ends can be joined tightly and permanently—until such time as you want to undo them.

Work Accessories

Typical "accessories" include the cardboard pot which can be used to hold paint and then be thrown away, vices to hold objects while you work on them, and workbenches to provide working surfaces.

The simple workbench made of bolted-together two-by-four stock and planks is worth its weight in gold at the recycle location. There are always a few jobs a day that go much faster on a bench, particularly if it's supplied with a good vice.

Vices come in many varieties: wood vices, pipe vices, etc. The best buy is the "combination vice" with a jaw that can be used to hold non-disc stock and a pipe vice jaw, for discs, underneath. To protect surfaces from jaw-marks, place scrap wood in the vice.

There are other vices: portable suction vices that you can stick down on any flat surface and portable combination vices you can clamp fast. There are also spring clamps, which look almost like scissors and which hold work in place instantly. There are

C-clamps made to hold several pieces together and corner clamps to hold right-angle corners together. Clamps can do a hundred odd jobs requiring positioning. They are inexpensive. We sometimes leave them right in place inside the walls—they work efficiently as fasteners and sometimes are the easiest fastener to place.

Another efficiency accessory is a ladder. Used wood ladders tend to break. Aluminum ladders are not that expensive, so we opt for aluminum. The steps in the aluminum ladder last forever. The disadvantage is that aluminum conducts electricity. Watch for bare electric lines overhead when you carry it around.

Tool Boxes

Other accessories for efficiency are tool receptacles. The familiar tool box is one variety. Our preference is for tote boxes. It's a more flexible approach. We'd rather work from a two-pound tote box than a ten-pound tool box. You can put a handle on an old drawer and have a tote box.

An efficiency accessory all professional carpenters use is an apron-with-pockets. If you are nailing, you can nail twice as fast picking nails out of a pocket as out of a bag or jar. And there's the hammer loop. It hangs on your belt and keeps your hammer at hand. It saves hours a week when you are doing heavy carpentry.

Another efficiency-maker is the common plastic pail; just a half dozen pails in the room will organize small tools and materials effectively. A good big-tool carrier is a wheelbarrow.

If you can keep your tools and materials organized and at hand, you work effectively. If you don't, you spend time searching and scratching instead. Center your tools in your working area. The tools can be then quickly and easily laid down and retrieved. If you can't find a pry bar you laid down two minutes ago and have to look for it, that is just so many minutes wasted. Efficiency isn't comprised of dramatic time-saving machines, but the seconds you save 100 times a day. The difference between an organized an an unorganized approach is the difference between barely making profit and making good profit.

Organizing Materials

The same goes for materials. There comes a point where you will get overwhelmed if you don't organize the materials so you can pick them up and discard them efficiently. You need a "used lumber pile," a wood scrap pile, a metal scrap pile.

This doesn't mean a "military appearance" in the working area. It's enough if you can separate the elements so as to locate each yourself. What may look like a mess to an outsider may actually be a well organized "floor plan" for recycling. Only you can tell; if you are spending time searching for things you had in your hand ten minutes ago, then you know that your system isn't working.

Allied to this is cleanliness. The recycler's clean-up hour is when he quits. Nothing is more discouraging than to come to work early in the morning ready to go, and then spend the first hour cleaning up. Cleaning up is routine work you can do when you are tired. You should save your fresh morning-mind for the hard-to-do or hard-to-solve.

Listing Work

Leave time at the end of your day for a thirty-minute reorganizing of material and tools, sweeping up of sawdust and dirt, trash-canning of the throw-away stuff. When we first hired help, we thought we'd give the clean-up job away. But, we found that we located our tools much better the next day if we had put our own tools away.

Before going home, list what you're going to do tomorrow. Not a mental list but a written list—one, two, three, plus the materials and tools needed to accomplish the listed deeds.

Trash cans themselves are a great organizing aid. Have plenty of them around. Discard into them directly rather than having to pick up after work. It keeps the floor clean.

Finally, clean your tools. Clean them up with rags. If paint splattered on them, use paint remover. If they have mastic or resin, swab with cotton soaked in acetone. After cleaning, don't throw the rags into the trash. (There's a process called spontaneous combustion which sets oily dirty rags on fire all by themselves.) Dispose of them in a fireproof can, an empty gallon paint can with lid.

Tool Maintenance

Let's switch to the subject of maintenance; in efficient work, there's always a quota of maintenance. The most important maintenance backup are your sharpening stones. There is nothing more frustrating than working with a tool that is dull. There's a quick way out: have a portable bench grinder available. We know how to sharpen any tool in a matter of a few second's work at the grinder. We finish off with a few strokes with an oilstone, hand-held. Sharp tools make a good carpenter. Dull tools injure a carpenter because when he bears down on a dull tool it slips or bends.

There's much to be learned about sharpening tools. Spend some time learning. Even hammers, for instance, need to be ground down once in a while. Every tool how-to manual has a long section on tool sharpening. Get one and read that chapter.

The grinder itself should be maintained. There's a procedure for "truing and dressing" the grinding wheel that is important for keeping it working well. Again, read about it.

Lubricating Tools

Some maintenance falls under "lubrication." One pail in your work area is the "lubrication pail." In it are a squirt can of household oil, a pump can of heavier oil, a spray can of penetrating oil (to loosen up rusty sticky tools), and a can of WD-40 (to dry your tool if your tool gets wet; WD-40 displaces the water; your tool won't rust). Finally, the pail ought to have a grease tube.

These lubrication devices work not only on tools, but on the job you are doing. Sometimes you will be nailing into a knotty piece, for instance. Greasing the nails will make them drive in much easier.

Every power tool requires some lubrication. You may ignore that if you have classed the tool as expendable, but otherwise not. The directions for the lubrication of the tool come with it, and you ought to save the directions in a folder you keep for that very purpose. Before you take a tool into action first thing in the morning, lubricate and *then* take the tool with you. It will perform better and last longer.

21

The Troubleshooters

We have been looking at tools, materials, and procedures to make work go faster and more efficiently. Here in this chapter we will look at tools, materials, and procedures that, by and large, make work go *slower* at first, but still produce efficiency in the final sense. Troubleshooters can be described as "measures, markers, retrievers, and safety implements."

Let's have a look at measuring first.

One of the least natural things to a person who is creative (and therefore somewhat impatient at times with "what is") can be meticulous measurements. If "genius is the infinite capacity for taking pains," a genius of a recycler takes pains with his measuring. If your measuring is consistently an inch off on the placement of studs, for instance, everything that follows can also be thrown off.

Measured Modules

Modern construction calls not only for measuring but for paying attention to the measuring of modules in which a building is constructed. One such is the "center" for studs. If you build with studs "on two-foot centers," each stud will have its center just two feet from the center of the studs on each side. This "module" allows you to calculate a number of things that follow so that you can always make use of studs to the best advantage, because you know exactly where they are. Say you want to fasten a fixture on a wall; you can confidently place it where you will get maximum support from the studs in back of the sheetrock covering the studs.

Another module is the four-by-eight-foot sections in which plywood (the most useful building material) comes. If you scale your plans to multiples of four feet or even divisions of four feet, you can reduce the number of cuts and of wasted lumber substantially. There may be good reasons for departing at some points from the modules used on a construction; but, you should think about such a move carefully.

Tapes and Rules

The most frequently-used measuring tools are tapes, rules, and straightedges, all marked in inches and feet. Tapes are soft and have to be wound back into their case, but are very compact, so you can carry a forty-foot tape in your pocket. Rules are semi-flexible and spring back into their cases automatically. Straightedges are rigid and are used to measure, but mostly to guide pencil lines and scribed lines (scratched into the material). In a pinch you can draw a line, or scribe one, using a rule instead of a straight edge, but it's not as sure.

The rule has a disadvantage, and so does the measure. They depend on a certain amount of tension or friction to hold them in place, which means for measuring long distances your tape or rule may more easily slip. A straightedge lies in place by its own weight more readily.

Straights and Squares

The elite class of all measuring tools carrying inch marks (or metric marks, or both), then, is the straightedge. If you are working alone, as we often are, then straightedges of three and six feet are handier than a tape measure or rule. We keep a couple of three- and six-footers around for just that reason.

The straightedge has a cousin, the square. One kind of square is the fixed or "try square." A fixed head sets at right angles to the longer straightedge part. Another kind is the combination sliding square, in which the head slides along the rule section; the head can set at forty-five degrees as well as at a right angle. (If you need a quick forty-five degree angle, just fold a square piece of paper in half.)

The *raison d'etre* of the square is to draw a line directly across the grain of a plank for a crosscut. The assumption is that the plank has been so well cut that when you draw at right angles to one side, you will have a line that meets the other side at right angles too. The whole plank as cut will then fit nicely into a rectangular space. Let us stop long enough at this point to say that the assumption about the accuracy of cut of the plank should be checked before you proceed. Simply check whether the lines of the sides are exactly the same distance apart all the way down the plank (in other words, check whether the plank's sides are parallel). If that is so, you may proceed with confidence.

In ripping, you use a chalk line. Measure down from the far edge the requisite number of inches—eleven—on the plank at both ends, stretch the chalk line between, pull it up like a bowstring, and snap! It lays a straight-as-an-arrow line down the length of the board, parallel to the far side. If you try this operation on a twelve-foot plank using just a six-foot straight edge, you'll see how hard it is to come out right and how much slower. You can, of course, measure anything with precision with almost any tool, no matter how inappropriate, but the idea is to do it fast.

Using Scrap

Here's a startling thought: the recycler is really not interested in the actual dimension! What he is interested in *isn't* the fact that it's exactly sixteen feet and three sixteenths inches from one point to the next, but that this is simply a length than you have to measure off, regardless of exactly how long it may be.

A couple of pieces of scrap wood clamped together with a C-clamp so that their combined length "takes off" exactly the dimension needed will be a lot quicker to use than a rule if you have to measure out the dimension five times.

What do we have to measure besides length and width? Well, there's diameter.

You have a tube and you want to plug it; how thick a plug? An "inside caliper" "takes off" or measures the inside diameter; then you lay the caliper on a rule to get it in inches if you want to. To measure the outside dimension of a rod or a pipe, there are "outside calipers," as well.

You may say, why not measure a pipe with a rule? It's pretty hard to make sure you are measuring the diameter. To do that, you would have to lay your rule exactly over the center of the pipe by eye. Of course, with a little finagling, you can probably get the diameter. Measure several times; the longest measurement should be very close to the diameter because a diameter is the longest possible distance across the circle. (Or, you can lay a string around the circumference, measure that and divide by pi, which is 3.1416.)

Measuring Angles

How about measuring angles? There's an angle measurer, called a T-bevel which "takes off" the angle so you can lay it on the piece of wood that has to be cut to fit the angle.

How about finding the center of a circle? You need to find that when you drill a screw hole to attach one piece to another. The "centering punch" will fit into the top hole, and when you hit it, mark the center position for an identical hole in the identical place on the bottom piece. This means that once you've drilled one piece, you don't need to measure up all the remaining pieces, but just locate the holes with a centering punch from the original piece.

(For drilling holes in general, there are prick "punches" that will make visible the spot where you want to drill; the punch will indent the spot enough so that your drill won't hop about during the first revolutions before it digs in.)

Measuring Holes

Besides width, length, diameters, degrees, and centers, there is also a need to measure the depth of a narrow slot or hole. You use a depth gauge; very simple. There are several types, depending on the size of the hole.

Suppose you want to divide a piece of wood exactly in half? This was one of the very ancient geometry problems; the solution is probably a couple of thousand years old. You take a "compass" or a "divider," as it's called, and draw two overlapping arcs, centered on each end. Rule a line through the two intersections of the arcs; that line divides the piece exactly in half. Euclid wrote it first. (You can also divide a piece of wood—roughly—by balancing it on the edge of your hand.)

A divider also can be used to "take off" a short dimension, a length you need to lay down repeatedly, as in sawing ten equal lengths, just in the way marked scrap lumber can be used.

You may need to know the size of a nail so you can order more—the length is easy, but how about the shank size? There's a "wire gauge," a board full of little holes that will do it for you. And the same for the shank size of a screw. There's also a "thread measure" which will take off the thread of a screw so you can see whether the hardware store has what you want in thread as well as size of shank.

The last item in our measuring discussion is somewhat ephemeral, but most useful: how to measure whether something is exactly horizontal and whether something is exactly vertical.

An age-old construction philosophy is that you do very well to have the sides of your house as nearly perfectly vertical as possible, and its beams and floor as nearly horizontal as possible. A wall which leans to one side has a tendency to lean more and more to that side as time goes on. A tilting floor is no fun either.

Even more than that, we want any wall to be parallel to any

opposite wall, so that we can safely estimate the length of planks for these two walls and the floor between. Gravity provides us with a great reference line. Anything that measures the direction of gravity exactly can provide us with a precisely vertical reference line anywhere in our construction job. This makes parallel wall construction much simpler to set up.

The simplest and oldest gravity-direction measuring device is the plumb bob, which is a shaped weight on a string. The string is by definition vertical (when it stops swinging).

The more usual tool for gravity-vertical, though, is a level, which is constructed so that a bubble floats in between the center lines of the tube when the framework around the tube lies exactly horizontal, or exactly vertical, depending on how the level is held.

(One of the problems, of course, with an old house is that a particular room or the whole house for that matter, may be "out of plumb." If you put up horizontal shelves in a room, it makes the room look askew. So you fudge a little.)

Troubleshooting

Let's go to another kind of troubleshooting; troubleshooting tools.

What happens when you drop an irreplaceable part down an inaccessible slit to a nearly irretrievable depth? If it's metal, get out your troubleshooting magnet and lower the magnet down on a string. If that won't work, they make something called "mechanical fingers" which has a set of small claws that will close around an object stuck in a crack. If you can't see down the crack to get it, then there's an "inspection mirror" that sits on a stick that will let you look into the crack to see it.

You may need some light on the subject. It's exasperating to have to work in poor light. Luckily, the cost of the extension cords and protected "drop lights" that go on them is not that much, so we always keep them in supply.

Another troubleshooting tool is a set of lock picks and skeleton keys for opening reluctant doors (our own). We nearly always have a couple of coat hangers around for bending into whatever shape needed to retrieve overhead lines, or wire dropped between studs, or even to get the door of our van opened when we lock ourselves out.

Safety Devices

That brings us to the last troubleshooting category: safety. Safety would be universally practiced if it didn't take time to do so. We take that time. The alternative smacks of eternity.

The most dangerous thing we deal with is height. We make sure our ladders are set sturdily and properly before we go up. We test a plank before we use it to walk from one beam to the next. We never assume that when we are working at height we have to hurry. That's one time when the most efficient person is the slowpoke.

Second most dangerous is electricity. A shock can interrupt your heartbeat and/or breathing impulse until and unless you get resuscitation. Even resuscitation may not help if electricity is coupled with dampness. The man who stands in wet shoes on a wet floor and gets a shock is a man in real danger of losing his life. Normally, the human body acts as a resistor to restrict the current that travels through, but when you have wet feet in contact with a damp floor, your body acts as an electrical wire, not an electrical resistor. Pow! When it's wet, we go around in rubber-soled boots if we're doing any wiring, and we handle wire with dry gloves.

If we're doing any work with power tools, we set up a "ground fault interrupter" (GFI) on the end of our power cord.

Another likely accident we are exposed to is getting hit by dropped material from above. When we're "working below," we put on a hard hat.

Vulnerable Parts

Fourth is eye damage. The eye is the most delicate irreplaceable organ that you have. We're cautious about exposing it. If we're using a circular saw, painting overhead, or mixing "hot stuff" we put on a pair of nonprescription glasses; they look just like ordinary glasses and yet are inexpensive. They give us a lot of protection. When using the bench grinder, we put on goggles or the full-length plastic face shield that is held in place by a headband. The sparks from the grinder could cause eye damage very easily.

The area next most vulnerable to the eyes is the lungs. There are new nose masks which will protect you from organic fumes as well as dust particles. We put on either a nose mask or one of the doctor's respiratory masks if we're machine sanding in close quarters and old paint dust is flying around. The dust may be leaded, and you risk lead poisoning by breathing it. There's nothing healthy at all about old paint in any form, and we'd just as soon smoke five packs of cigarettes a day for a year as stand in a spray of old paint dust for an hour without protecting our lungs. The same is true of using spray paint cans or paint sprayer.

The most frequently hit part of the anatomy, of course, is the hand. What should you do to prevent scratches, abrasions, and the like, which while not lethal can be damaging enough to cut your working efficiency? Use gloves. We use gardeners' gloves a lot. If we mix paint, we use rubber gloves. We like to come back home without having our hands look like they have been in a shark's mouth.

One more vulnerable organ is the ear. Whenever we cut with a loud circular saw or disc sander for more than a couple of seconds, we wear earplugs or earphones—which look big, but are really very light and comfortable. Continuous loud noise can damage your hearing. We want to keep our hearing unimpaired, thanks.

No one can lay down a complete set of safety rules for every situation; use your head. Don't be misled into bravado. You're in business to take business risks, not health risks.

part 5

Installing Basic Value Raisers

22

Insulation: Foam, the Magic Money

There are four basic value-raisers in recycling.

First there is insulation, which is the one basic in which most older houses and many new ones are woefully deficient. It is almost a byword in recycling that where you insulate you make value.

The second basic which most older houses lack is plumbing for a decent number of bathrooms in the house. New bathrooms, which are a common recycling addition, each require new plumbing. And the old plumbing may not be working well, either.

Then there is heat: a summer house with potential for becoming year-round is a sure money-maker. Here, a whole heating system has to be put in. Also, the old house may have no central heating, or the heating system that is installed may not be working right.

Finally, electricity. There's often not enough capacity in an older house for 1979 kitchen, bath, and appliance needs. Here

167

is one place the recycler can modernize appreciably.

We'll start with the first of these; ways of insulating an older house.

The chapters in this section, incidentally, like the preceding section, are fairly technical. There is a good amount of basic theory, and there is also a good amount of detail pertinent to recycling. For those who would rather not get into such detail at present, it would be advisable to turn to the section beyond this one, part 6, rehabilitating interiors and exteriors, which may be more relevant to those having no experience in working with insulation, plumbing, heating, and electrical systems.

However, once any of these jobs are to be tackled in a house, the reading of the chapters in this section will prove very helpful. There are a number of technical handbooks and how-to books dealing with these subjects (the best of which we've listed in the appendix), but a look at basic theory and a look at the facets most directly connected to recycling will help the recycler read the handbooks with more understanding.

Cutting Energy Consumption

As the energy crisis continues, all of us have become more aware of how directly energy consumption affects our personal pocket-books. "Insulation" is the magic word relevant to the enormous waste of energy that takes place in the average American home. A year ago, an article on our recycling operation ran in the Sunday *New York Times;* the reaction was unbelievable. Scores of people called us from places such as Oregon, Arizona, and Michigan to ask about recycling. The single most common question had to do with reinsulating their homes. They felt they were losing money in wasted heat. (They were undoubtedly right.)

Take a look at the home maintenance and do-it-yourself building manuals of five years ago. Note what a minor place insulation occupies. A couple of inches here, a couple of inches there. Heat was cheap. If you turn to the section on heating systems in those same books, there's lots of advice on how to pour on the heat. The books could have been written by the fuel companies.

A building contractor starts from scratch to decide, within his budget, what kind of insulation he wants. He designs and constructs the house with that in mind. A recycler is given certain fixed spaces; he must fit his insulation to those spaces. The result must make sense in heat savings versus time and money spent.

Pioneering Reinsulation

Recyclers, appropriately enough, have thus become pioneers in the art of reinsulation. The United States is trying to make both fuel and housing stretch. Reinsulation is a great stretcher on both counts. As an added inducement, there's a tax incentive program. Before you reinsulate, check with your local or state government; in many localities, there's either a rebate tax deduction or low-interest loan for reinsulation projects.

The insulating that a recycler does is his second most frequent source of added recycling value. It ranks in frequency right after installing good central heating. Nobody today wants to buy a house not centrally heated, nor well insulated.

We have taken huge mansions and run our "insulation drill" on them, with the result that we can show prospective buyers a fuel bill in line with the cost of heating a smaller modern ranch home. A two-story Victorian house is more economical to heat than a ranch, because any two-story home uses only one roof to cover double the room space of a single-story ranch home. Even disregarding that advantage, we have learned how to do a job of insulation in a Victorian house that is more efficient than the insulation you'll find in most modern ranch-style houses.

Our work as house recyclers has given us an education in the basics of insulation. We do not just apply somebody else's formula. We innovate, and we know what we are doing. We know the basic heat-energy theory as it applies to practical situations, and know what insulating materials are available.

Let's start with fundamentals: heat is a form of energy.

Broadly, energy is what the universe is made of. Solid matter, as Albert Einstein was the first to point out mathematically, is at bottom simply a very concentrated form of energy. The essence of the modern nuclear plant is that it converts matter (uranium) into energy.

It follows, from energy's universality, that energy must have the ability to go anywhere, and that nothing can stop it. Energy travels through solids (by conduction), through gasses (by convection), and even through a vacuum in space (by radiation).

Your purpose is to prevent heat from escaping from your house. The one thing to remember, however, is that you cannot completely stop energy (heat) from moving. To move is the nature of energy. All you can do is slow it down. That's the art of insulation.

Slowing Heating Down

There are many materials that slow down one or more of the three forms of heat transfer—conduction, convection, and radiation. These are mostly fibrous or spongelike materials in a "sandwich," with air or gas occupying the role of the meat between two slabs of bread. Given any type of insulation, however, the total effect depends on how thick the particular material is laid in. The thicker the barrier, the more time it takes a given amount of heat to transfer. Double the thickness equals double the conservation of heat.

Let's say it takes ten minutes after the furnace has been shut off by the thermostat until it turns on again. If you double the insulation, it takes your furnace twenty minutes to cool down before it turns on again.

Conduction-Convection

Conduction is the process of heat passing through a solid. Heat one end of a brick and the other end gets hot too. Houses are constructed of solids, so there has to be some conduction going on all the time. Energy is unstoppable. Thus, if the inside face of an interior sheetrock wall is hot, heat will conduct through the sheetrock to the "insulating" space between the inside and the outside wall.

At this point, convection takes over. Convection is a fancy name for a draft. Warm air is lighter than cold air; therefore any warmed-up air rises (convects). Heating systems have their heaters on the floor to take advantage of convection. Between an interior wall and the exterior wall, there is air. The interior wall heats up, as we've said. This, in turn, heats the air next to it. That hot air rises to the level of the ceiling inside the wall, and then it's gone as far as it can go. As it hits the barrier of the ceiling, it cools off somewhat, and the cooling air drops down next to the exterior wall, still warm enough to warm up the exterior wall.

As soon as the inside of the exterior wall warms up, the exterior wall conducts this heat to the outdoors. So you have conduction-convection-conduction.

The central idea of insulation is that the best way to slow down the between-the-wall air is to keep the air from moving. If very little convection is going on, you have a very good insulation system.

This way of looking at insulation doesn't seem like such a great leap of imagination, yet it took a long time for this idea to get across. Joule identified heat as energy transfer way back in the 1700s; 200 years later, at the end of the 1800s and even thereafter, builders were trying to "insulate" by stuffing walls full of bricks! Granted, this hindered convection somewhat, but solid, dense brick is a good conductor, and conducted heat passed through the dense brick rapidly. The *density* (weight) of a material doesn't have much to do with insulation. Thickness insulates. Weight does not. A thick layer of airy foam, or even just still air, insulates well. The confusion of thickness with density is what made the Victorian home a cold one.

Density

Density is often thought of as preventing movement. It works out quite the opposite when it comes to insulation. The more dense a material, the more quickly it conducts. Wood is relatively light compared to stone, and thus stone conducts heat more quickly than wood. Iron is heavier than stone, and iron conducts heat more quickly than stone.

When you get to the very light materials, such as a gas (air, oxygen, helium, etc.), they conduct heat very, very slowly. If you could keep gas from moving, within itself, it would be a nearly perfect insulator. But all gasses will move about in currents, just like smoke does in a room. And that is how heat starts moving through air.

Modern builders learned from nature's furred and feathered animals that what works best is to fill any between-wall space with soft, light, *air-encapsulating* material, such as foams and fibers. Any substance that keeps air from moving about is air-encapsulating.

This is the key. How much air is trapped? And how well? Any fibrous or scrap material will trap a layer of air (stratify it). People have successfully used the following materials for insulation: cotton, wood shavings, shreds, human hair. These materials, however, do not come neatly packaged.

Modern insulation materials are those that are handy to use. Modern insulating foam, for instance, can be "foamed into place" from a tank. Modern fibers such as rock wool and fiberglass come in batts, rolls, or bags that can be brought to the spot and the fibers quickly put in place between walls or floors.

K and R, and U Values

There are at least twenty modern insulating materials. Each has an "R" value, also expressed as a "K" value ($=1/R$), a measure of how much it slows down the heat transfer. Four to six inches of fiberglass or two inches of polyurethane or urea foam gives sufficient "K" value to make a home comfortable and economical to heat.

When you add the "K" values supplied by a plaster or sheet rock interior wall and a wood outside wall to the "K" value of the insulation, the total, or "U" value, for all the materials taken together is what counts. Every book that deals in depth with insulating materials provides such tables of "K" and "U" figures. You might think that your upper basement wall, for instance, can be successfully insulated with a few inches of fiberglass, but that would not be the case. The "K" value of cement is very low, compared to wood. You therefore need more "K" value in your insulation because of the material with which it is combined.

Get tables of specifications at a building supply store or from a˙library reference shelf. You can figure how much each of the possible options is going to cost for a given amount that you plan to cut heat loss.

Now let's get into specific materials.

The most satisfactory insulating materials all around—if you leave aside cost and the trouble to install it—are the foam-in-place materials. There are three reasons for this. One is that the foam-in-place materials eliminate "exterior convection," or in layman's terms, "wind blowing through the walls." Second, foam eliminates most of the water vapor condensation problem. Third, foam is a good air or gas trap. An inch of foam is worth three inches of the most common fiber insulation, fiberglass.

Currently, there are two foam-in-place materials that are widely used: polyurethane and urea formaldehyde.

Foam is a spongelike collection of millions of separate air or gas bubbles trapped within a light solid. The air or gas cannot escape its bubble. The air entrapped within each bubble can at most carry energy from the warmer side of its little bubble a short distance to the colder side. That bubble does not connect to any other bubble. Therefore, the heat transfer *between* bubbles has to be by conduction. Foam material itself is a poor conductor, so foam is a poor conductor allied to a poor convector—a super-insulator.

Foams are expensive, but new owners, especially in the northern climates, are calling for houses sheathed in foam from rooftop to cellar floor. Extra good insulation pays for itself in a few years at current fuel rates.

Polyurethane Foam

The   first   insulating   foam-in-place   on   the   market   was polyurethane foam. Polyurethane comes out of a tank through a hose which sprays it into the closed wall space, or if one wall is down, in between studs where it will stick to the standing wall. As an insulator, it has a few drawbacks.

First, when you have to spray it between two existing walls— working blind—you can only fill successfully and completely a limited amount of "blind space" between the walls for each hose position. You have to cut a hole for the hose every few feet up the wall between each set of studs.

A more crucial objection is that polyurethane will often resist fire, but if it "catches," it blazes like fury. Building codes require a good fire barrier between any polyurethane and the interior where you are living. Sheetrock, of course, is a fine fire barrier. Using polyurethane behind sheetrock paneling is perfectly okay. But many old Victorians have a wood panel interior, and that eliminates polyurethane from between-the-walls consideration, because you want to leave the wood paneling in place.

Basement Insulation

Suppose you wanted to insulate your basement. You could spray three inches of polyurethane over the whole inside of the basement, but you would have to cover that again with a facing of sheetrock or stucco. In many cases, this is well worth doing. Say you wanted to do the outside basement wall, the foundation wall, in polyurethane. You would then want to coat the foam with a fireproof barrier (such as stucco) because you would otherwise be creating a combustible foundation.

We use polyurethane-plus-stucco outside of the foundation walls in many of our recycles. It's one place you can quickly cut down heat transfer without much cost. (The basement is where you ought to start, since that is where your heating starts, and where all your vulnerable water pipes are.)

Polyurethane has a certain amount of structural strength. You could, in theory, build a complete polyurethane house. (In fact, someone did, by spraying polyurethane on the outside of a huge twenty-foot diameter weather balloon.) Sometimes a wall or ceiling hasn't been properly cross-braced to keep the beams or studs from sagging ("racking"). By insulating with polyurethane, we have avoided laboriously nailing up cross-bracing.

Before you decide to use polyurethane structurally, however, make sure that the local building code or inspector will accept that solution. There is literature available from polyurethane makers that will back you up, but that doesn't mean it will convince the building inspector.

Urea Foam

The second kind of foam-in-place material is urea formaldehyde, which contains formaldehyde gas bubbles rather than air bubbles. Urea formaldehyde foam is a good fire retardant. Its stickiness makes it fill cracks and cling to walls, the same quality that makes polyurethane so good.

There is, however, the same hassle of "filling a blind space" where both interior and exterior walls are in place. You have to cut through from the outside wall by first removing the exterior siding (shingle or board) and then cutting a hole in the underlying sheathing (board or plywood) every four feet from floor to ceiling between every set of studs. Once you do that (and there are companies who specialize in doing it), you have the most complete heat transfer slowdown you can have in this day and age.

Take a urea foam machine and fill the walls of an old Victorian and—presto!—a heat transfer reduction of 50 percent. You've cut your fuel bill in half.

In a typical case, it might cost $1,200 to heat a big three-story Victorian without good insulation. It would cost $2,000 to "foam" it—but you save $600 a year. You pay for your insulating job in three and one-third years. From then on, you coin "magic money."

Foam manufacturing or foam-insulating service people do not claim "50 percent" savings because there are too many variables in insulation to make blanket claims. However, we have on numerous occasions done just that: cut heat bills in half. So we know it can be done.

Foaming a house isn't a typical do-it-yourself operation, but we had so many houses to do once, a few years back, that we bought a foam machine. At that time, polyurethane was the only foam on the market. By the time urea formaldehyde came on the market, we were in a position where our time was better used on things other than foaming. We now leave that to the specialists. Whenever we see a situation that needs it, we call "the urea foam man" in. Urea formaldehyde now is said to cause noxious fumes if not properly sealed. Check this out with your local insulation materials supplier.

There's one more form of foam, and that is foam "boards." These can be styrofoam, polystyrene, or polyurethane boards. You can place them relatively more cheaply than the "foam in place" materials before your interior wall goes up.

You can use foam boards between the rafters or joists where there is no roof or ceiling in place. Foam boards, however, are combustible, so you must have interior sheetrock between them and you.

There are some fiber-type boards available now that are made out of wood particles. These can be used either to insulate inside the basement walls (instead of foam or fiberglass), or they can be used under siding, as a layer between sheeting and siding. There are polystyrene boards that can be used between the shingles and tarpaper on the roof. Such boards can burn, but here they are located outside a fireproof ceiling of sheetrock.

If you are redoing any wall or roof, always put in as much insulation as you can afford. Fuel bills are going to be higher as time goes on. The new homeowner will want to use much less fuel. The prospective buyer, from now on, is going to be looking at insulation value as well as land value.

Foam is great, but cost alone can rule it out. One thing is sure: we are going to see more and more foam in new constructions because, inch for inch, nothing beats it. When you can afford it, and it suits the situation, foam will eventually pay for itself, which is why we call it "the magic money."

23

Insulation: The Economical Fibers

The much-used fiber insulators include fiberglass, processed paper, rock wool, and vermiculate. These are all less expensive than foam and can be less trouble to put in. If you have space enough to allow sufficient thickness, a fiber will do almost as good a job as a foam.

Fibers insulate by presenting such a formidable number of little "blocking strands" that air has a very hard time stirring itself through the fiber material. Air eventually *does* move through by convection, but it takes a long time. The air in a fiber insulator is said to be "stratified," that is, kept in layers so that the air layers mix very, very slowly. Therefore, heat is transferred quite slowly.

As for conduction, the fibers themselves do conduct heat, but they do so primarily in the up-down direction in which the fibers lie. Thus, for a unit of heat to conduct through the wall space, it would have to travel through many, many yards of fiber, a very slow process. Therefore, we again have a situation of poor conduction linked to poor convection, or a good insulator.

Fiber Drawbacks

Before we get to the materials themselves, let's examine two universal drawbacks to using any fiber. The first drawback is that the fiber does not automatically close off the cracks in an exterior wall, as does foam-in-place. Nor does it seal the interior wall the way foam will. The recycler, to insulate with fiber, has to figure out first of all how to keep the wind from "blowing through the walls."

The second problem is vapor. All air carries with it invisible water vapor or "water gas." Vapor always moves *toward a cold surface.* Its pressure rushes it from warm to cold. Water vapor will then deposit itself as droplets on the cold surface.

Warm air from inside a house will first tend to work through the interior wall and deposit water on the insulation fiber between the walls and then on the sheathing or outside wall. Besides the rot problem it creates, there is as well the more lamentable fact that water short-circuits the insulating properties of any fiber. Wet fiber conducts heat like crazy. The water bridges from fiber to fiber. As a result, heat can conduct directly through the fibers, rather than running up and down. (This problem doesn't arise with foam because foam is impenetrable to air and, consequently, has no vapor condensation problem.)

Solving the Drawbacks

Let's start solving fiber's drawbacks. First, the wind problem. The main culprit in letting wind into the space between the walls is, obviously, the exterior wall comprised of sheathing and siding. Victorian house construction called for a sheathing of boards, on top of which was laid a decorative siding of shingle or clapboard.

Modern houses use plywood sheathing. Obviously, a Victorian board sheathing has a larger number of cracks per square yard of wall than does plywood. (Plywood comes in four-by-eight foot sheets, whereas boards are seldom more than eight to ten *inches* wide.) In addition, unless boards are exceptionally well cured, they tend to shrink with the years and leave cracks.

Finally, particularly with summer houses, the Victorians would sometimes dispense with sheathing altogether and nail up a siding only. This is not very windproof.

If the exterior wall isn't windproof, the minute the wind outside stirs, it's going to stir right through the siding and sheathing into the space between the walls. Then, no matter how thick a layer of fiber you install in there, it's not much better than no fiber at all. Convection is going on in the wall space at a great rate, regardless.

Even if your *interior* wall is perfectly wind tight, wind coming through the exterior wall will rob your house of heat. The space between the walls gets cold, and the interior wall then conducts heat out from your rooms at a very fast clip. The conduction-convection chain will not have been broken.

The amount of heat going through by conduction in any situation depends on the difference in the heat level at the one side versus that at the other. If there's a big difference, the heat will conduct through much faster. Thus, on a cold, windy winter day, your leaky outside walls will cool down the house in minutes.

Solving Wind Problems

The simplest way to attack the wind problem is to spackle the cracks in the siding of the house with exterior spackle. Check especially under the eaves, where there are often large cracks. Granted, this is somewhat crude and time-consuming, but you should get a satisfactory enough result. If there are not too many cracks in the siding, the time involved isn't too much.

While you're at it, check the sills, the lowest of the wood construction elements of the house proper. They are the units that rest on the foundation walls. Often there are big gaps between the sill and the foundation wall, adding considerably to the heat loss.

In the case where old siding looks bad, you may decide to replace the siding. You then have a good chance to really do a job: put in plywood sheathing over the current board sheathing, and put in a "wind barrier" of tarpaper between the sheathing and the siding. (Victorians had neither plywood nor tarpaper, so you can't blame them for not using them.) Sometimes there are so many cracks in the siding that what makes most sense is to take the siding off, put up tarpaper and new sheathing, and then replace the siding. Now the older interior wall isn't necessarily windproof either. Use interior spackle to fill out any cracks or crevices, not only for cosmetic reasons but to keep the warm air inside from seeping through into the wall space.

Vapor Condensation

"Vapor" can be divided into two problems. One is the acute problem of keeping the air from the interior of the house out of the space where the fibers are. (The warmer the air, the more vapor it carries. The moist indoor air *must* be kept away from the fibers in the wall space.) The solution is the "vapor barrier," a substance that bars moisture.

If you use fiberglass rolls or batts, the fiberglass comes made up with an aluminum sheet on one side. This sheet is the "vapor barrier." The fiberglass has to be hung so that the sheet is *toward* the warm air of the house. That is, as you nail fiberglass rolls up between studs, you nail it so the sheet faces *inward;* this keeps warm moist air inside the house from reaching the fiberglass. If you use a loose fiber, such as rock wool or vermiculate, then you nail up a polyethelene sheet on the *inward* side of the space between the walls. Remember: no vapor barrier, no insulating effect.

Wall Snare Vapor

The second, less pressing form of the problem is wall space vapor. The cool air of a well-insulated wall space always carries *some* water vapor. This will not deposit as moisture, *provided* there's some way for moisture to get outdoors. Therefore, you must not completely seal the wall space from the *outside.* If you did that, you would not allow the small amount of vapor in the air between the walls to work its way into the outside air. Instead, it will condense inside the wall space on cold days.

The exterior wall has to be *windproof*—but it should not be *vaporproof.* This seems like a tough problem, but it's not. All wood allows moisture to pass through. The only real moisture seal in any exterior wall construction is the tarpaper. If you notice, all such tarpaper has little holes in it. That lets moisture from the wall space come through the wood sheathing and go through to the siding and into the outdoors. The eager amateur builder who seals his wall on the *outside* by putting in a polyethelene sheet between the sheathing and the siding will keep all the moisture *within* the wall space *locked in.* Every time the weather gets cold, vapor trapped in the wall space will immediately deposit on the insulating fibers, and—poof!—there goes the insulating value of the fiber, just when you need it the most.

Cold Attics

It's worthwhile at this point to go into the special case of the "cold attic." Many attics are left unfinished and unheated. That's okay, provided you take care of the insulation problem and vapor condensation problem.

To solve the first problem, you insulate the *floor* of the attic, facing the aluminum sheets or the polyethelene sheets toward the rooms *below,* so that no air with moisture comes up from the heated part of the house into the insulation fiber lying on the attic floor. Now all you have to do is let the air from outside come inside to pick up any excess moisture that does get into the attic. Vent the attic with little vent holes at each end, so that you have some air circulation. Otherwise, when it's cold outside, the moisture already in the air in the attic will condense on the attic rafters and roof; and if that roof is plywood, it will rot out fast.

Fiberglass Insulation

The most convenient fiber to install and the least expensive to put in, provided the interior wall is down, is fiberglass. So cheap and handy is fiberglass that it's sometimes worth pulling off the inside wall just to put it in. Fiberglass comes in rolls and batts. You staple one end of the roll or batt at the top of any space between the studs. Let the batt hang down to fill the space, then cut off the excess. One man with a ladder and staple gun can insulate a whole house this way. That's ideal for recycling.

Six inches of fiberglass, when you can fit it in, does as good a job as needs to be done. You get more for your insulating dollar with fiberglass than with any other material. That's why fiberglass is our material of choice, provided the right combination of factors exists.

When it comes to insulating, you may not have six inches depth between the studs (studs are usually four inches deep) or beams (they may also be four inches deep). Nothing prevents you from nailing an extra layer of fiberglass *outside* the studs, rather than between, to get your six inches.

Do not compress fiberglass to get "more" into a given space. Compressing fiberglass reduces its thickness, so nothing is gained, and money is lost.

There are, of course, fiber insulators other than fiberglass. Rock wool is fiberglass's predecessor as the cheap all-purpose insulator. Rock wool, however, comes loose and can't be handled as easily.

(Both fiberglass and rock wool, to digress, but especially rock wool, have little fibers that come loose and settle on your skin. Depending on how sensitive you are, they can either annoy you or drive you crazy. In any case, a good shower is called for, the hotter the better, to open your pores after handling an itchy fiber. If, after a shower, you find yourself still bothered on the exposed areas of wrists, neck, and face, next time buy a "protective cream" to put on before you start work. When you wash the cream off, the stray fibers come off with it.)

Using Rock Wool

We use rock wool in only two situations. Where we have an attic floor to be insulated, we simply buy bags of rock wool (or vermiculite) and empty the bags to fill the space between the attic joists. (Vermiculite is as good as rock wool and not as "itchy" to work with, but it's more expensive.) The advantage of rock wool and vermiculite in the attic floor situation is time: you can do the job faster. Both cost more than fiberglass, but may be worth it.

There is one situation, however, where loose fiber is the best solution regardless of cost. Let's say you have exterior and interior walls with *no* insulation between and you *don't* want to go to the expense of foaming. Any loose fiber can be dropped into the space between from the attic level until it fills the entire wall space. (You can have a "rock wool man" come in and do it professionally with a blower, if you prefer.)

If your house has the Victorian "balloon construction," you can fill the walls from cellar to attic in one trip. Balloon construction means that the floors do not extend beyond the interior wall into the wall space. Therefore, it's a clean drop down inside the walls all the way to the cellar.

If you don't have balloon construction, your trip to the attic will fill only the second floor wall space. Then, you have to go down to the first floor, go outside, and, using a ladder, remove the siding and cut a slot into the sheathing between each set of studs to drop in the necessary amount of rock wool, vermiculate, or processed paper (the least expensive loose fiber), to fill the first floor wall space.

A recycler's insulating material is determined by its price. Anything you do to cut costs along the way ends up in your pocket. The trick is to cut costs as you go along.

There's one more loose fiber to consider: recycled paper. It's inexpensive. It has a fire-retardant mixed in with it. All you have to do is drill one-inch holes in the center of the wall space between studs and blow recycled paper into the space. If you insulate with loose fiber between the floor joists of an attic, however, you do not have to fireproof (sheetrock) the ceiling below.

24

Insulation: The Finishing Touches

First, in this chapter let's deal with heat transfer at the windows and doors. This can be caused partly by "radiation." This is a mysterious process which shoots energy across empty space where there are no solids to conduct energy and no gas to convect it. Luckily for us, it happens. Otherwise, the sun's rays would never get here through the vacuum of outer space. Not only does the sun radiate heat to us, the earth and all things in it radiate heat back out toward space. Everything—vegetable, animal, or mineral—radiates some of its heat outward in the form of "heat waves."

These heat waves are a part of the spectrum of "electromagnetic waves," which also include light waves, radio waves, and X-rays. Heat waves are shorter than light; heat is "infrared" and invisible, but only just. They lie very close in the spectrum to visible light waves. In fact, light waves do carry some heat and can be thought of as "long heat waves." The practical point is that anything that blocks light *also* blocks heat radiation.

Radiation Blocks

A solid wall, then, does a pretty good job of blocking heat transfer through radiation. Walls and roofs are no radiation loss problem. Windows, however, are another story. Heat radiates through from the sun, and at night, heat radiates out.

Even so, radiated heat loss accounts for only 10 percent of the heat loss of a given house. (Convection and conduction are the big villains.) Ten percent is nothing to sneeze at, though— real estate brokers and literary agents have grown rich on 10 percent.

You have a net heat *gain* through the windows during the day in terms of radiation, so the way to cut radiated heat loss is by blocking windows at *night.* (Conversely, in summer, keep sun radiation out to help your air conditioner cool your house by blocking the windows during the day.) To get the ultimate in slowing down heat transfer, therefore, design your house with curtains that pull all the way across glass windows and doors. That takes care of the radiation loss, right there.

Back to convection and conduction, again, this time related to windows and doors.

On your nonthermal sliding glass doors and picture windows, you can estimate that roughly 10 percent of your total heat loss through windows is by conduction-and-convection. Plain window glass conducts heat at a much faster rate than the wood walls. Just put your hand on the inside face of a window pane on a cold day, and you will feel the difference between the temperature on the pane and that on your interior wall. The pane is much colder, and that means it's conducting heat out at a much more rapid speed.

Insulated Glass

The answer here is thermal "insulated" glass. Thermal glass, of which Thermopane is the best known brand, is simply a "sandwich" of two panes of glass locked tight to each other along the edges with an airspace between. There is some heat loss, of course, even through a thermal pane. The inside pane conducts some heat into the airspace, and the air picks the heat up and convects it over to the outside pane, which then conducts it to the outdoors. But a thermal pane provides a much, slower heat transfer than a single pane.

There is a way we've frequently used to turn ordinary windows and doors into thermal pane windows and doors. You take the "tape" used by auto repair shops to install auto windshields and run the tape all around the edge of the pane. Then, you take a second pane, cut to the same size, and press that on top, exactly congruent. Use silicone rubber cement to seal the edges completely and—presto—a thermal pane. At first, you ought to try it on something that doesn't matter, because it takes practice to do it neatly enough to make it visually acceptable. But practice will lead to a payoff. Thermal pane—whether homemade or not—really cuts your heat bill.

A second way to achieve a slow-down transfer is to get a set of good tight storm windows for the outside. Combined with thermal pane inside that, you then have a triple layer that cuts heat loss through door and window glass by two-thirds—up to a 7 percent savings on the whole fuel bill.

Heat loss *through* a pane by conduction is usually less, by far, than heat loss *around* the window itself.

Sealing Windows

As we mentioned earlier, our first house at 18 Beach had leaky windows. We replaced them with tight new windows at great cost. Later, we found we needn't have done that. We could have stopped the convection around the windows with about twenty minutes' work on each with the Weir Window Special. We simply caulk the upper sash in place with a caulk gun, making sure that there are no chinks left. And that is that.

A bottom sash has four sides to deal with. Weatherstrip the vertical sides by nailing the stripping into the slots on each side in which the window runs up and down, making sure that the stripping bulges out enough to contact the vertical sash sides all the way down when the window is moving. Two sides to go.

To seal the top horizontal frame of the lower sash, first open the lower sash. Spread low-conduction silicone rubber caulking on the inside face of the bottom frame of the *upper* window; then, cover that with a thin sheet of Saran Wrap, and close the lower sash. Lock it. Let the silicone harden so that it takes the exact shape of the space in between the upper and lower sashes. When we open the lower sash after the silicone has hardened, we remove the Saran Wrap. What results is a perfect conduction-proof and convection-proof seal between upper and lower sashes. We do exactly the same thing to seal the bottom frame of the lower sash, only this time against the window sill. This Weir Window Special has given us a lot of inexpensive airtight windows.

Basement Heat Loss

Let's look at one other conduction trouble spot: basements. Basement walls are made of dense stone or cement, and so they definitely conduct heat out faster than a similar structure of wood. If you have a cold basement, it is definitely robbing heat from the rest of the house.

The first option in cutting basement conduction heat loss is to spray an inch-thick coat of foam on the outside foundation from the ground up to the sills (the lowest horizontal members of the house structure). The junction of the sills and the foundation is often not tight; this is where the basement can lose a lot of heat by convection over the top of the foundation as well. Covering the outside face with foam, you slow the conduction through the foundation, as well as slowing convection "over the top" between the sills and the foundation. Finish the outside of the foam off by fireproofing with stucco; it trowels on with little trouble; and, it makes a nice touch in the exterior design of the house. Now you've cut your basement heat loss by two-thirds.

One of the alternative ways to insulate a basement is to put studs against the inside wall as "furring strips," then hang fiberglass insulation on the studs. Another way is to spray polyurethane foam in the *inside* basement wall and put up sheetrock or stucco right over that as a fire barrier. In either case, you need only to bring your insulating material down two to four feet from the level of the ground outside to the "frost line" in your region. The ground outside the basement below the frost line doesn't get very cold; therefore, there's not much heat flow through the lower part of your cellar wall, and very little at all through the cellar floor.

Balloon Construction

One final convection trouble spot. Believe it or not, some of the fiercest convections that can occur is *between* the walls. Many Victorian summer houses (and some later non-Victorians, too) used a sort of natural cooling system. Instead of having each floor extend into the space between the studs at floor level, the builders ran the studs all the way from basement to attic without a break. Cool air, collecting in the cellar, would flow up the cellar from between the studs. The air would keep going up between the studs, sucking more cool air from the basement after it.

Cool air would thus go "up the chimney" to the attic, through attic vents to the outdoors. This "air-conditioned" the walls, and drew the heat out of the house. Great for summer. Terrible if you want to use the house in winter.

Given such a "balloon construction" house, we close off the "bottom of the chimney" by stuffing paper up into the space between the studs in the cellar. These spaces are often hard to reach. Stuffing newspaper up is often the only solution, short of tearing things apart. Next, we go up to the attic, as we said before, and drop recycled paper, vermiculate, or rock wool down until the space between each set of studs is filled from cellar to attic. That does it.

Sometimes a house will have an "inadvertent chimney effect." The house builder "forgot" to seal off the space between the studs at the cellar level. This is a place that we always check. Even if the house is not balloon construction, the fact that cellar air can go up between the walls of the first story will cause the insulation in the first story wall space to lose its ability to stratify the air. Even though it's air from inside the basement house that is going up, the convection lowers the insulation value of the wall space insulation drastically. So, one way or another, this space between the studs at cellar level has to be blocked.

Sometimes you have more or less the same situation in the attic, with somewhat the same effect. The space between the attic studs has not been closed off. If air can rise from between the studs into the attic, then that will tend to suck air right through the walls below; the chimney effect is quite powerful once it gets going. You have to fill with insulation until you close off the space between studs at the attic level, too.

Insulation at 18 Beach

Let us give you the benefit of some of our negative experience with 18 Beach at a time when we were naive about insulation.

Because it was a summer place, it had no insulation. We therefore decided that we had to insulate it. Since the only insulation we knew about was fiberglass batts, we tore off the inside plaster wall (destroying it in the process) and stapled up fiberglass batts between the studs. We then installed a new interior wall. We didn't know that air was still coming up from the basement between the studs and circulating through all the fiberglass. It was also coming in through cracks in the sheathing and siding. So, after spending a lot of time and money insulating 18 Beach, we still had a very cold house!

Today, we would—as one possibility—have had a foam man come in and foam the walls as they stood. (This would have been a lot less expensive than what we actually did.) Foaming would have solved all the problems at one fell swoop—the cracks in the walls and the chimney effect, as well as the lack of any insulating material between the walls.

If we'd wanted to do it more economically, we would have blocked the spaces between the studs in the cellar with news-paper (or cut boards to fit, if we could reach in) and drilled one-inch holes through the outside sheathing to blow recycled paper or rock wool between the studs until it filled up the space all the way to the top of the second floor walls.

The recycler's job is to know the options and to use the one that makes the most sense. The developments in insulation in the next few years are certain to be many, given the urgency of the fuel situation. It's likely, therefore, that new options will be available. Even at the present state of the art, reinsulation is probably the prime stratagem in the recycler's bag of tricks. As we pointed out, it pays for itself in savings on heat bills in a remarkably short time. And once it has paid for itself, it goes on earning dividends in continued savings.

25

Plumbing: Fixing What's There

Plumbing is an extensive but not complex subject. There are many ways of accomplishing the simple, logical organization of a plumbing system. You can't become expert in every possible approach.

Plumbing is logical and straightforward in outline; you *can* get lost if you focus on detail first. After having read these two plumbing chapters, you might look through the sections of home improvement books that go into much greater depth. Jackson Hand's *Complete Book of Home Repairs and Maintenance* (Harper & Row, New York) and *Manual of Home Repairs, Remodeling, and Maintenance* (Fawcett, New York) are recommended.

Our advice is to use plastic and copper pipe. Stick to one way of working with each. For instance, you can become a "pipe threader" and do all your own thread cutting. We think it much simpler to avoid threading—less tools, less time. We use non-threaded couplings, and on the rare occasions we go for threading we let the hardware supply store do it for us.

Our philosophy is fix what's there, rather than replace it. There are exceptions. A rusted, clogged galvanized pipe is better removed and replaced.

Another way to enlightenment is to hire a plumber, have him do a simple job, and see if he is willing to answer questions. Certainly you can learn from watching him work.

Plumbing Tools

We'd like here to list the plumbing tools. Pipes are round; it's hard to get a grip on pipes. That's one reason for specialized plumbing tools. Pipes are often located in places that are hard to get to with ordinary tools; e.g., the back of the wash basin coupling requires a "basin wrench."

The basic tools are two pair of pipe wrenches, with cunningly designed jaws that lock on when you turn the handle.

"Pipe wrench" is usually used to mean the Stillson wrench. There are a number of other types: as alternatives for the Stillson, including the chain wrench and the strap wrench. The chain wrench is a neat gadget with a chain that wraps around the pipe and holds the pipe very firmly—it's great for hard to turn pipe (worn or rusty threads). The strap wrench does the same, not quite as firmly, but without leaving marks on the pipe, if you're doing chromed fixture pipes. Both are great for getting at pipes laid against a wall.

The most specialized pipe wrench is the basin wrench. It's a T-handle with an automatic pipe-grabbing device on the other end. It lets you unscrew pipes from the fitting embedded in the back of a wash basin.

The vise grip is not specifically a pipe wrench, but if it's all you have on hand, it will do quite nicely.

There are also nuts to be turned: the channel lock plier is a useful nut-turner since it can expand easily and quickly to accommodate any size, yet the jaws always stay parallel to fit flush against the sides of the nut. It can grab a nut where the normal wrench has to be adjusted, pulled out, readjusted, and so on. The channel lock does not have self-gripping or fixed position jaws; so, you have to hold it on the nut by hand pressure. In normal situations where the nut is free of obstructions, you use the adjustable wrench, which locks in place.

The basic list of wrenches: Stillsons, chain, strap, basin, vise grips, channel lock, and adjustable.

Plumbing Systems

Now let's get to the theory of a plumbing system. Plumbing, like ancient Gaul, is divided into three parts. First, there's the incoming system. This is a system of relatively small "pressure pipes," which bring in and distribute the water from the outside under pressure and deliver it to the fixtures.

If you go to the basement of any house, you can see where the pressure pipe comes in from the water main or the water pump. From there, the pressure pipe system divides so that the pipes going upstairs can shoot straight up inside the walls to feed the bathrooms, laundry, and kitchen. The least expensive way to lay pipe, of course, is in straight lines. The fewer the bends, the quicker the installation, and the less the chance of leaks developing.

Second is the outgoing system. These are the "drains," which bring the water after it's been used in the fixture down into the basement and outside the house again, under gravity pressure only. Drains are highly visible in the cellar, coming down from above, collected by a larger drain, and finally run through the "house drain" to the sewer or cesspool drain outside the house. The drains, unlike the pressure pipes, have "cleanouts" at intervals; you see little Y-sections with a screw-off cap into which a plumbers snake can be inserted to clear any part of the drain that's clogged. Drains are relatively simple to clear.

Each of these two parts has its typical problems.

All water that comes in must go out. Using a little logic with this concept, you can often come up with ingenious solutions that make the difference between a recycler and someone who "goes by the book."

Venting System

The one thing you can't see in the cellar is the components of the venting system, the third system. The visible components are the funny looking U-shaped pipe sections, the "traps" outside the fixtures. Up on the roof are one or more "vents" which are connected to the drain pipes. This "vent piping" is all hidden in the walls.

Here's how the vent system works: the U-shaped traps are set to hold enough water in them to block any air returning up the drains from the sewer or cesspool. This means that bad air can't get into the fixtures. What happens is that any bad air goes up to the roof level in the vent pipes and is dispersed in the atmosphere.

The vent pipes have another related function. When a slug of water starts going down a drain, ordinarily that means suction develops behind the slug of water. But the vent pipes do let air in behind the slug of water. Therefore no suction develops. What's bad about suction? Well, it would take all the water out of the traps, and thereby destroy their odor-blocking function.

Thus, the venting system, the least understood of plumbing's three parts, is connected to the drain system, but doesn't help carry the water. It just carries air, lets bad air out and good air in.

We've had a friend install a sink and drain with the U-shaped trap and all, but without a vent pipe. He didn't realize that there are more than two parts to a plumbing system. (In fact, a sink doesn't really need a vent pipe most of the time because the overflow pipe acts as a vent.) But, once our friend's overflow clogged, and at the same time the sink drained; zap! All the water sucked out of the trap and sewer gas came floating back up to tell the world something was not working right.

No Vents

An old house may not have any vent pipes at all. Sometimes, oddly enough, this doesn't seem to matter. Air is getting drawn into the drain system somehow and all is fine. Sometimes you can unmistakably tell all is *not* fine, because there's a rank odor in the house from time to time. In that case you have to figure out how much it's going to cost in time and labor to put in vent pipes. (On the back or side of a house, you can run vents *outside* to save money.)

Strange as it may seem, some of the Victorian summer houses we bought did have an odor: this problem had had nothing done about it. Maybe the Victorians were more robust or less sensitive.

Since sewage odor may not always be present, the only sure way to tell if there's a venting problem when you inspect a house is listen to the drains working. If the vent system is not functioning, you hear a horrible gurgling as the water is sucked out of the traps. This is a certain sign. (A seagull once built a nest on one of the vents on the roof of our shore house. When the third floor tub emptied, it sounded like a giant snoring.)

The easiest way to solve the venting malfunction problem if it's "localized," that is, affects only one or two traps, is to install "one-way valve traps" that defy suction and keep their quota of water regardless. If it is a toilet, since the trap is built into the toilet, there's no way but to install a second valved trap in the wall. (You tear out the wall.)

The Pressure System Problems

Incoming system problems:

Most of the problems in the pressure side come from "leaks" where the faucet or the joint leaks. If a joint leaks, then you treat it as you would when installing a new pipe. Take the joint apart and refasten it with the appropriate technique, i.e., gluing for plastic pipe and soldering for copper, etc.

If it's a leaky faucet, then it's the washer that is the problem. You turn off the water. (If you are lucky, there are turnoffs right under the fixture, otherwise you may have to turn off the whole system in the basement.) Then take the faucet apart and replace the worn washer with a new washer. All this sort of thing is illustrated for various types of washer and faucet combinations in all home maintenance and repair books.

Every fixture can be considered "an interface" between the pressure and the drain side. For instance, the standard toilet tank has an incoming pressure pipe, then a drain at the tank bottom, and an overflow drain at the top of the tank.

The usual trouble with the toilet is "running toilet," which means a malfunctioning float valve (designed to close the pressure pipe when the water in the tank reaches a set height). The water comes in and then goes out the overflow drain continually. Usually the float itself just needs to be slightly adjusted.

Or, the drain side is at fault; the ball valve that's supposed to close the bottom drain at the end of the flush isn't seating right. Water, thus, continually runs out the bottom drain. Hardware stores sell kits containing a ball-valve guide that causes the ball valve to seat more certainly than does the standard ball valve set-up. Once the ball-valve guide is installed, your toilet will stop running.

Failing Drains

Don't knock drain problems; they can make money for you since they are not that hard to fix, but the present owner may not know that. In the case of our dramatic second house profit, we can say that we got halfway rich on one drain problem. Our second house was a beachfront property that we converted into a two-family. The basement had a problem that had to be solved before anybody could safely live in the house. The sewer was backing up into the basement. The previous owner figured he couldn't do anything about that so he felt he had a big problem.

What it was—we found out—was that during any spring floods on the heels of a heavy rain, the city sewer system (which also serves as the rainwater discharge system) flooded. Because the house was on such a low site (a few feet above high tide) and because there was a drain opening in our basement *floor,* the water level of the flooded sewers was higher than our basement floor. Ergo, the water came backing in.

We solved the problem by installing a house drain—higher than the existing drain plate—in the opening. We turned a liability into an asset with minimum work. (That is a short definition of recycling.) The other lesson to learn from this is that the drain problem isn't necessarily originating *in* the house.

Outside Sewers

There's an outside cleanout plug in most city sewer systems at the curb to take care of the part of the sewer drain *outside* each house. Since it is the city's system, they are responsible for the sewer drain; anything *beyond* the cellar wall your taxes should take care of. If the outside clean-up plug is flooded, that means the problem is *outside* the cellar wall, and it's up to the city to do something. However, if this cleanout is *clear,* then the problem is *inside* the walls, and it is your problem.

The first sign, of course, of a clogged drain somewhere is an overflowing fixture. The problem could be in the fixture drain, in a cellar drain, or in the house drain.

A fixture signals a cellar drain problem if the fixture is the lowest in the house—therefore it will be the first to overflow from a general drain back-up. If a second floor fixture floods, you can be sure it's the fixture drain and not the cellar drain.

The first line of defense against drain clogging, is the plumber's helper—the foot soldier of plumbing. This simply is a large suction cup on a large broomstick. You put the mouth of the suction cup over the fixture drain opening and push down hard on the stick. Then jerk upward. The theory is that as you pull up, you create suction (air cannot get under the sides of the suction cup), and that, in turn, pulls the clogged material back a few inches and dislocates it. As you repeat the plunging a few times, the clogging mass breaks up and begins to run down the drain pipe.

Knowing this much, you can see it's important, first of all, to make sure the cup covers the drain hole completely. Second, if you have sink or bath trouble, it helps to fill the sink or tub with a few inches of water to increase the air seal for better suction. Third, if there are any holes in the cup, it's not going to do much good. One more tip: on the sink situation, plug the overflow drain cover with a rag to keep air from coming in there to spoil the suction.

Chemical Warfare

If the plumber's helper doesn't work, what next? Chemical warfare, usually Drano or another liquid chemical mix. Follow closely the directions on the bottle. Pour the stuff into the pipe, where it drops through the water to eat a hole in the clogging material; then you can flush the whole thing out. If it doesn't work, then the chemical lies there, and it goes very hard on anything that comes in contact with it later, such as human hands. Even so, the percentages on chemical warfare are good enough so it's worth a try.

Suppose that doesn't do it? Then you take out your trusty snake. Snakes come in various sizes. The size for the fixture drain is pretty modest, but snakes for the cellar drain are larger, and huge for outside cellar drains. (If you have a cesspool, you may have to rent equipment and go after the sewer drain yourself, or get help to come in.)

A snake has a head which is made to rotate by the flexible segment behind it, which in turn is being fed through a crank, which turns it as the operator turns. The snake burrows through the offending material, and water starts running and clears out the rest of it.

Even if it fails, the snake will tell you right away whether or not the problem is in the trap under the fixture, because if it is, then the snake will penetrate only a short distance.

If the blockage is in the trap, there is often a bottom plug on the trap that can be unscrewed to let the chemical previously dropped into the pipe drain out before the recycler takes the trap apart to clear it. If there's no cleanout plug in the trap, then before you disconnect the trap, you should spoon or suction pump out the liquid in the trap, because the chemical in it will eat right through the cotton gloves in a hurry, not to mention human skin (wear rubber gloves).

Let's say that the blockage isn't in the fixture drain. Then it's very likely down in the cellar. All drains drop straight from the trap through to the cellar, and a drain isn't likely to clog in the vertical part.

In the cellar, however, your drain turns a corner as it goes horizontal, finally exiting into the house drain. Assuming you've checked to make sure that the problem doesn't lie outside, you proceed to take off the caps of the cleanouts in the cellar. Starting with the cleanout nearest the house drain, go back to the next cleanout, and so on. Somewhere in there is the block, and your snake probably can clear it—if yours can't do it, then the professional equipment used with the bigger snakes by a plumber can. At least you will have located the problem.

Plumbing is as logical as a mathematical equation. You have straight lines, you have corners, and you have incoming and outgoing; it all fits together. It's not mysterious or illogical. There are obvious solutions to most malfunctions.

26

Plumbing: Adding New Features

The recycler isn't looking to replace those usual old grey galvanized pipes with shiny new copper or clean plastic just to improve the look of the cellar. But sometimes old pipe is deteriorated to the extent that it's much more sensible to replace it than to try to clear it. So new parts are added. There are many many times where we know that to make a house marketable we have had to add at least one more bathroom. You will have trouble selling a five-bedroom with only one bathroom in it.

Actually, the cost of putting in new plumbing is 80 percent labor. The cost of the pipe and fittings isn't that much. There-fore, we usually buy our pipes and fittings new at cut-rate outlets. If you start having to go back and repair used pipe after you've installed it, you have blown a lot of the profitability of adding plumbing.

What materials do we pick, when we're buying new? If we are replacing a good portion of the system, we pick plastic. It's inexpensive, light in weight (easily handled), and connects by gluing (rather than threading which takes more time). It can be bent flexibly into position, so that you don't have to come out exactly where your next connection is.

Plastic Plumbing

Plastic is fairly new on the market and somewhat controversial. Its advantages are being recognized, though, and it is the material of the future. Plastic pipe cuts quickly with a hacksaw into the lengths needed (so you can do it right on the spot) and is so light a man can carry an armful.

What's controversial about it? Two things.

First, there is the political opposition. (You thought there were no politics in plumbing, right?) This comes in the form of persistent attempts to block inclusion of plastic pipe in the local or state building code. The idea of a householder installing plumbing without recourse to professionals is not a welcome one.

This brings an important facet of plumbing into focus: you do have to conform in materials and procedures with the local building code. Before you do your own plumbing, you ought to know what materials are allowed, what, if any, layout is mandatory for a plumbing system, and what kind of inspection is necessary once you finish in order to get "certificate of occupancy" or whatever papers are needed to give you a right to sell or rent the house.

The first plastic was soft—polyethelene—as in plastic garden hose. Soft plastic had only limited value in plumbing. Most plumbing pipe has to be hung, and it's difficult to hang soft plastic. Second, polyethelene did not stand up to hot water. (Soft plastic pipe does have some uses. For instance, we use it to connect other pipe in an emergency; you can just tighten hose clamps on both ends of a soft plastic connector to get a tight connection.) In addition, soft polyethelene tends to deteriorate after a time. This is the ultimate objection.

ABS Pipe

Soon, stiff plastic piping came along—ABS, and then, even better, PVC (polyvinylchloride), which was the first that could take hot water. Environmentalists soon pointed out that PVC was potentially a cancer-causing agent. A spokesman for the Environmental Defense Fund told us he'd never use PVC in *his* house. It gets into the groundwater of well systems and into the rivers and lakes and oceans. Now the manufacturers have come up with "polybutelene," which is environmentally safe. One way or another, plastic pipe is here to stay.

The advantages:

First, in cutting. Plastic pipe cuts almost like wood. You do a better job with a fine-toothed saw, such as a hacksaw. Take the time to cut clean; you'll have no problem thereafter joining the end to a coupling, and then the coupling to another pipe. The joint is made permanent by previously applying a solvent, which actually dissolves the surface layer of the plastic. When the surface layer hardens again, it forms a permanent bond with any like plastic next to it. However, you *can not* use the same solvent for different kinds of plastic. If you want to join polybutelene and ABS, for instance, you have to have a special connection made for the purpose, or use our standby, the flexible polyethelene hose with clamps.

There are tools for bending plastic pipe, but we don't bother with them because you can make a shallow bend simply by bending the pipe in your hands. We make a right angle by gluing in an elbow coupling. There are also plastic pipe threading tools for making tight threaded joints, but gluing with solvent is faster.

The only operational drawback to plastic is that you have to support it for thirty minutes or so while its solvent is being dried, and you cannot turn on the water until the glue *has* dried. Therefore if we only have, say, one pipe to replace, it's quicker to do it in copper. You simply solder the couplings and turn the water pressure on immediately. You then can go on to something else.

If we have to replace any large drains, we prefer ABS plastic because it is lightweight and less expensive. To connect plastic to existing metal pipes you need special connectors sold in hardware stores. (You can't use a plastic solvent to connect to a metal pipe.)

Copper Pipe

Copper piping is expensive. We use copper for a "quick fix" where we're doing only a new pipe or two. In connecting copper to galvanized, use a special connector. Any metal, when wetted down, will set up an electrical current with another different metal it contacts. Contact sets up a corrosive (or galvanic) action that will eat through the joint. Galvanic action is the same thing that makes a battery work. (You know how fast a battery can wear out if left on.)

Copper is the lightest metal pipe. That is why we like working with it. With copper, you can work on the material with fairly light tools; you do not need the giants that the larger galvanized pipe calls for.

There are basically two kinds of copper pipe: the *flexible* and the *rigid*. The flexible costs twice as much, but there are times when you need to be able to bend the pipe a little to make the connection.

You can go even farther. If you have a "bending spring" inside to keep the sides of soft copper from caving in, you can bend a soft copper pipe to a right-angle curve. Usually, though, we put in an elbow coupling for a right-angle turn. Rigid copper pipe can also be bent, with the help of a bending rig. But a bending rig is expensive; we let "elbow" connections plus slight bending by hand do the work.

Threading Pipe

One way to join copper pipe is by threading. Soft copper pipe can be joined by flaring one of the ends with a flaring or flanging tool. The flare then holds a nut in place. This nut screws onto the other end of the pipe which is threaded. Such work calls for threading with threading tools, which takes time. We'll only go for threaded connections if we have a joint that for some reason has to be constantly coupled and uncoupled.

Soldering Pipe

It is easier to join copper with solder. The art of soldering is not picked up in a minute; but it's a skill that's very handy to have, since copper is widely accepted, widely available, and long-wearing. There are times when you will want copper, so there are times when you will want to solder.

To solder, first sand the ends of pipe and fitting to be joined. Then coat those sanded places with a paste called "soldering flux." Hold a propane blow torch flame to the middle of the fitting (not to the juncture line at which the fitting joins the pipe). Now apply solder wire (50 percent tin and 50 percent lead) to the line where the fitting and the pipe join. The heat generated inside the fitting sucks the solder up into the crevices between the fitting and pipe. Some solder will flow out again at the bottom of the junction line, so take a rag and "wipe" the joint, bringing the excess solder up around the sides and top of the junction line. That helps seal the fitting-pipe connection.

If you are holding the fitting as you solder, lay it down gently, because solder takes a little while to solidify. Any thumps will cause the fitting and pipe to part again. Once it's cool, the soldered coupling is as solid as it's ever going to be, and you can turn on the water to see that all is well. You can cool it in seconds by dabbing it with a damp rag.

If soldering doesn't appeal to you (it's kind of fun to do), there's a third type of fitting somewhat more expensive and not as widely available—the squeeze or compression fitting. This is a double-threaded collar which seats watertight over the end of the pipes when forced with a hex nut.

Working with Copper

A copper tube cutter is a sharp, hardened metal wheel that fastens to the tube and turns round and round it, scoring it until it cuts through. It is a worthwhile investment. Copper tubing should always be cut with a tubecutter. This leaves a clean beveled lip. A hacksaw will tend to leave a ragged lip.

Fittings available for copper include an "elbow," for right

angles. You can add another pipe at right angles to an existing pipe, and a forty-five degree fitting to branch at that angle. There's also a "saddle," which you can fasten right to an existing pipe without cutting it to make a ninety-degree branch. Simply fasten it on, drill a hole, and you are in business.

Copper, like any other pipe, requires hangers or some sort of support when you run it horizontally, or it will get little sags in it which cut its efficiency and present opportunities for sediment to collect. A stiff copper pipe needs a hanger every six feet, while a soft copper pipe may need a hanger more often. You have to look and see how many it takes to keep the pipe from sagging.

Copper pipe is especially prone to "sweating," just about its only bad habit. In summer, moist air comes into the cellar. As it strikes the copper cold water pipes, it condenses, often so profusely that the floor is covered with water underneath. The quickest way to combat this is with a brush on insulation that leaves a thin coating on the pipes. If this doesn't work, you can use insulating tape or regular insulation. (Avoid asbestos insulation, though. That is one building material that has definitely been tagged as cancer-causing. Asbestos particles are easily absorbed by the body.)

Pipe Sizes

This brings us to pipe sizes. The smaller the pipe, of course, the less it costs. There are minimums. The usual sizes for the pressure side are ⅜-inch, ½-inch, and ¾-inch copper. We figure, as a rule of thumb, that a ½-inch takes care of the water to one bath and one kitchen, while a ¾-inch will feed two baths and two kitchens. Drains have to be much larger, 1¼ inches to four inches in diameter, depending on how many drains feed in. Four inches is standard for the final house drains in cast iron, three inches for copper or plastic.

You can get a table of specifications for your pipe diameters from a local town or building inspection office. It's usually imbedded in the local building code. The code may seem complex, so have a knowledgeable person point out what the provisions mean in regard to plumbing. Your hardware or plumbing supply specialist or a friendly plumber may be able to give you a digest of the code's plumbing requirements. Since he works with it every day, he can separate what is important in it from what is not.

Galvanized Pipe

Now we come to galvanized pipe (and ungalvanized "black iron pipe.") Galvanized is pipe with mottled light lead-grey coating. It was used extensively up to twenty-five years ago. After that, copper became king until plastics came in just a few years ago to challenge copper.

All galvanized pipe is joined by threading. This means that if you are going to take apart a galvanized joint, you have to hold the fitting still and turn the pipe, or vice versa. It also means you may have all kinds of problems putting it back together, because galvanized threads notoriously are easily worn and damaged.

Galvanized pipe is heavy. The six-foot length of galvanized pipe you need two hands to hold, you can hold in one hand in copper pipe.

We replace galvanized (or ungalvanized "black iron pipe") with copper whenever we have to make a quick replacement in an older system, using an adapter coupling to join it up. There is one exception to replacing iron pipe with copper; that is where you have gas pipes. City gas comes in under such high pressure that building code specifications usually call for black cast-iron pipe, which is more rugged than copper. The chance of a gas leak is much more to be feared than a water leak. We always replace black iron gas pipe with the same stuff.

Black or galvanized iron pipes are connected by male and female threads. By measuring accurately the length you want, you can have it threaded at the store where you buy it. (Add ¾ inch to the male pipe, because it screws in that far.)

Before you thread iron pipes, smear the threaded parts with

pipe dope, or use a new threading tape that's come on the market (less messy). Either seals the connection.

If you have a short break anywhere in galvanized pipe, you can cut out a piece, borrow a threading die, and insert a coupling. Galvanized can be cut with a handheld hacksaw, but you are in for a long job. We use our reciprocating saw with a hacksaw blade in it.

Cast Iron Pipe

Even on houses where the plumbing is copper, there is often a black cast-iron house drain.

Cast iron is something out of the dark ages. It used to be required for the strength it gave to the four-inch diameter house drain. If the building code still requires cast-iron and you have to reconnect a house drain to it, you are in for making a "cast-iron connection," which is not easy. The cast-iron drain is joined to the smaller drain by having a wider aperture than needed, which is then stuffed with oakum. On top of this is poured hot lead.

You can break the cast-iron connection by melting the lead with a propane torch and then ladling it out. But you have to be careful; hot lead can really burn. Dress in heavy clothes and use heavy gloves. To reverse the procedures, you have to melt lead and ladle it in. Unless you have a lot of time to spend on this, you are better off getting a plumber to do it, or at least a friend who has done it before. There's also a new T-Y seal that lets you avoid most of this procedure.

If luck is with you, the building code will let you use an ABS drain instead of the cast iron, and you can connect ABS to the adjoining pipe easily by comparison. It's just a question of cutting ABS to the right length, coating it with solvent, and then holding it to the adapter connection.

Planning Plumbing Additions

When all is said and done, your plumbing additions are easy or hard depending on how well you plan your new plumbing layout.

First rule is to make the additions so that you can come *out* of a wall pipe *to* the fixture with a few short connecting pieces of pipe. The new bath or kitchen *should* adjoin a wall that already has plumbing big enough to take the additional volume both coming in on the plumbing side and going out on the drain side. That holds the job to just hooking up a little bit of piping. This is making best use of what is already there.

If you are going to put a bathroom in a place where you cannot reach it very easily from present plumbing, you better have a very good reason for doing so, because you are going to have to bury a lot of pipe in a lot of wall.

Planned right, your job in adding fixtures is to simply go into the wall to join old plumbing to your new fixtures, close up the wall again, patch the sheetrock or plaster, and you are in business.

If you are lucky, you will find a "union connection" in the pipes in the wall. Replace that with a T-joint for your new pipe. Alternatively, find a place to fasten a saddle fitting that lets you tap in on the old line easily.

We find that we spend, on the average, one plumbing day out of every two weeks spent on a recycling. Of course, that can still be quite a bit of plumbing. If we work on the house six months steadily, it's twelve days worth of plumbing.

We've learned to make the best use of what is there; we buy the easiest, quickest pipe material to work with; and a good layout plan allows us to put it in fast—and get on to other things.

27

Heat: Wise Recycling Choices

If a house doesn't have central heating, the asking price is low. A house that sells for $30,000 without central heating will sell for $40,000 with. It's *not* going to cost $10,000 to put central heating in. More like $2,000 to $3,000. You triple your money.

The running efficiency of a heating plant per dollar spent on installing it depends on a few things. One is the heat at which the fuel burns. Another is the exchange efficiency between the "flame," the burning fuel, and the "carrier" that distributes the heat around the house.

Efficiency also depends on absorption efficiency of the carrier. How much heat per unit of volume can the carrier take with it? If the carrier has good absorption, then you can buy a smaller, more compact unit for the given amount of heat needed.

Eight Fuels

Today we have eight different fuels to choose from: three liquid, two electromagnetic, and three solid.

1. *Liquid*
   Natural gas, low pressure gas (LP gas), and oil
2. *Electromagnetic*
   Electricity and solar rays
3. *Solid*
   Wood, charcoal, and coal

Five Carriers

We have five different carriers: two gasses, two liquid, and one electromagnetic.

1. *Gasses*
   Air and steam
2. *Liquid*
   Water and "refrigerant"
3. *Electromagnetic*
   Radiant heat

Matching Fuels with Carriers

Match the best fuel to the best carrier for the circumstance—an interesting problem. The systems haven't been developed for all possible combinations. Today the systems that are available are:

Natural gas fuel with the following carriers: hot water, steam, air, and radiant.
Oil fuel with the following carriers: hot water, steam, and air.
Electricity as fuel with hot water, air, refrigerant, and radiant heat as carriers.
Solar rays as fuel with air, water, and radiant heat carriers.
Wood as fuel with water, air, and radiant heat carriers.
Coal as fuel with water, air, and steam carriers.

Notably missing from our fuels is LP gas, which is very expensive for room heating, and charcoal, which doesn't offer anything significant over coal. Both LP and charcoal are used for back-country cooking and LP for residential hot water in situations where natural gas is unavailable.

The practical combinations are used under varying circumstances.

Hot Air Systems

These are the most easily maintained and the least expensive to install, regardless of the fuel. Also, hot air lends itself to winter trips or summer vacation homes. A hot water system with its piping has to be off if the house has to be left cold for the winter.

Air as a carrier is fail-safe. Nothing can really go wrong. If there is a leak in a hot air duct, then there's some hot air going out and heating up a room, that is all. Hot air ducts also can be used for cool air if you want to put in central air conditioning.

The hot air furnace is relatively bulky, though, and is less preferable than hot water systems if the installation has to be on the first floor because of a small basement or no basement.

Natural Gas-Hot Air Combination

This is the cheapest hot air system to install wherever you have natural gas. Cheapness of installation is important. For instance, if you save $1,000 installing natural gas-hot air over, say, oil, you can put the $1,000 in the bank and get more than $80 back every year in interest, which you can count as $80 saved off the fuel bill every year.

Oil-Hot Air Combination

This is the usual choice where there's no natural gas. Oil and hot air cost twice what gas-hot air costs to install, but runs more efficiently. The reason it runs more efficiently is that oil gives out more heat per dollar spent, simple as that.

Electric-Hot Air Combination

These are competitive where there is a moderate climate. If the temperatures regularly fall below ten degrees centigrade in the winter, electric-hot air is too expensive. But installation is cheap, and electricity is a clean fuel.

Solar-Hot Air Combination

The heat from radiant light rays is collected by solar panels in liquid that runs over the panels. That, in turn, heats up a storage system such as rock or a water tank. From here, hot air is blown through ducts into the rooms. So far, solar-hot air is not competitive economically.

Passive Solar Systems

One of the more fertile fields of house design recently has been that of using "passive solar" heating, that is, setting up your windows and skylights so as to make maximum use of the "greenhouse effect." The heat from incoming electromagnetic waves (light) will be trapped inside any glassed-over areas. Anybody building a new house should be thoroughly familiar with the advantages and recent designs of passive solar heating. Unfortunately for the recycler, he is often working with houses designed with no idea of what passive solar heating was all about. To convert part of such a house to solar costs more than is saved by the increased heating from the sun.

Wood-Hot Air Combination

There are today wood furnaces so efficient that a couple of logs laid in the furnace will heat a small house simply by letting hot air raise through the house from the basement where the stove is heating up.

Coal-Hot Air Combination

This method uses a hot air chamber just as do oil and natural gas. It costs about the same as oil.

In general, hot air systems are cheap to install and easy to maintain, but air is not the most efficient carrier in distributing heat. To get the heat out of the "hot chamber," lots of heat is lost up the stack. Also, using the enclosed "hot chamber" to heat up the air to be blown through the system is not an efficient heat exchange for a second reason. Air does not draw heat from the metal hot chamber surface as readily as water draws heat from heated pipes in the hot chamber.

Hot Water Systems

The second most popular way of distributing heat is to use water as the carrier. Water picks heat up fast and divests itself of heat fast, so you need a smaller volume of water than air. This means saving space for starters. A smaller room unit provides more heat.

The disadvantage is that any hot water system is not failsafe. If there is a leak, there is loss and expense to repair it. Another disadvantage is that the cost of installing pipes for a hot water system is much more than installing air ducts and registers for a hot air system.

Let's look at the individual combinations with hot water.

Natural Gas-Hot Water

This one is the least expensive of the hot water systems to install. And the price of natural gas at this writing makes it the most economical of all the hot water house heating systems.

Oil-Hot Water

This is the modern oil furnace heating system. Oil is more widely available than gas, and in some places is competitive with natural gas.

Electric-Hot Water

This is an extremely unusual system, but is very compact since you are using electric heat wiring wrapped around metal pipes.

It is more expensive. The only thing you can say about it is that we will probably never have a long, long interruption of electric service because too much depends on electrical power, whereas in an oil shortage, oil may be cut off.

Solar-Hot Water

This is the most popular of solar systems for house heating. Water—fortified by antifreeze, usually—is run across the solar panels and through the house in hot water pipes. Like solar-hot air, solar-hot water is not yet economically feasible in most parts of the country. You may buy solar heating as a way of making a political statement, and that has certain value. However, if you put in the bank the difference between what yo᾽ would pay for solar and what you would pay for hot air or hot water combined with any other fuel, you would find that the yearly interest on that amount banked (when subtracted from your fuel bill) would give you lower fuel costs than with solar. In other words, you are, in solar, investing your money uneconomically at present.

There is this, though: particularly in milder climates where house heat isn't a matter of survival in winter, solar heating insulates you from the vicissitudes of the Near East and U.S. national energy policies, whose ultimate thrust no one can predict.

Solar Write-offs

There may be for solar power investment write-off tax advantages to consider by the time this is published—in your particular area. There is no question that local and federal governments could easily convert the nation to solar heat in private dwellings if they had the conviction that such is a national priority. That day may come yet.

However, as long as the coal and oil industries have all the leverage nationally that they do, such legislated tax advantages are not likely to become overwhelming. So, with the solar option, in any location in the U.S. where you really *have* to have reliable heat all winter, you are faced not only with a solar installation that is expensive, but with supplying some sort of standby heat.

Coal-Hot Water

This has declined in favor as the less burdensome gas and oil furnaces have appeared. Coal had to be shoveled once a day. The latest generation of coal furnaces, however, are almost as care-free as gas and oil. All you have to do is carry out the ashes once a week. Coal is, in some parts of the country, cheaper than oil per unit of heat given out.

Steam Carrier Systems

These are the older houses' standard systems and have a number of problems which make replacing them inviting. Steam systems are almost never installed now. They have big disadvantages compared to hot water and hot air distribution systems.

In the first place, there is the safety problem of having to have a pressure boiler in the house. In the second place, steam is not as economical. In figuring the efficiency of heat exchange, one factor is the difference in temperature between the burning fuel and the carrier. The greater the difference, the greater the economy. Steam, at 250 degrees centigrade, is closer to the temperature of a gas flame or oil flame than either hot air or hot water, which are both heated to about 180 degrees. You are behind with steam, right from the start.

The one advantage steam heat does have is that a very small radiator heats a very large space because of the high heat of the radiator itself. However, space is rarely at such a premium that hot water pipes or air ducts are a significant disadvantage.

As with other carriers, the natural gas-steam system is more economical than either oil-steam or electric-steam.

Refrigerant Systems or "Heat Pump"

The heat pump warms a house through the use of an electric pump and has as a carrier a refrigerant, which is alternatively compressed to a liquid and expanded to a gas by the pump.

A heat pump can be viewed as being the exact opposite of an air conditioner. If you have ever held your hand near the outdoor exhaust side of an air conditioner, you have felt heat. This heat is generated by the compression of the refrigerant to a liquid. The refrigerant in an air conditioner is allowed to expand inside the house, cooling the interior of the house. If you reverse this, compressing the refrigerant *inside* the house and letting it expand *outdoors*, you get the heating effect inside. This is how you "pump heat" into a house.

The disadvantage is very large installation costs. If you want *both* heating and central air conditioning (a change which the heat pump can accomplish at the flick of a switch), then your heat pump installation is fairly competitive.

Another advantage of the heat pump is that it uses electricity for its pump—no fuel has to arrive via gas pipes or an oil truck. As long as you have electricity, you have heat, distributed by hot water.

Radiant Heat Systems

To use radiant heat, some object has to be raised to such a temperature that it radiates a substantial amount. This means you have to have a very hot object somewhere in the room, a "radiant heat panel" that has to be shielded from the touch.

The only two practical radiant heat fuels are gas and electricity, with electricity predominating by 98 percent.

Radiant heat cost-of-installation is low, because all you do is run wires from panel to panel. The efficiency is relatively high, because radiant heat travels in electromagnetic waves. The heat goes directly to all the objects in the room, heating the objects, without having to transmit the heat by heating the intervening air (although, of course, the air does get some heat).

At the current cost of electricity, though, radiant heat-electricity is not the way to go, unless you simply prefer it as the cleanest of all possible systems.

What is left now is to relate all these considerations to practical recycling, which the next chapter proceeds to do.

28

Heat: Making It a Bargain

Ideally, there ought to be *both* good central heating and good insulation in your house, but when all the factors are considered, you cannot price yourself out of the market. In estimating costs for redoing a house, you have to balance heating and insulation against each other.

For instance, an insulation-minded person would insist on changing all the windows in the house to thermal windows, but the cost would in most cases not be reflected sufficiently in increased market value, and could send the price of the house beyond that which will give you a good fast sale.

Getting stalled because you overdid it on heat would be too bad. Just because you recycle a house doesn't mean the house has to be perfectly insulated or perfectly heated. You have to be judicious. In your heating installation, you are talking about a large sum in comparison to other things you are spending money on in the house.

In recycling, you have two basic cases facing you in a given house. In the first case, there is no central heating at all.

To take the first case:

If natural gas is available, then that is the first choice. Where there is no natural gas available, make an oil furnace your central heating plant. Where natural gas *is* available but there is very little space to install, choose natural gas-hot water.

Hot Water Advantage

As your fourth choice (where natural gas is not available), you take oil-hot water. The extra expense of water pipes is offset by the fact that your hot water furnace is a much smaller piece of furniture.

A very practical further advantage of hot water pipes is that you can have "zone heating," keeping different parts of the house at different temperatures by installing thermostat valves on the pipe. The bedrooms can be kept at sixty degrees while the rest of the house is at sixty-eight. Over a year that can be a nice saving.

Where there is a call for central air conditioning, as there might be in the Sun Belt, a heat pump installation makes sense.

Where there is a country property with plenty of wood available at reasonable prices, you could consider a wood furnace with hot air—either passive hot air, rising from the basement furnace, or with a regular blower and ducts.

If there is a real trend in the neighborhood to solar heating, you may want to put it in *if* the house has the right exposure, and *if* you are reroofing it anyway. In that case, installing solar panels isn't such a big deal.

Existing Heating System

Let's take the case where there *is* a heating system in place.

If you can make it work, then let is stay. That seems like common sense, but we've seen more than one recycling project go bust because the recycler decided that *his* recycled house *must* have the latest in central heating, rather than simply adequate central heating.

It's probably *feasible* to replace a present system if you don't have much other work to do and still have a low enough market price, but then you really cut into your profit. You have to ask yourself whether that is what you want to do or not. The latest in modern heating systems doesn't raise the market value of the house all that much over an adequate older heating system. Central heating is central heating for most people.

Our suggestion is to consider first cleaning up the present system and go with that.

On oil systems, you can clean the burners, adjust the flame precisely right, and achieve wonderful economies compared with the cost of heating under the previous owner.

Changing Filters

If there is a hot air system, changing the furnace's duct filter makes a big difference. It's pretty hard to push hot air through a filter that's clogged because it was not replaced for two years. Buy filters two at a time, and check the present filter every six months or so. Changing the filter is like changing the oil filter in your car: every so often it just has to be done.

Gas furnaces seldom need adjustment or cleaning. But, if it's an air carrier, then change the duct filter (do this for oil-hot air too) and vacuum the blower motors to get all the dust out of them. They will work better clean.

If you have a hot water system and it's sluggish, you may want to run a decalcifying detergent through the pipe system to cut down on the calcified "scale" that accumulates in water pipes in areas where the water is hard (has lots of minerals in it).

Let's just take a look at a few specific heat system recyclings we have done.

18 Beach Street

We put in gas-hot water because we were cramped for space and couldn't fit in a hot air system. The basement would flood in a very high tide, so we put the furnace in the kitchen. Using a hot water system allowed us to "zone" the building so that we had one heat for our own apartment upstairs and another for the apartment downstairs. No one minds if the landlord turns down his *own* heat.

265 New Ocean

We had room in the basement so we put in gas-hot air, but with a new wrinkle. Since the house had two chimneys, which could be used as stacks for furnaces, we found that it was cheaper to put in one furnace for each stack! Each furnace heated its own end of the house. The cost of ducting for a one-furnace system was that much *more* than for a two furnace system: fewer ducts.

32 Riverdale

We bought this house partly because it had a gas-hot water system ideal for rental apartments, which was the use we had in mind. All we did was clean the gas burners with a brush.

5 Griffin

Here, there was one apartment that was small and one that was big. It was obvious that separate heat controls were needed, so we put in gas-hot water with a thermostat for each apartment.

71 Victor

We put in gas-hot air because there was room in the basement to do it. We had a centrally located chimney, so we only put in one furnace and ducted from there.

The previous heating system at 71 Victor, if you can call it that, had been gas burning space heaters—that is, a burner for each room. They risked freezing their basement water pipes because there was no basement heat. We never use space heaters as a way of heating a house. Particularly if you are going to be a landlord, you should know that replacing frozen pipes is a very expensive proposition. When there is a frozen pipe incident, it's going to be in the dead of winter, when your tenants will be very unhappy.

Desirable Installations

In order, the desirable installations are (1) natural gas-hot air, (2) oil-hot air, (3) natural gas-hot water, and (4) oil-hot water. Special situations call for carriers such as radiant or refrigerant or fuels such as wood and solar.

Don't get carried away by the solar-heating fad. When the U.S. government makes it profitable to install solar heating, do that. Until then, avoid such expensive installations unless a client offers to pay the extra cost.

Don't get carried away by the utility advertisements for the "all-electric house." The all-electric house is turning out to be the "all-time expensive house." People who have electric heat have been reconverting to other heat in recent years as the price of electricity has risen—and risen.

There is a legitimate electrical back-up system that you can install when redoing a house in the Snow Belt for someone who wants a heat pump: at ten below, the heat pump doesn't work very well, so you have to augment the pump heating with a little radiant heat.

If you are rewiring a hot air-ducted house, anyway, you might want to install radiant heat panels in a bedroom which has lots of exposure—two or three sides—particularly if the room is on the prevailing wind side of the house. It's hard to heat a "cold" room if you don't have zone heating, unless you turn up the thermostat and overheat the rest of the house.

In conclusion: if there is no central heating, then it will really pay well to put an economical system in. Yet if there is a system, you have already paid for central heating. Anything you add, substantially, comes out of your pocket.

29

Electricity: Basic Thinking

Two generations back, the usual house electric system was rated at 40 amps. The amount of electricity flowing (when everything was turned on) was something less than 40 amps of electrical current. Thirty amps would light up two or three dozen 40-watt bulbs (the biggest they had in those days) and take care of the electric refrigerator besides.

Today most houses are rated at 150 amps, four times the rating of fifty years ago. This requires bigger and more "channels" (wires) for the electric current to flow through, and a bigger utility line from the outside electric utility pole to the house.

Put more and more appliances on a house wired for only 40 amps, and you are going to blow a fuse or burn up a wire. Overloaded wires can get hot enough to set fire to whatever is near. Once an electric fire is started, it's like any other fire, disastrous.

The first no-no in basic electrical systems, then, is to overload wires.

The second no-no is to block the wire channels for the electrical flow, by allowing corroded wire to remain in place. Any wire that corrodes not only blocks the electricity, but as the electricity tries to push through the corroded section, it heats up the wire, and again, you are playing with fire. Copper wire corrodes at the terminals and connections if the terminals and connections are loose, or if exposed to corrosive liquid or fumes. If you see corroded wire, replace it!

The Nature of Electricity

Let's look closer at the nature of electricity for a moment. You can say that electricity is a flow of "electrons" (from a Greek word meaning "wanderer"). The electrons stream down a wire which "conducts" electricity. Plastic or fibrous substances, called insulators, do not. Thus, all wires are insulated outside by a coating of fibers or rubberlike plastic.

The electron streams run into the house from outside in the utility cable's "hot" wire and flow out of the house again on the utility ground wire. There has to be *flow* for the electrons to do useful work. No flow, no work.

In this way, electricity is like water. If water is flowing, it can be made to do useful work. If not, it cannot. There's another waterlike property that electricity has by nature. Electricity needs a certain "drop" or descent to *make* it flow. A drop is called, in electrical terms, a voltage drop. Voltage is a measure of the drop, or the "push" behind the flow. Some flow is gentle, of low voltage. Sometimes the flow is fierce, of high voltage.

The utility's generating plant supplies the voltage. In a "hot" wire, all the electrons are full of energy, needing only a place to jump to. A ground wire is just such a place.

A hot wire can be considered a "high channel," and a ground wire a "low channel." If you connect an appliance between the high channel and the low channel, the electrons flow through from high to low, performing useful work in the appliance. Electrical systems are simply variations on this theme of electrons pushing from high to low, from a hot wire to a ground wire.

Three-Wire Systems

You'd think that all the electrical system needs then is two wires, the hot and the ground. Actually, that is so; but modern electrical systems are "three wire" systems. Look at your appliance cords: they have three-pronged plugs almost universally today. Each prong connects to a wire inside the cord. The third wire of the modern three-wire system is protection against the third no-no. This no-no is called "shorting the circuit," or a short circuit, or simply "a short."

A short circuit is something that supplies the electricity with an *easier* way to flow than going through an appliance, doing work. (Electricity is basically lazy.)

Let's say that a wire corrodes inside an appliance, and the wire heats and melts so that the wire now also touches the outside metal case of the appliance. You get a shock because the electricity enters your hand and tries to push through your body. If you are standing on something dry, the body resists becoming a conductor and all that happens is that the hand gets a mild shock.

Let's say you are standing on something wet and the wet goes through the skin of your feet. Then the whole of *you* becomes a conductor, and the whole current goes through your body, out through the moisture at your feet and across the floor into the pipes or whatever metal is around, down the pipes into the moist ground outside, which is a low channel. The route is actually a "long circuit" in distance, but a "short circuit" in terms of how little resistance it meets. In running through your body, the electricity did not meet much resistance at all, nor did it in the plumbing pipes, nor the moist ground outside. It found an easier way.

When there's "low resistance" as the current comes through the wires, it surges in volume. The volume or "amps" become more than the wire can hold. A fuse blows or circuit breaker trips and saves you from any more pain. But it may not have been in time. A shock which goes through you can stop your heart, or at least knock you out.

The short circuit does not necessarily include a human. An

overloaded wire can burn through its own insulation in the appliance cord and "short" to the ground wire in the appliance cord without going through the appliance at all. There is a surge of current. Your fuses blow or your circuit breakers trip; the power is cut off. You restore the power by replacing the fuse or resetting the circuit breaker.

The heat thereby generated in the wire can be considerable, enough so that if the fuse or circuit breaker is the least bit faulty, then you can get an electrical fire in the cord, and anything around it.

Minimizing Short-Circuit Hazards

The three-wire system is designed to minimize these hazards. The third wire in an appliance cord or an electric cable is a second ground wire, "the house ground." It's a bare wire, without its own insulation, laid in beside the two insulated wires to the appliance, connected to the outside case of the appliance, and to the "house ground terminal," usually a pipe driven deep into the moist ground. The moist ground outside the house acts as a "reservoir" drawing off all unwanted current, storing it in a placid "pool" where the electrons have nowhere else to flow to. That's why the bare ground wire leads, literally, to the ground.

When a hot wire "shorts" and melts inside a cable or against the case of an appliance, the "house ground" draws the current into the moist ground outside, instead of letting it burn through the cord or shock you. You might feel a slight tingle, or the insulation on the cord might melt a bit, but the current won't be on long enough to burn things up or hit you strongly.

Of course, the electrons will surge through the bare ground wire and a fuse will blow or circuit breaker trip, but in the meantime, there's been no real damage.

Two-Wire System

In a two-wire system, if there is a wire that is getting *too* hot in a cord, then before there is a short, the heat first has to melt through the insulation of the utility ground; only *then* does the fuse blow. By that time, there may be a fire. With a bare house ground added, the surge occurs right away, and occurs in the house ground, not in your hand.

The bare house ground never has any current at all, except when there is a short circuit. Therefore, the house ground can be left bare, without insulation. Adding the bare or house ground to any electrical system increases the system's safety, considerably.

Enough on safety. It is sufficient to know that, although electricity has its dangers, a properly set three-wire system will not seriously malfunction and will give years of faithful service. Thus, it's worth going to the three-wire system, if you rewire a house.

The 20-Volt Option

A second solid reason for rewiring is that the new systems have the 240-volt option that older systems do not. What comes into the house today from the utility pole is three wires: two of them are 120-volt hot wires, and the third is the insulated utility ground. (There is no bare or house ground because that is only strung inside the house.)

The two hot wires are carrying in alternating current. This kind of current switches direction sixty times a second. (This is the sixty-cycle current we use in the U.S.) The direction the current flows at any given moment is either positive—toward the utility—or negative—toward the house. The extremely rapid switches of direction are undetectable by most appliances—it's just as if the current were simply flowing through in one direction. The advantage of alternating current is that it can use transformers. (Transformers are big boxes on the utility poles which often make a buzzing noise.) Transformers step up the voltage to travel long distances (on high tension wires); then they step down the voltage to 120 volts to go into the house.

As the two hot wires come into the house, their electricity is phased. The electrons in one wire are going toward the *utility* whenever the electrons in the other are going toward the *house*. The one wire is "plus" whenever the other is "minus," and vice versa. Thus, each wire swings from 120 plus to 120 minus. Anytime you connect these two hot wires, you get a 240-volt total voltage drop, because you are connecting 120 plus to 120 minus. It's very clever.

So anytime you want to push current through an appliance at 240 volts, you connect the appliance between the two hot wires. Anytime you just want 120 volts, you connect from *either* of the two hot wires to the utility ground, which is at zero voltage. Then you get a drop of only 120 volts. (The utility ground is sometimes called the neutral wire since it works with *either* hot wire.)

There's some safety here. If you grab either of the hot wires alone, you can get only a 120-volt shock; however, if you manage foolishly to grab both hot wires, you can get a 240-volt shock. A 120-volt shock usually will give you a shock; a 240-volt shock is almost guaranteed to do real damage.

Before you start to work on any circuit, then, *test the circuit*. Use a simple device called a voltage tester. It is a light between two prongs, one for each wire. If the meter lights, there's voltage, and you should shut the current off before commencing.

Ground Fault Interrupter

Before winding up the basics of electricity, we ought to mention that there is a new safety device called a Ground Fault Interrupter, or GFI. This is a device which senses when there's any current in the house ground (which means there's a short somewhere). GFI then shuts off the circuit much more quickly than does a fuse or circuit breaker. In modern main panels where all the safety devices are, there is now sometimes a GFI for the bathroom circuits and the pool light circuits, those places where your wet feet make you a perfect potential short circuit and where a few thousandths of a second can make a difference between damage and none.

You *can* put a GFI on all the house lines, but GFIs are very expensive: $25 apiece, compared to $2 for a regular fuse or circuit breaker set-up. GFIs are very sensitive and are likely to go off in a storm when there's change of electric potential outside, or if there is even a very, very slight current running through the house ground. For this reason, the main incoming circuit isn't usually supplied with a GFI. You'd be resetting the main circuit breaker all the time.

There is, however, a portable GFI that can be plugged in; it's a very good thing to use with any shop tool that you use outside, particularly if the ground is moist or you are near a body of water.

For further study of the basics, and of the many ways in which the ingenuity of man has elaborated these basics, there are many reasonably good books on home electrical work. It isn't our intention here to displace them. We wanted merely to set up the basics (which we think we've done here more clearly than in any other book we know about), so you can understand the books in the first place.

This basic knowledge also has practical value. Knowing what you know now about circuits, you are not likely to commit the common sin of inserting a copper penny into a fuse box to replace a fuse which keeps blowing. If a fuse blows, you know now that there is a wire heating up somewhere, and you are playing—literally—with fire.

We are now ready to take on electricity as it relates to recycling. That is what our next chapter does.

30

Electricity: Systems in Recycling

Electrical work in recycling can run all the way from a complete new service down to a touch-up job, adding a few outlets to the existing sufficient system.

Generally, you leave well enough alone if the system is adequate, and spend your money somewhere else. If you have to rewire and put in a new service, then you do a complete job and put in a full modern service, including, say, air conditioning outlets, electric hot water, electric stove, and a couple dozen new appliance outlets.

In order to sell a house at $60,000 or more, you should figure that you have to have a pretty complete modern electrical service. If you can't afford to put that in, then maybe you'd better not recycle that particular house. You will be competing with other houses that do have washer-dryer, hot water electric heater, air conditioning, etc., and you have to be competitive.

Cooking and Hot Water Electric

In general, if natural gas is available to the house, we prefer that, since it's cheaper to run. If natural gas is not available, then electric hot water and cooking is the choice, because it costs the least to install. If you have a low cost of installation, you can reckon the money saved as being banked at 8 percent, so you still have an effective low annual electrical cost.

A new hot-water heater and electric stove usually calls for a new service, meaning you have to go back to the utility and tell them you need a bigger line coming to the house. In addition, you have to redo the main panel, the distribution center for the current coming to the house.

A new main panel not only has capacity for more 120-volt lines (for ordinary appliances), but has lines for 240-volt appliances as well. Instead of the screw-in fuses that were standard in the old main panels, you have the modern circuit breakers. A circuit breaker which trips has only to be reset by switching its lever from "off" back to the "on" position. A blown fuse has to be replaced.

Putting In a New Service

In putting in a new service, you or (if the code requires, or if you prefer) your electrician have to work with the local utility company. They give you the new meter and a new service entrance line. You put the meter on the outside house wall, run the service entrance line up to the top of the house wall, and the utility connects its line there, at the service head.

The service head consists of the fastenings for the non-electrical suspension cables holding the utility wires. There is a "drip loop" in the utility wire which keeps rain water from running down onto your house wall. From the meter, there's a connection through the wall of the house to the main panel.

Your planning of an electrical system really starts there, at the panel.

The panel has a main circuit breaker through which all the current comes in. If that is tripped, then lights and electricity are off throughout the whole house. The panel has small circuit breakers for the current to go through after it divides up into smaller circuits to go to various parts of the house.

Before you get your panel, since it comes with circuit breakers all set up, you want to have an electrical diagram for the house which tells you how many circuit breakers you will need and of what voltage—120-volt or 240-volt. The diagram is a sketch of all the circuits in the house, how many appliances and outlets on each circuit. In making a diagram, you have to figure how the wires are best threaded through the walls, floor, and ceiling from the main panel to the eventual appliance or "load." Once you have your diagram, you know how to have your main panel circuit breakers set up.

You will want to run 240-volt lines to your stove, hot water heater, air conditioner outlets, and dryer in the laundry. Although all these appliances can be bought in 120-volt models, the 240-volt models are faster and more efficient.

Single and Multiple Lines

There are two kinds of 120-volt lines: single appliance and multiple appliance. You want single appliance lines for stuff that either draws a rather heavy current, or where you want to make sure that the appliance keeps on going regardless of what happens to other appliances. You have single appliance lines to the heavy loads on the toaster, curling iron, hair dryer, and, in fact, all bathroom outlets since people are likely to plug a hair dryer into any of them. You also need single lines for each kitchen outlet for blenders, etc. You want single appliance lines for your shop tools. When electric motors start up, they draw a heavy starting current. You want your sump pump, furnace, refrigerator, and freezer on separate lines because you want them to work at all times.

All other appliances can be ganged up four or five to the circuit, which makes for less wire and less expense. On such multiple outlet circuits, you will want to have the light fixtures in the same room split up between two different lines, so that if one fuse blows, there is still a light working in the room.

15-Amps and 20-Amps

All the lines have either a 20-amp circuit breaker, or a 15-amp circuit breaker. (In older main panels, there are 20-amp fuses and 15-amp fuses.) The 15-amp breakers trip a lot faster than the 20-amp ones. A short circuit on a 15-amp line will cause a shut-off in time to save an appliance which otherwise would have burned up on a 20-amp fuse. You have to match loads and circuit breakers. (That is also why, after a system is set up, you do not switch fuses around in a fuse box, so that a 20-amp is put in the place of a 15-amp.)

In a circuit breaker panel, make sure that there are 15-amp circuit breakers for all the "light load" lines. You want to cut current out before the appliance starts to burn. Of course, in a three-wire system, the house ground is carrying off the shorted current, but even so, if the current surge is a little too much for the appliance, it will cause it to burn out.

(As we've said before, in old fuse boxes, the practice of shorting out a fuse receptacle by inserting a wire or a copper penny is a terrible idea because then there's no way for the current to cut off if it does surge. So you then have a situation where fire can break out anytime there's an overload.)

Threading Wires

Once you've made your electrical system plan, you are ready to thread those wires around through the house, leading out of the main panel you have bought.

Usually you can lead the required wires from the basement and *up* into the rooms, or from the attic and *down* into the rooms. If you are unlucky, you are going to have to break into walls to get your wires through.

To go up from the basement, start where the new outlet is to be, take off a baseboard (floor molding), punch into the wall at the point where you want the wire to come up, drill down through the floor *inside* the wall, and then thread the wire up through the hole from the basement below.

Once you have brought the wire up for one outlet, you can run the wire from outlet to outlet behind the baseboard by gouging out a channel in the wallboard or plaster back of the baseboard. Then you cut all your necessary holes for your outlets through the baseboard, pull the wire through each hole in the baseboard, and then nail the baseboard back onto the wallboard.

Surface Wiring

There's another approach. If the local code allows, you can use "surface wiring," which is a fancy form of extension cord that can be nailed on the surface of the baseboard, and still look decorative. Provided that you have wired to the room sufficient capacity for current that could be drawn, you can add outlets on the surface wire until you have all the outlets you need along the floor. You don't have to remove the baseboard at all.

To go down from the attic, take a chain or weighted string and drop it down inside the wall. This can be reached by a "fishing tape." Or simply bend a coat hanger into a hook. The hook is thrust in through the opening punched in the wall for the receptable, and the hook grabs the string or chain and then pulls that out through the receptable hole. The person in the attic ties the end of the new wire to the string so the wire can be pulled through.

There are many variations. There's getting from a ceiling light down to a baseboard outlet, and vice versa—all are detailed in the handbooks. By using the attic, cellar, and interior walls, you can get an electric wire nearly anywhere in the house that you want it.

Kinds of Wires

Until recently, copper wire was the only wire used. More lately, some builders have used aluminum wire. There have been some unfortunate results, because aluminum wire has to be properly installed to work. It has to have cadmium wire nuts (splice nuts), not the regular brass or copper wire splice nuts. Otherwise a galvanic process sets up that heats aluminum wire and melts it, or causes it to start a fire. Secondly, aluminum must be covered with insulation right to the connection; it can not be left bare, or it oxidizes, blocks the current, and heats up.

So although it's cheaper, aluminum is also trickier to handle. Some codes have outlawed it. But there are special nuts and special kinds of boxes with terminals made for aluminum. It can be done right and work well.

There are special considerations in electric systems for a rental house. If you have a rental house, it's worth making sure that there are baseboard outlets every six feet or so (some building codes require that). This means the tenants aren't going to put in long extension cords, which are an invitation to burning. Extension cords fray; they get stepped on by sharp high heels and crushed under furniture legs. They are likely to be overloaded by too many appliances and start burning.

Safety in Electrical Work

All electrical work carries risk. Most recycling electrical work is done with the appropriate current breaker shut off, so that there is no electricity in the line. But some of the circuits are on; make sure that the line you are working on isn't "live." The quickest way to test is with your voltage tester, which, in its simplest form, is simply a light with a couple of prongs that can go from the hot wire you are working on to the ground wire. It will light up when there is voltage there. This means your hot wire is "live."

In your first wiring, it is often advisable to get an electrician to come over and do some simple stuff for you. It is not very expensive and you can learn a lot from it.

part 6

Rehabilitating for Maximum Profit

31

The Exterior: Making It Sell

Here in this last section are six chapters on what most people may think of as the whole of recycling. Of course, it isn't so. There's much more. But working with interiors and exteriors, and in the case of the advanced recyclers, with large, mansion-size houses, is very much at the heart of the matter.

There's nothing really to compare with the exterior of a house for bringing in buyers. The term for it in the real estate trade is "curb appeal." The reason for drop-in business is an attractive house with a "For Sale" sign on the lawn.

Interiors are no less selling points, once the potential buyer is inside. The thought and imagination that goes into an interior are almost surely going to tell, once the potential buyer is in.

Then there are the special cases, the mansions, in which restoring becomes a big point. The question is: how much to restore and how much to make up to date?

We will start with exteriors. Although exterior changes are expensive, they are sometimes the key to the recycling of a

house. The most important consideration lies in the neighborhood. The house must be competitive. If it's really below the
standard of the houses roundabout in outside appearance, the
appearance has to be upgraded. On the other hand, it's not a
good idea to "outbuild the neighborhood," because then money
spent on the exterior will not be reflected in the market price.
Your house has a top price limit in any neighborhood.

We regularly look for "noncompetitive" exteriors in a given
neighborhood. We know that then we can add value to the
house through exterior changes, as well as interior.

Exteriors Are Money

The exterior is what people see. It can make the difference
between a house that sells for $10,000 and one that sells for
$50,000. We find that in large, older houses we often get a good
buy because the exterior looks grim, while the interiors are
relatively sound. We fix up the exterior; that in and of itself
raises the price tens of thousands of dollars. The buyer often
makes up his mind before he enters a house. The exterior is
what *he's* going to show people. If he can show it with pride,
he's going to buy it, provided the interior is reasonably good.

The last of our recycled houses in our "ten-year track record"
was a good example of adding value through exterior changes.
This was 25-29 Monmouth Road; a property with three houses
on the lot, two very close together and one smaller separate
building. We subdivided the lot and sold the smaller house to
one member of our recycling community. We gave the remaining
two houses a "condominium" look by roofing them both with
the same mansard roof, giving each house matching siding and
front decks, which made the two dwellings look like twins. We
tripled the value of the property when we'd finished recycling.

Beforehand, both had been quite a bit below the neighborhood standard, low cost rentals; the owner had neglected the
exteriors in order to make a profit. We made the two modern
and desirable. In the end, we jumped the value of the property
from $44,000 to $172,000.

This shows what can be done by exterior work. It shows, too, the unique kind of solution that a recycler with experience can come up with, something that no contractor would have the time or patience to puzzle out.

Order of Work

Let's get into the subject. First, let's consider the order in which you tackle the large jobs in recycling in which there are both exterior and interior work.

This is the order (after cleaning the house):

1. Roof first. Refinished ceilings and walls won't get ruined by roof leaks.

2. Replace windows and exterior doors. You won't have to go back and rip out new or restored siding to replace them later.

3. Plumbing. Do this before you put in any interior or exterior walls or refinish old ones. Otherwise you have to disturb already finished work.

4. Heat pipes and ducts, for the same reason.

5. Insulation; again, the same reason.

6. New interior walls.

7. Refinish interior ceilings, then the walls, and then the floors.

8. Siding. Parallel with (7), whenever the weather is good, you put on new siding or refinish the old siding.

9. Landscaping last, so your supply vehicles won't destroy the landscaping already in place. In good weather, you can start landscaping that is out of the way anytime.

Frequent Exterior Jobs

Now let's consider the frequency of the exterior work of different kinds. Most houses, first of all, need paint, assuming the exterior is otherwise largely sound, which it often is.

The second most frequent job is replacing the existing siding: putting up pieces to fill in for missing house molding, patching the siding, restoring gouged and scarred window moldings. We replace partially rather than go for whole new moldings or replacing whole sidings; it's much less expensive and much less time consuming. Old moldings are very high quality.

Third most frequent job is roof patching. Often there are at least a couple of leaks, usually in the "valleys" where two sections of roofing meet an an angle. Fourth, putting on a partial new roof or a whole new roof.

Fifth is putting on *new* siding or molding either to upgrade the house or to replace siding and molding too damaged to fix, or where we have to fill "holes" left when we have closed off the front doors, moved windows, or put in a new front door to form a new traffic pattern for the house.

Sixth is changing ordinary doors to sliding glass doors to give more light. Seventh is adding porches, decks, and upstairs shed dormers.

Eighth is landscaping—fences, foundation planting, regrading the lawns, moving hedges.

Let's take these in order.

Painting

This requires scraping down to remove old loose paint and adding one or two coats of new paint. It takes some time, but painting is the most profitable time you spend in terms of return. It upgrades and keeps the siding from rotting or discoloring. You can scrape and paint a big house in two weeks, a small one in a week or less. The paint cost usually runs from $1,000 for a mansion to $200 for a smaller house.

Replacing and Restoring Molding and Siding Sections

Lots of times the owners have simply picked up fallen pieces and stored them in the basement, attic, or out-of-the-way halls. Be vigilant; spot these pieces. They are almost worth their weight in gold compared to the time and expense of replacing a molding section with new lumber. The work of putting up an old molding that already fits is very little.

Roof Patching

You can usually look at the interior ceilings and tell whether or not the roof needs patching. Leaks discolor the ceiling underneath quite quickly. If the leak is in a valley, you may have to replace the aluminum flashing underneath. The flashing may be bent out of shape or torn. Each valley (and around each chimney) has flashing under the shingles. These aluminum pieces protect the roof sheeting under the shingles from water. A much greater amount of rainwater comes across these valleys in the roof and at greater speed. Water here can force passages in the shingling. Hopefully, the flashing is okay. If not, remove flashing and check the sheeting underneath to see if the sheeting has rotted. If it has, you may have to replace a section of sheeting, caulk it, then replace the flashing and finally the shingles immediately above. It is a job.

Most of the time, happily, all that is needed is to go over the leaky section of roof with a tar brush and a gallon of tar. Then you wait for rain to see if you got the leak or not.

Of course the tar patch leaves a tar spot; and if the spot is in sight of the ground, you should paint the roof as a whole with oil base paint, sprayed on with a gun. The roof, if it's discolored at all by aging of the asphalt shingle (most roofs are asphalt) can be greatly helped, cosmetically and practically, with such a spray paint job. This may keep an older roof going for another two years, and then an additional paint job for two more, and so on.

There is a limit to how much a paint job can cover up. There always will be a slight difference between the tar spot and the asphalt shingle even after painting. Rather than spot a roof with tar to cover a multitude of leaks, we replace the roof, that is, reshingle it. If there are lots of leaks now, more leaks are likely to develop in the near future.

Professional Roofers

The cost of professional reroofing depends on whether or not the house has "one or two roofs." A first reroofing can be laid right on top of the original roofing. But most building codes will not allow more than two roofs, because of the weight build-up. Therefore, to reroof a house with two roofs on already, you have to tear up both roofs, take up the underneath roofing felt, lay bare the sheeting, and start over again. This is a messy job. Asphalt shingles come with underlying tar tabs (to make the lower edge stick).

The professionals around us charge $10 "a square" for a first reroofing (a square is a ten-foot by ten-foot section), and an additional $10 a square for tearing up the old roofing. So for a first reroofing of a small roof, say fifty-by-forty, 2,000 square feet, or twenty squares, you are only into $200 or so. For a tear-up and reroofing, you are into $400 or so, or $1,000 for an average medium size house roofing job.

Other Roofs

There are other roofings besides asphalt shingle; the second most popular around our part of the country is cedar shake (shingle). If a cedar shake roof is "gone," and there are lots of leaks, you are in for money. Say an asphalt roof costs $1,000 to put down; a same size cedar shake roof would be $5,000. So you should think twice about recycling a house that has a bad cedar shake roof. Very likely a cedar shake roof is what the neighborhood "requires." It's not always feasible, therefore, to replace cedar shakes with asphalt shingles and still have a competitive house.

If you repaint or reshingle a roof, do it when there is a forecast for good weather. The paint will take four hours to dry in summer, and longer in winter. We once painted a roof in the morning and it rained at 2 P.M. By 3 P.M. the paint had all washed off, down the drain.

If you reshingle with asphalt, the soft tar tabs under the lower edge of the shingle have to dry to "seal" the roof. You don't normally have to nail the lower shingle edges, but should you get a good strong wind, as once we did, before the tabs are dry, your shingles may "tear off." On our house at 1 Ocean, Sam had to get up on the roof at night in a near hurricane and nail the lower edges of all the asphalt shingles to keep them from blowing off—not a particularly nice way to spend a night.

But Sam saved the roof.

32

The Exterior: Upgrading the Value

Sometimes the house looks so "down" compared to its neighbors that you have to add something special to the exterior, rather than replace or restore. At minimum, this is simply new "trim" to the corners (corner moldings) of the house. At maximum, you replace the siding along one whole face or several faces of the house.

We have sometimes added nothing but new molding and repainted the existing siding to have a house that looks almost new. This is lots cheaper than replacing the old siding. New corner trim is just primed and painted new boards. We added trim to 71 Victor, 477 Ocean, and 32 Riverdale in a darker color than the siding, brown for the first two cases, and black for the last. These were colors that were popular trim colors in the vicinity for these kinds of houses, and they all very much needed to come up to the neighborhood standard. We didn't try to make a "stand-out designer house" of any of them; they were modest structures in the first place. Your buyer wants to keep up with the Joneses; he doesn't, in spite of everything, want to put the Joneses down too much, either.

New Siding

There is a lot you can do with new siding—almost so many different things that it's bewildering. There is a siding in almost every color and quality you can think of in your lumber supplier's store or his catalog. To find out what it's going to cost you, go to your supplier and price the stock available. New siding can make an old house look as up-to-date as anything around, a real face lift. Residing a single face of a house can run from as little as $200 to as much as $1,000, without even getting into the really fancy stuff with which catalogs like to tempt you.

We reside no more than three sides of any inexpensive house. We *paint* the back of the house the same color. Sometimes, when there's a short side facing the road or street, just residing that one face will do it, provided you cleverly match the other three sides in paint, and put on new trim.

Types of Siding

Let's look at the simple siding choices commonly available.

Cedar plywood siding comes in nice designs, and we like it. We decided to take the cedar shakes off 1 Ocean because the shakes had been painted so many times the paint was peeling badly. It would have taken forever to scrape. We replaced the shakes with cedar plywood siding, much quicker to put on than cedar shakes, and still maintained the requisite quality for the location.

Plain cedar boards give a very nice effect. Cedar is particularly weatherproof, and it slowly darkens, though not nearly as much as cedar shakes, which go dark much faster, and make a house look old and weathered.

(Of course, you may want the look of cedar shakes. If you are recycling in a vacation colony, often cedar shake is very much the fad; why fight it? When all the houses look weathered, the weathered look is nice.)

Our favorite new siding, though, is rough sawn Vermont board. It's relatively cheap for us since we get it from Vermont ourselves. We put it on vertically or diagonally, and it makes a house look very woodsy. Great for mountain resort areas. We resided our Vermont house in rough sawn Vermont board because it was inexpensive locally. Later we used the rough-sawn in some of our other, not so rural recyclings, as in our complete residing of 25-29 Monmouth Road.

Aluminum Siding

Aluminum siding can look good, if you can afford a good grade of it. The drawback is that it dents; and then it makes the house look rather like an old kettle. We bought a new aluminum siding for the short, street face of 32 Riverdale, where we'd closed up several windows and a door to form a new traffic pattern. It wasn't that expensive and went on very fast, because it comes in such large pieces.

We enclosed a porch at 477 Ocean with board and batten siding. It suited the house and the location. Board and batten was the best looking siding available for the money. We'd already used board and batten on our first house, at 18 Beach, with good results. It was faster to put up and cheaper than replacing the cedar shakes that had been there originally but which were now weathered, split, and coming off.

We restuccoed part of the siding at 71 Victor, where we closed off windows and a door, to match the stucco already there. That worked fine, and was lots better than replacing the whole siding of the house.

Asbestos shingle is less expensive generally than cedar shake, and where the house already has asbestos shingle, this is easy to fit into the sections of siding that have gone bad. Asbestos shingle has to be distinguished from its poorer cousin, asphalt shingle, mostly used on roofs except in less affluent sections of a town; even there asphalt shingle used as siding looks ugly.

Wood bevel is what the pre-Victorian houses used. It gives an "antique" look, and we only have used this to replace missing siding.

There are many more kinds of siding available. The only way to convince yourself on a choice is to go down and look up the price at your supplier and have a look at the houses all around to see how that kind of siding weathers as the years roll by.

New Windows and Doors

Where you are selling the great outdoors, as on a beach or in the mountains, have plenty of picture windows and glass sliding doors. Windows and doors are not hard to add; you knock holes in the siding and the sheathing.

Our most extensive big glass window-and-door jobs were on our beach houses (which we still keep to rent out because the land is appreciating so fast). One Ocean and 477 Ocean are right on the Atlantic Ocean. Nothing like seeing the steamers heading out to Europe or fishing trawlers setting out nets from your dining room window.

New Shed Dormers and Roof Additions

To put the dining room on the second floor at 1 Ocean, we ran floor joists out from the roof rafters to build a sort of "super dormer" with a fifteen-by-twenty-foot floor, but usually we are content with smaller "shed dormers" where we want to make more bedrooms in an attic—as we did at 5 Griffin Street and our Vermont house. We can put a dormer in, flash, and reroof in a day.

Porches and Decks

At 12 Main Street and 25-29 Monmouth, we built decks to enhance the value of the house. A deck seems to add a whole room to the house. To make a deck, you have to pour some concrete "feet" or foundations. How many and how far apart is something that a good home remodeling book goes into at great length. Don't guess at it, because you are talking engineering type stresses here. Just digging holes and running posts into the soil won't do it, either, because the posts can sink slowly under the weight of passing feet. And a slanting deck adds nothing to a house.

Concrete footing has to extend below the frost line. It's two feet into the ground in New Jersey, three feet in New York, and it goes deeper the farther north you get. If you don't get the footings dug down below the frost line, you get a "frost heave."

Landscaping

Sometimes an outbuilding is the thing. We put in a swimming pool bathhouse at the Lindens, a very rustic little shed, just set up on bricks dug slightly into the soil. It isn't so important to make sure the particular outbuilding here is absolutely level, and it sits there of its own weight.

Another alternative is to build from the ground up out of "prepared lumber," which is rot proof. But, this costs two times ordinary lumber, and you have to have at least the first two levels of board prepared.

Fences

Most often we've used this to divide the property from the neighboring land, to "show off the property" as it were—show the size and extent of it. This is particularly effective where you have a fairly large but somewhat irregular plot where the boundaries are not readily distinguishable.

Once or twice we've used a high fence to "hide the neighbors" in areas where we were building inexpensive rentals. We never had trouble renting these houses because of the neighbors. Otherwise, the neighbors could have sent the house value down.

Plantings

You surely don't have time to grow a hedge, but often moving one that isn't particularly prepossessing where it is to some more prominent location will improve the look of a piece of land. Hedges are good for killing traffic noise.

Lawns

We usually just have some topsoil trucked in and rake it level, add grass seed, and let it go at that. In one case, we had a place with a retaining wall out front, and it made the house look odd by comparison with its neighbors who all had lawns sloping right to the sidewalk. We regraded that lawn to look like the others on the block, and that brought the house back into the neighborhood.

If the house doesn't have any plants nearby, you can use foundation plantings, bought from the local plant nursery to soften the foundation lines and the corner lines of the house. Shrubbery make the house look like it belongs on the land.

Exteriors, in General

This subject is diverse and extensive enough to fill a book by itself, with another couple of books on landscaping. We've sketched here some exterior changes that have particular relevance to recycling. The nub of exteriors is, "fit the house in." That's true whether it's fitting the house to the neighborhood (we are not talking about mansions now), fitting the house to the landscape, or fitting the house to the land. There's a kind of "recycler's eye" that you develop to enable you to see what a weird old crumbling-porched house with sagging window sashes will look like when it's upgraded, updated, and correlated with the surroundings. You can make, well, if not a swan, a reasonably proud looking duck out of an ugly ducking.

33

The Interior: Conjuring Ceilings

For some people, renewing interiors—redecorating and remodeling—is what recycling is all about. If so, they are going back-end first. Our remodeling and renewing hinges on the recycling, rather than vice versa. We are considering the whole house in recycling. Say it needs lots of exterior work; this then has to come first (nobody is going to inspect a house with a bad exterior, much less seriously consider buying). The redecorating and the remodeling of the interior will have to be done at a cost lower than if you had no exterior changes. It's the whole house that sells. If you have bad siding and a beautiful master bedroom, that isn't going to do it.

We prefer to call the whole renewal process "rehabilitation," which means making a house a fit place to live. The basics, such as watertight roofs, modern wiring, and an efficient kitchen, come first. After that comes what people generally refer to as redecorating and remodeling.

Again, the kind of job you do on a room, given a certain size, depends on what is happening to the room in the whole recycling scheme. If nothing is being changed in the room, then the best approach is to leave the room alone in every way possible. If, on the other hand, we are taking out a wall, and in so doing will be ripping open the ceiling and marking up the floor, then that room will get a real ceiling and floor treatment while we are at it.

Kinds of Houses

There is also another set of parameters. This set concerns the kind of house in general that is being recycled. They fall broadly into three categories:

(1) Utilitarian

This is a house not particularly distinguished in any way, being recycled for straight money value, very often as a rental. Here "economical" is the byword.

(2) The Half and Half

This is a house with some very good features from its heyday and with some very bad features in relation to modern standards. We aim to keep the best of the old and put in the best of the new.

(3) The Period House

This is the most fun, even if we don't get to make as many changes. The challenge is to disturb the evident beauty as little as possible while making it marketable for those who live well, but in today's "live-well" style, without a squad of servants.

Those are the parameters. Now we go to the specifics. What do you do to what under what circumstances? Do you wallpaper the room, refinish the floor, wallboard the ceiling? Or paint the room, carpet the floor, and paper the ceiling?

Let's list all the possibilities.

Permanent Changes Possible

1. Walls
   (a) subsurface—spackle, Structo-lite
   (b) surface—paint, wallpaper, wallboard, cork, tile, paneling, moldings, wall strips, shelving, wall columns, wall beams

2. Floors
    (a) surface—hardwood, linoleum, tile, stain
    (b) platforms
    (c) wall-to-wall carpeting
3. Ceilings
    (a) subsurface—spackle, Structo-lite
    (b) surface—paint, cork, wallpaper, wallboard, tile, paneling
    (d) moldings
    (e) beams
    (f) fixtures
    (g) hanging or dropped ceilings

Removable Changes

1. Walls
    (a) mirrors
    (b) pictures
    (c) hangings, drops, curtains
    (d) sconces
2. Floor
    (a) area carpeting
    (b) furnishings
3. Ceilings
    (a) hanging plants

Outlining Needs

This is a list we work from. It may not be complete or the same as someone else's list. By filling in the blanks—what kind of carpeting, do we need sconces, and so on—we outline in advance what we need for a room, and then we get all the lists for all the rooms together and we can start thinking about where to get what we don't already have.

It's super fun to go to a big flea market, say Englishtown, New Jersey, and pick up—in one day—almost all that we need to finish off a house. There comes a point where you are so familiar with the house that you can start with its basic plan and modify in your head as you go along, changing sometimes the entire concept of a room because of a series of finds you make.

Of course, whenever possible, we use what we already have stored in the attic of 91 Rumson. While our recycling is in progress, we keep a sharp lookout for estate sales, auctions, and even lawn sales in our area.

Finding Wallpaper

The idea is to make the recycling as efficient as possible. We haven't the time to go to the ends of the earth to find just the right wallpaper. It would be fun to be able to do that once in a while. But we almost never can. We find good quality things, and we make a quick mental match to see if it would go in a given room. If not, we go on until we find the closest thing we can to the ideal. We've nearly always been able to come close enough to make our "class recycles" really special places.

The challenge is to make a recycle work when it gets down to the bottom line, and yet make it something we point to with pride. We do make it, both ways, time after time.

Let's get back to our list. We take ceilings first. Once you finish a ceiling, you don't have to go back there. You clean up the mess your ceiling work made of the walls and floor and go to them, in that order.

Ceiling Surface

What are the choices? Well, ninety percent of the time what is there is wallboard and paint or plaster and paint. If we are lucky, what's there in the subsurface, be it wallboard or plaster, is good enough so it can be repainted without much preparation. Such is not usually the case.

The one thing about a big flat surface is that any little unevenness shows up glaringly. Even if there are no holes or cracks, the lumps and bumps look terrible even when painted.

If the dents in the plaster or wallboard existing in the room are reasonably shallow or confined, then we go after the surface with spackle and Structo-lite. Spackle will fill in shallow indentations quickly. But one of spackle's properties is that, when laid on in depth, it takes forever to dry. So the fast-drying Structo-lite is our deep-hole ace-in-the-hole.

Making an even surface takes a trained eye. Until your eye is trained, you are going to have some uneven ceilings. That's all in the game. It's a good reason not to start out with a fancy first recycle. In our own case, 18 Beach was a kind of house that anything you did to it either improved it or made it look as lousy as it did before you started. There was no way to lose. That's the perfect kind of first recycle.

Often the damage to the ceiling is beyond reasonable repair. This is especially true of plaster ceilings on the first floor. Today there are few plasterers of real ability. Even professional restorers, willing to pay nearly any price, have a hard time finding plasterers who can do a decent job. We simply cover really bad plaster with a sheetrock wallboard (the old name is "drywall" to distinguish it from plaster, which went on wet). Then you spackle out the small unevennesses that even new wallboard has, tape over the intersections with a good tape, and then you are set to paint.

An alternative—which may be more expensive but has advantages—is cork. Squares of cork can be glued to a ceiling easily. Cork can survive wetting down which wallboard cannot. Say that you are recycling a rental and redoing a room under an upstairs bathroom: inevitably somebody will let the sink upstairs overflow. If you have cork on the ceiling under, you simply reglue any squares that the water has loosened. Water will darken cork but not damage it otherwise. It will ruin wallboard, even so-called waterproof wallboard.

Ceiling Tile

A more expensive alternative to wallboard is ceiling tile. You can make a ceiling look beautiful—but if it gets wet, you have to take down at least some of the ceiling tiles, because they are interlocking.

When all is said and done, sheetrock (wallboard) is the usual answer. If wallboard is ruined, you replace it. It's the cheapest surface that exists.

Stucco painting the ceiling is done to give a Tudor look. It takes some time to learn to stucco paint efficiently and esthetically, but it can be learned.

Stucco will—if it's in the proper kind of house—make fine finishing of the ceiling surface unnecessary. Stucco is cheap: fifty pounds in a barrel for a few dollars. But it's labor-intensive. At 1 Ocean Avenue we had plaster ceilings that looked just terrible, but the house was right for stucco so we went in with five friends one day and did all the ceilings in the house that day. Stucco has water resistance, since it's a ceramic product. This means you don't have to worry about spilt sink water from above.

You *can* wallpaper a ceiling but you need lots of hands. Somebody has to hold up the initial end and the middle while the far end of the paper is being pasted up. Wallpaper is more expensive than anything else you can put up except tile, so you should do wallpaper only for a special effect. Do it where you won't have to worry about an upstairs bathroom spill.

Wainscot Ceiling

There's another kind of ceiling altogether, the wood ceilings of the best Victorian houses. Often they were wainscoting. Obviously, this is something that you want to restore, if possible, because then you are offering something unique to any buyer.

If you are able to afford oak wainscot ceilings today your name should ring with those of Rockefeller and Onassis on the social register. It's what you get for nothing in an old house or that you find to fit for next to nothing in a flea market that often constitutes your strongest selling points.

The Victorian wainscoting is a type of wood panel ceiling. There were other types: straight oak paneling, inlaid oak paneling, raised oak paneling, etc. In today's rooms, you sometimes see a modern equivalent: plywood panel ceilings and knotty pine board paneled ceilings.

We mostly stay away from either plywood panel or the

"rumpus room" look with knotty pine or cedar paneling. It's not appropriate for the kind of houses we do in the "class recycles." Plywood panel or board ceiling would be much too expensive in the utilitarian recycle. Panel and board are the kinds of materials that you see in "home improvement," and it's great there, as a hobby. In recycling, paneling does not add a tenth of the value of the materials used, let alone pay for the labor. To put in wood panel ceilings is just outside the bounds of recycling.

Moldings

Any ceiling looks better set off from the walls with molding. But if you have a Utilitarian recycle it's okay just to have the painted ceiling meet the top of the wall without any molding at the juncture.

In a Half-and-Half house, we always restore the moldings that are there or buy some new ones. Reasonably priced new moldings are a proper investment. You are trying to sell a house in the $60,000-plus range. You are usually talking about buyers with some taste.

In a Period House, the full restoration situation, you often have fantastic original moldings. If you have the same moldings in two rooms, you can find enough good molding between the two to do one room. Then you buy Victorian molding at the flea market for the other, or get it at an estate sale or auction. Finding a molding that fits the spirit of the house is a challenge.

Strips and Battens

Sometimes you can liven up a ceiling by putting strips across it, or "battens" as they are called. We have even used battens and rough-sawed Vermont lumber to give a board-and-batten ceiling that is not expensive. It's the only time we put in a board ceiling. Strips or battens allow you to put in overhead light fixtures without going up through the ceiling to put in the cable.

Beams

Sometimes a ceiling has a structural beam across it. You can match these with "false beams" or box beams: three sides of plywood with a hollow center. This gives you four or five beams across the ceilings, often a very fine effect. Even less expensive and not quite as convincing are the styrofoam false beams that weigh next to nothing and are easy tc put in place.

We often use beams in a Half-and-Half recycle where a room has no other special character. We feel that in a Half-and-Half recycle, *every* room ought to be reasonably interesting. Beams are particularly effective if you have a ceiling where there are small cracks and some unevennesses. These are often hard to completely hide. Beams draw the eye away from them, the conjuror's trick.

Stucco Paint

Another thing you can do if there are cracks is to stucco paint, but not all houses are right for stucco. As an alternative there are other strong texture paints, like sand paint. They usually do the trick. But again, sometimes beams are just the right touch and nothing else would have looked as good.

Cathedral Ceiling

A final solution of sorts, where you have a bad ceiling in an upstairs room or in a ranch house, is to take the ceiling out completely and wallboard the now-exposed attic roof to create a cathedral ceiling. That way you get to start new.

34

The Interior: Wall and Floor Facelift

The walls we face are 90 percent of the time either wallboard or plaster. Since we favor Victorians, plaster is the usual. The other 10 percent of the time is solid paneling in oak or mahoghany.

Plaster walls, as plaster ceilings, are in conditions ranging from nearly-all-there, ready to refinish or paper over, or "30 percent missing." If a wall is only flaking or a little discolored, all we have to do—this is our best case—is wash it down, let it dry, and repaint or wallpaper.

Wallpapering walls is much much easier than wallpapering ceilings. You wet the wallpaper strip with paste and press it in place; gravity lines it up. One person can do it.

The advantage of wallpaper over paint is that wallpaper lasts longer without renewal. You can buy—and we always do—vinyl wallpaper which is eminently washable. Wipe it down with a slightly soapy cloth and a year of smudge disappears, just like that. If cost weren't a factor, we'd always vinyl-wallpaper a room.

Vinyl wallpaper is roughly $8 a roll versus $2 for your average wallpaper. If you hang it slightly askew, you can strip it right off without tearing it—which makes it twice as easy to put up. (Regular wallpaper has to be steamed off, even while it's still drying, for fear of tearing it if you pull hard on it.)

Paint is ten times cheaper than vinyl wallpaper. And it takes less skill to put on. Almost anybody can paint a wall. Wallpapering takes experience.

Wallpapering for Class

We always wallpaper all our "class recycles," houses we plan to sell eventually for $60,000 or up. Wallpapering means we can rent the house while the price of the house escalates; then come in and clean down the walls in a hurry to get the house ready for showing for sale.

We paint when we have a Utilitarian recycle, an inexpensive rental, or an inexpensive house. You can cover the walls of a room with good paint for $6; a vinyl wallpapering job (the only kind worth doing) will cost $100.

Wallpapering is the way to go if it's going to be special. We key our redecorating on the wallpaper; we keep buying good wallpaper in odd lots at sales whenever we can. To wallpaper a house is a way of saying "top quality."

We have treated the best case, when the wall is ready almost to go. What if it has cracks and really deep discoloring? Our first thought, in a Utilitarian situation, is texture paint—sand paint, stucco, or whatever. If the wall is flaking badly, it not only has to have the cracks spackled first, but also has to be thoroughly scraped. Where the discoloration is, you have to "size" the spots and paint over with cheap paint first, so that the spot won't show through the final overall coating. If the wall is "porous" so that it soaks in paint, you follow the sizing with a primer coat of paint.

Wallpapering Preparation

We don't escape any of the above by wallpapering; the wall still has to be spackled, sized, scraped, and primed. If the wall is really bad and we are putting on very expensive wallpaper, we paper with a "liner" first. It's got to look good when it's all finished.

Unfortunately, there was no vinyl in the days of Queen Victoria; instead of stripping it off, as with vinyl wallpaper, you have to steam off old wallpaper—and it's a *messy* job. We won't do it unless we have to. If the old wallpaper has a fairly smooth finish, seal it with a paint coat, pick a wallpaper that will go over without the underwallpaper showing through, and use that—keying the rest of the room to that wallpaper. (Incidentally, you cannot wallpaper over vinyl.)

Let's go to the worst case: the wall has flaking paint, cracks, discoloring, and big holes as well. Call for Structo-lite. If the wall has holes so deep that the lathes (wood strips that hold the plaster) are also missing, you have to put a metal mesh into the hole so the Structo-lite will have something to hang onto.

Now, the very worst case is wall surface more than thirty percent missing. Here you simply wallboard the entire wall and begin over again. If the wall is so shot that part of the surface is missing from top to bottom, you fill out the missing part with wood so you have something solid to nail the wallboard to at that point. To stay flat, wallboard has to be nailed up tight all the way across and up and down, too.

Then you tape the wallboard sections, one to another—we use a porous tape that doesn't "make bubbles" and which makes taping easy—and spackle the tape. You are in business for paint or wallpaper, whichever is appropriate.

Cork

For the right house, a cork wall works well in some rooms (certainly not all). Particularly in a bedroom, which could be a kid's bedroom—anything can be pinned onto cork. Cork is two times as expensive as paint, but less work. Your wall does not have to be smooth.

In a really classy bathroom, we dispense with the usual utilitarian fiberglass molded shower stall and do the stall in bathroom tile. But, of course, the molded fiberglass shower stall can also be dressed up. For the inexpensive recycle, bathrooms are painted; for expensive houses, they are tiled to waist level. Bathrooms really have been written about so much that we haven't much to say about them that hasn't been said—except, watch the cost! Next to the kitchen, the bathroom is the most expensive room in the house, ordinarily. Even if it's only a plain old everyday bathroom. To go beyond the standard low toilet, fiberglass shower stall, and vanity sink you have to have good reasons.

Veneer Paneling

There is some very tasteful plywood available in veneer paneling, and it's not more expensive than good wallpaper. We like wallpaper because it's easier to clean; but for some houses, the veneer panel is right.

Modern paneling definitely is *not* right for a Victorian house. It's too slick. Wallpaper is much better. For a good solid house that you want to sell, but which is not Victorian, plywood paneling is a definite contender. Some of the modern plywood paneling is positively beautiful.

Solid Paneling

What we have here are two things: one, the house has solid paneling already; and, two, you decide to put in solid paneling where there was none before.

In the first instance, you want to preserve, restore, and reassemble any solid Victorian paneling that exists. It's priceless; it's going to twist the arm of any buyer mightily.

Sometimes we put in our own solid paneling. It's always rough-sawn Vermont lumber, the only kind of new solid paneling we really can justify financially. Sometimes we alternate narrow strips with the Vermont rough sawn boards to give a board-and-batten effect.

Before we get into things like strips, battens, and moldings, you may have noticed that there are lots of "decorator effects" such as textured wallpaper, and so on, that we have not gotten into. We save that for the mansions we redo. When it comes to recycling houses, even a good Victorian, we cannot afford the costs incurred by the professional decorator.

We don't compete with decorators. Sometimes after we sell a house, the owner likes it so much he's willing to go ahead and spend more; he calls in the decorator. In that sense, we provide opportunities for decorators.

For many families a decorator house is not comfortable; they have kids and kids don't know decorator effects from Monopoly. If they are made to mind the walls too much, kids are uncomfortable. At our own place, 91 Rumson, we would have been perfectly in tune with the house to have put up textured wallpaper such as burlap, or "padded wallpaper"—but we didn't do it because we didn't want to stick Charlie and Chris with the burden of never smudging a wall. We opted for vinyl.

Strips and Battens

We put up one-by-twos over unfinished plywood in Utilitarian houses to give a very nice effect. (A Utilitarian house should look *good*, but inexpensively.) Battens and plywood are tough. You never have to do anything with it. It's more expensive than wallboard but takes less time to put up and finish.

Moldings

We always put moldings around the bottom of walls because that is the part of the wall that takes an unholy beating, even by adults. Furniture bumps it, people kick it, pets scratch it—you name it, and it happens to the lower couple of inches of a wall.

Sometimes (when we have some left over) we've used rough sawn Vermont lumber for floor moldings. Other times we just buy inexpensive floor moldings—or if the house calls for better—expensive floor moldings.

If you stain inexpensive floor moldings, they look good—quite contemporary. If you paint floor moldings, the nicks and scratches show up easier.

Windows and Doors

We always use moldings—even if only one-by-threes—around doors and windows. Otherwise, the room looks unfinished.

Fireplace Moldings

If the present fireplace moldings are crummy, we rip them out and replace with old brick around the fireplace, which always looks good.

Victorian Floor Moldings

We make a big effort to save on the floor moldings by patching or cannibalizing, using molding from two rooms to finish one, and then finding a like molding for the second room.

Shelving

For sure, built-in wall shelving is beautiful, contemporary, and all that. But it usually limits the room to use as a den, library, or living room. Built-in shelving is something we let the buyer add—rather than add it to the cost of his house when he buys it. We don't want to lose the buyers who don't want it where it is. We want a house to be flexible.

A bachelor friend of ours redid an old house, ripped out the walls, and built in everything right down to the beds. If he were going to try to sell it tomorrow, he'd be trying for a year. Every room has its use already dictated, and it certainly wouldn't work for a family with kids. He would have to find a counterpart bachelor with his means—and that buyer might be elusive.

Wall Columns and Beams

Every structural beam has to have "legs" on each end to hold it up. If we put in a structural beam, we make the legs into wall columns and match that with a series of false wall columns. That is, if it's less expensive to do that than burying the structural legs inside the walls.

With that we can go on to what's under the walls, namely the floors.

Hardwood

We almost invariably have a hardwood floor to deal with. It may have old tattered carpet or linoleum on it, but under that is hardwood. (If we did have a softwood floor we'd be tempted to lay hardwood or linoleum over because of the quick wear that characterizes softwood floors.)

The worst problem we run into is a sloping floor. There are two main cures: one is to fair the floor out with plywood overlaid with linoleum. Just gauge the underneath supports to make the plywood compensate for the slope. The second way is to have professionals come in and do a "wet setting," something like cement, into which goes floor tile. It's guaranteed level, after that. But it's not cheap, just quick.

Let's assume now that all the floors are level. Then let's take the best case, where the floors are only in need of a sanding, at most, and they are ready for their new coat of polyurethane clear varnish which outlasts the old nonsynthetic varnish four to one. From there on, you can warm the room up with area carpeting if you need to.

Carpet

Let's take the case where there are cracks and deep discoloring. Here you have no choice: you have to wall-to-wall carpet. To bring a bad hardwood floor back is a long labor.

You might want to carpet wall-to-wall anyway, even if the hardwood floor is perfect parquet. One of the minus qualities of Victorian homes, particularly mansions, is that they were cold, echoing places. On the other hand, in dining rooms, and smaller rooms, a parquet edging with small area rugs is often very nice.

Laying wall-to-wall is a pro job; the pros handle such a

volume that it's not expensive at all. It costs about $40 a room to have them come "stretch it" professionally—something you need special machinery for. Add to that the cost of the rug— roughly $200 minimum, probably, for an average 15-by-15 room.

If you have a bedroom, you definitely want wall-to-wall— unless it's a very inexpensive recycle. A hardwood floor is cold and, in the morning, it's *very* cold. It is a big selling plus to have carpeted bedrooms.

There are two kinds of materials sales we always try to get to: one is wallpaper and the other carpet. We buy inexpensively for the future. Between the carpet and wallpaper, we make any house a home. You can deduct from the price of the carpet the $50 it would have cost you to sand and polyurethane the floor.

Let us say that you have decided not to carpet wall-to-wall. One way to keep from having to sand off discoloring is to stain the floor. You may want to stain anyway; a light wood stain is really very up-to-date. Make sure the stain is compatible with the polyurethane that is to go on top. Your hardware store will know which stain you should use. And let the stain dry well before urethane is applied. If you ignore either, you will end up with "polyurethane mush." It's hard to get off the floor.

Always use linoleum in the kitchen, unless you want to go to the expense of kitchen floor tile, which is very "in" these days. But it's very expensive (at least $56 a square foot). We've nothing against tile, we just want somebody to give it to us free.

Platforms

This can dress up an otherwise dull room. A half floor or quarter floor raised three or four inches is a really inexpensive way to achieve a rather stunning effect, if you have a "designer's eye" and you know what you are doing.

At this point we are into the area of interior decorating, an area we approach with trepidation, because of its dangers to recyclers. Decorating can be a "Bottomless Pit." When you think decorating, think price; think final market price of the house;

think bottom line. Don't let your fantasy go wild—unless you've already got a buyer, he wants to pay a lot of money, he's signed on the dotted line, he's crazy about decorator effects, and wants you to go worldwide to find the right touches.

What you do otherwise is let your fancy tackle the problem of finding "decorator effects" that are not "slick" and not expensive. That's what our "signature" is: you can tell when we've done a house because we use some special effects over and over in various ways—such as rough sawn lumber. There are so few that are not expensive that we treasure each one we invent. Our decorator effect may be no more than an unusual wallpaper we picked up for a song. Simple is best.

There are whole college level courses on interior decorating. We're not going to presume to teach that subject within the bounds of this book. We are pointing out how it relates to recycling: money.

All the "Removable Changes" listed in the previous chapter fall under interior decoration, more or less. For ceilings, hanging plants; for walls, mirrors, pictures, hangings, drapes, curtains, sconces; for floors, area carpeting, and furnishings.

If you are a good interior decorator, you have a great recycling future ahead of you, because you can turn all your designing talent to finding designs that stay within the rough estimate for the house. It is a real challenge.

35

The Challenge of the Mansion

Why do a mansion?

First of all, because it's bigger. That means it presents different kinds of challenges. When you've done a number of houses, it's great to do something that isn't a repeat. And a mansion *is* more interesting, definitely.

Second, you make more money. If you are scraping and painting in an older house, you might be making $40 an hour, figuring your eventual return. If you recycle a mansion, you could be making $200 an hour scraping and sanding.

Third, it's more fun. It's more fun working on leaded windows, restoring wood paneling, a graceful banister, or refinishing a parquet floor than doing run-of-the-mill windows, stairways, and floors. You work among beautiful artifacts, the kind of thing nobody can afford to put into a house anymore.

Last, there is the great joy of knowing you have saved a gracious house from decay.

What are the special challenges of recycling a mansion?

We have figured out that there are five *Special Challenges of a Mansion.*

The first challenge of a mansion is to complete the complex financing, so that the house can be bought and sold without pulling you under. You need financial depth; you need a reasonably quick turnaround. Carrying costs are usually very high.

What all this adds up to is that you have to do it right; it has to sell fast. You can't rent it; your rents will be too high to be reasonably sure of getting tenants.

Our second "big" house, 78 Ocean, is what we call a "mini-mansion." It's on the borderline between a big house and a mansion. The house today would be worth $110,000 or so. In a house that expensive, rent is about $2,000 or so a month at 1978 prices. That's way up there. Not impossible, but not probable. Somebody who could pay that much would probably be looking for a house to buy. Why not?

We rented 78 Ocean at first. It was our first one-family expensive house, and we did not know as much about the economics of renting then as we do now. We had trouble finding tenants at what we had to charge.

Cleaning It Up

Then there was cleaning it up. We had to spend a good three weeks getting the place back in shape to sell as a luxury house at the end of four years of renting it out. We saw that we could have made at least as much money by selling it the minute we had recycled it, and reinvesting the profit in our next recycle. When you are recycling a mansion, you are in it to sell.

The exception to this is the mansion that is appreciating at a higher rate than inflation, a Type V (Type I plus Type III). Then it is worth the bother of renting it, just to hang onto it to get the appreciation. But 78 Ocean wasn't a Type V. It was only appreciating at 7 or 8 percent. Not enough to warrant keeping it just on that account.

The usual big house or mansion is not "investment property."

If it were, the land would have been bought for investment and the house torn down long ago, in most cases. Another reason you recycle mansions to sell.

There's an out, incidentally, if you are thinking about a sale of a mansion putting you into a big capital gain for the year. You can give back a mortgage to the buyer and he will pay it off gradually. It's like renting, except you don't have the bother.

In recycling, make sure you're ready for the financial challenge before you take on a mansion.

Second Challenge

The second challenge of a mansion is to restore the architectural detail authentically.

Our second house, at 265 Ocean, was an "almost-mansion." It was big enough, but it didn't have the beautiful detail—the moldings, the intricate ceilings, the parquet floors. They just weren't there. In defining a proper mansion recycle, you include the idea of restoring past graciousness in architecture and past luxury of interior design. A big house built in Victorian times almost inevitably had both architectural detail and interior luxury. Very few *ordinary* large houses were built. They built mansions in every sense of the word.

Recycling a mansion is a peak, not a beginning. If you get in over your head, skillwise, by trying a mansion too early in your career, you are not doing yourself or the mansion any favor.

Can you find out how to refinish a balustraded stair to original luster? Can you find out how to relead windows, reconstruct carved plaster ceiling designs, repair damaged oak paneling? If your confidence in these tasks is justifiable, it's because you have a wealth of experience in various processes of refinishing and remodeling behind you.

Our house at 78 Ocean, the "mini-mansion," had eighteen rooms, some with beautiful carved plaster ceilings and wain-scoted walls. The bathroom walls were pressed tin. The mansion doorways had the most gorgeous door moldings that we had ever seen.

The 78 Ocean ceilings were the kind of job we had not tackled before. But we had worked with plaster and we had retouched wood and were confident we could find out how to restore the carved plaster ceilings and beams. It took us only a little while to figure it out. We sanded off and retouched the oak beams. We took plaster and "sculpted in place" to restore the damaged parts of the carved plaster ceiling flowers. We built up the missing spaces layer by layer and a new carved plaster flower bloomed.

Be sure you can handle the skill challenge before you take on a mansion.

Third Challenge

The third challenge of a mansion is successfully combining the old and the new.

There have been some really bad results from people attempting to "modernize" old Victorians. What is missing from the result is an appreciation for what was "fun" about the old houses and what worked, esthetically. If you don't keep the fun and reinforce the old esthetic, you have a rather unprepossessing Victorian, however solidly built it may be.

This doesn't mean you can't mix occasional contemporary furniture, for instance, with Victorian. We have a great Victorian fireplace room at 91 Rumson where we've got weapons on the wall and a 300-year-old fireplace front, and use contemporary leather and chrome furniture around the fireplace. We aren't really hung up on making a house a museum.

In our work at 78 Ocean, we modernized several things: the kitchen on the first floor, and on the second floor, we built a new bathroom, to give the house three. (Old houses are always "one bathroom short" in relation to the number of bedrooms, by modern standards.)

In 78 Ocean, we did partially restore the two existing bathrooms, keeping the lovely pressed tin walls and the marvelous cast-iron Victorian tubs (clean and repainted). We added modern toilets, because the originals were not functional by modern standards, and we added shower heads over the bathtubs and shower curtains.

Outside of that, we stuck mainly with straight historical

restoration. The rooms were large, and there were enough of them so that we could designate uses and provide a good traffic pattern without tearing down any walls or adding exterior doors. That's one of the advantages of a big house.

In the wainscoted bedrooms, we stripped the old wall finish. The varnish had darkened with the years. We revarnished with a semigloss to lighten the bedrooms' atmosphere.

In the downstairs rooms where there was paneling, we let the darkened varnish stay. It looked good down there, very Victorian and shadowy, not the way you'd want your bedroom to look, but the right "atmosphere" for downstairs rooms where you have nooks and crannies that serve as delightful retreats. We washed the paneling and lemon-oiled it so the dark varnish glowed.

Where the walls had been painted, we chose to wallpaper. Our vinyl wallpaper would only have to be washed down every few years; it would last twenty years.

Notebook Files

Where did the ideas for all these combinations come from? Our heads. And our notes. Mary carries a "house notebook" for every house we do. The notebook has a section for each room of the house we are restoring. In each section of the notebook, we put our ideas for a particular room, and what materials and furnishings we need to carry out the ideas. Then we go looking for the necessary stuff at estate sales, flea markets, our own attic. It's like a great chess game. The squares are the rooms. You have to make a coordinated attack on all the rooms, considering carefully how to make best use of the existing situation.

The notebook charts the possible moves to make the coordinated attack work. This furniture piece goes here, and that one goes there; this finish goes here and that wallpaper there—and it all has to come out reinforcing the final result. The final goal is a house that looks, feels, and lives like a comfortable Victorian, except for easier upkeep, modern appliances, and heating.

That's exactly what 78 Ocean became.

Needless to say, when the house was put on the market, we

had no trouble whatsoever selling it very quickly. Where else would you get carved plaster and beam ceilings, glowing dark oak paneling, and a 1978 modern kitchen all under the same roof?

Before you recycle a mansion, be sure you can meet the design challenge of combining old and new.

The fourth challenge of a mansion is the skill in picking a mansion that is in reasonably good shape in spite of appearances.

Fourth Challenge

In a mansion, you have big carrying costs. Time used in turning the house around is of the essence. There is so *much* in a mansion just in concrete physical wall space, ceiling, and floor that, if it all needed extensive repair, you'd be in for a ten-year recycle. Being fundamentally sound and easily restored isn't as important on a relatively small place like 78 Ocean, but in a place like Goldencrest, our first big mansion recycle, it's crucial.

What we found at Goldencrest was that the house had been abandoned and was dreadfully dirty. But under the dirt, the plaster and wood was still in good condition. The surfaces looked bad; the essential structure was sound. Foot for foot, the mansions we pick are far easier to recycle than an ordinary house. They had better be!

Goldencrest was designed by Stanford White, one of the greatest turn-of-the-century American architects. We were really getting up there among the restoration elite when we took this one on.

We were amazed to find that the price was not all that unreasonable. What people who looked at it through the years thought was, "How could I ever manage to have this place put into shape?" Well it wasn't so hard, after all.

The mansion was built between 1901-1904, all forty-six rooms of it, by the Dixons of Crucible Steel. It was named Goldencrest because it was the fiftieth wedding anniversary present of Mr. Dixon to Mrs. Dixon and, as such, was one of the greatest showplaces of the Jersey shore back when the Jersey shore was the East Hampton and West Hampton of its day.

There's a nice little anecdote about it. As it was being built, Mrs. Dixon, who had not been told it was for her, would ride by in her carriage, exclaiming over its beauty and wondering who would be living in it. On the eve of her fiftieth anniversary, her husband handed her the keys.

Goldencrest's Details

The house had eleven master bedroom suites, each with its own marble bathroom. The living room, fifty-by-seventy-five feet, had three fireplaces, seventeen windows, and was supported by eight carved Corinthian columns.

And it was ours—to save. The quicker the better.

We jumped into the cleaning job with our fingers crossed, putting the salvageable stuff in the basement and throwing the rest out the door.

The first thing we had to do was redesign the traffic pattern because the kitchen was way off in one wing. We solved that by setting up the kitchen in what had originally been the dining room, creating a new dining room in a set-off part of the living room. This traffic pattern worked out beautifully. Best of all, we didn't have to take down any walls.

We insulated the house and replaced the third floor balustrade railing with a railing from another house—we could have had new balustrade railings milled at $25 apiece, but that would have come to $1,750 for the whole thing. We did something better than restoring, we replaced with something just as good, in the period, and yet which did not add appreciably to the price of the house.

We cleaned and restored the Napoleonic bathtubs in all eleven master baths—they had been ordered especially from France in 1901. We polished up the gold leaf sinks in the bathrooms. The toilets rods we kept. They were wonderful overhead "water closets" that still worked with great vigor. We added brass-plated shower curtain rods to each bathroom and replaced the rusted

Victorian plumbing in the walls with parallel pipes of modern plumbing.

Besides that, except when it came to furnishing, we didn't do all that much. A little Structo-lite and spackle and some Old Dutch Cleanser and we had it 80 percent "renovated."

Fifth Challenge

That brings us to furnishings, which is what the Fifth Challenge of a Mansion is about:

The fifth challenge of a mansion is to refurnish and redecorate it so that the beauty of the mansion will convince a potential buyer on the spot.

Because 78 Ocean was a relatively small mansion, the price on it was relatively modest, too, as mansions go. Although we did redecorate and refurnish, the part that this played in the eventual sale was, relatively, not that big. When you get up over $150,000, as in a project the size of Goldencrest, then the part played by furnishings and decor is vital in convincing the buyers. They are, in all probability, people of taste and well-traveled. They know a striking room when they see one.

We'll get into just one facet of this challenge in Goldencrest and then elaborate on it in the next chapter. The parquet floors at Goldencrest were magnificent. We spent two weeks off and on sanding down the wood inlays in the first master bedroom we tackled. (All the bedrooms were twenty-five-by-thirty-five.) But, when the whole floor had been done, it shone cold as a sheet of ice to the eye. And would have felt so to the foot. In spite of all our sanding, the bedroom had to be carpeted to make it reasonably inviting. We carpeted *all* eleven bedrooms. Downstairs, we ended up carpeting all the rooms, leaving the edges with nine different kinds of wood inlay exposed.

The emotional impact of a house has to be warm and inviting. Rather than restore completely, we made a restoration in which the furnishings, beginning with the carpets, were warm, original, and striking.

We never go by the old Stanford White house now without feeling a shot of pride. Not many grand old houses do get saved. And this one, *we* saved!

36

Home Sweet Recycled Home

After Goldencrest, we took on two more mansions, in fairly short order. One was the Lindens, and the other our own current home, 91 Rumson, The White House.

The Lindens was a gorgeous neo-Georgian built at great expense near the Jersey shore about 1900. The front porch particularly was a marvel, and the house a great gem of the summer colony. The house had been allowed to fall into disrepair. The front porch railings were falling off; the exterior paint peeled away. It was a sorry sight.

We had a look and found, to our joy, things were not as bad as they seemed. This is not, we were beginning to realize, an unusual case where mansions are concerned. Passersby seeing the falling porch must have said to themselves, that place is really coming apart! But it wasn't.

Another plus was that the kitchen had been redone in 1950, so that the plumbing, unlike the antiquated piping at Goldencrest, was quite up-to-date. We put in new cabinets, appliances, and tile, and had the kitchen renovated in a jiffy. The Lindens did not need a new traffic plan, either.

Every other year the Monmouth County Junior League picks a "Designer Show House," which is an outstanding home turned over to a dozen outstanding interior designers who each take a room and redecorate in their own style. The resulting house is then opened to the public and admissions go to the Junior League charities. We were asked to donate the Lindens as the Designer Show House. We agreed.

In all, it took us a year of planning and work, and a good bit of our own cash, to help keep the project going to opening day. But, the 1975 Designer Show House was a great success. Twenty thousand people filed through and the Junior League had $50,000 to give to charity.

What was obvious about 91 Rumson was that, when we first saw it, the house looked dreadful. The six-acre site was full of weeds, the drive impassable, the windows broken in, and the interior vandalized. During our first visit, we detoured over to a neighboring house and asked who owned 91 Rumson. "Oh, that belongs to millionaires," said the lady. "You could never afford it."

Well, with a little imagination, you could see that it had been a millionaire's place. It was called "The White House" by all the neighbors because of its resemblence, faintly, to the U.S. Presidential mansion. Right then, all that frequented it were rats and vandals.

Nothing—but nothing—had been done to it since the house had been built; all the original decorations were still in place. The original hand-made Belgian curtains hung in shreds on the rods. The original rugs, some in tatters, were still down. And the woodwork was all peeling, but had never been given a second coat of paint. What was showing was bare wood.

It all added up, once we'd inspected the place, to another mansion in really good shape under the superficial scratches, vandalism, scars, and dirt.

We looked up the owner on the city tax map. Our timing was great. The house had recently passed into an estate, and the heirs were willing to sell at a very reasonable price. The house had been built around 1915 by the Ceasar family of New York City, and they had spared no outlay to make a grand establishment for themselves as their "country house." But they sold in the 1940s to another owner who only used it summer weekends, and then it was allowed to go entirely into disrepair after he no longer came.

We bought it and moved in. But, for a longer spell, this time, than has been our habit. We were going to live here, permanently, at least for now.

We started in on it and did our usual tricks.

We moved the kitchen from the servant's quarters to a central location off the main entry. We renovated the bathrooms, cleaned off the beautiful *boiserie*—moldings which divide the wall space into squares—and restored the plaster moldings in the ceilings.

It was great fun furnishing The White House. We've collected a great number of interesting things in our sweeps through the flea market at Englishtown, at estate sales, and leftovers from other houses. Here we had a chance to put some of our gleanings on display.

For instance, there is a prize marvelous brass chandelier over the ballustraded staircase at one end, and carrying through from the entryway up the ballustrade and into the second floor is a green pattern flock (textured) wallpaper that sets off both the chandelier and the original alabaster wall sconces. We put a huge table in the middle of the entryway; it's such a big room that it needs large scale furniture. All in all, we enjoy just coming into that scene every time we come home.

(The overall effect is sometimes spoiled when we have a project underway: packages and furniture and bolts of cloth lie strewn around. We still like to have room for our projects.)

Fun with Rooms

One of the really fun things is the "billiard room" off the entryway. It actually was just that. We wallpapered in red and gold to set off the oak paneling, restored the billiard table, and put in a curved Victorian glass china cabinet in which we have the family sport trophies. It breathes Victorian male. It's sort of amusing.

The living room is our "Gilded Age" room. We used a light gold vinyl wallpaper and there's a gold and white wall-to-wall rug and gold and white striped overstuffed furniture around a grand piano at the far end where Mary has her singing lessons.

The dining room is big. We tend to eat mostly in the modern kitchen we put in the solarium, but the dining table is huge, and often we sit in the big carved walnut chairs and spread out one of our projects on the table. (The latest project was pictures for this book.)

To say that we enjoy the house—we're still working on it from time to time and will be—is an understatement. We love it.

Occasionally we take off the work clothes and put together a big wingding, just to use the house the way a Victorian mansion should be used. Last January we invited a houseful of guests, practically everybody we knew, and had a choir which sang eighteenth century madrigals and a chamber music ensemble in alternation. We put on a great show: it's the kind of thing that rewards you for the time and effort put in making a place like The White House reflect the grand life style, which ours is only very briefly, from time to time. It's almost like putting on a play to go all out once in a while.

Finally, after moving from house to house for eight years we have a home. People who come into our "gilded" living room still ask, "How did you do it?"

You know how we did it!!!!!